Jossey-Bass Teacher

Jossey-Bass Teacher provides K–12 teachers with essential knowledge and tools to create a positive and lifelong impact on student learning. Trusted and experienced educational mentors offer practical classroom-tested and theory-based teaching resources for improving teaching practice in a broad range of grade levels and subject areas. From one educator to another, we want to be your first source to make every day your best day in teaching. *Jossey-Bass Teacher* resources serve two types of informational needs—essential knowledge and essential tools. Essential knowledge resources provide the foundation, strategies, and methods from which teachers may design curriculum and instruction to challenge and excite their students. Connecting theory to practice, essential knowledge books rely on a solid research base and time-tested methods, offering the best ideas and guidance from many of the most experienced and well-respected experts in the field.

Essential tools save teachers time and effort by offering proven, ready-to-use materials for in-class use. Our publications include activities, assessments, exercises, instruments, games, ready reference, and more. They enhance an entire course of study, a weekly lesson, or a daily plan. These essential tools provide insightful, practical, and comprehensive materials on topics that matter most to K–12 teachers.

Math Essentials, Middle School Level

Math Essentials, Middle School Level: Lessons and Activities for Test Preparation

Frances McBroom Thompson, Ed.D.

JOSSEY-BASS
A Wiley Imprint
www.josseybass.com

Published by Jossey-Bass
A Wiley Imprint
989 Market Street, San Francisco, CA 94103-1741   www.josseybass.com

Jossey-Bass books and products are available through most bookstores. To contact Jossey-Bass directly call our Customer Care Department within the U.S. at 800-956-7739, outside the U.S. at 317-572-3986, or fax 317-572-4002.

Jossey-Bass also publishes its books in a variety of electronic formats. Some content that appears in print may not be available in electronic books.

ISBN: 0-7879-6602-9

Printed in the United States of America
FIRST EDITION
PB Printing   10 9 8 7 6 5 4 3 2

About This Book

Math Essentials, Middle School Level is designed to help students review and master all the mathematics concepts they are expected to know and understand by eighth grade. It takes a developmental approach, incorporating manipulative and pictorial lessons, followed by independent practice, and often including multiple-choice exercises that provide practice in standardized testing. *Math Essentials, Middle School Level* covers thirty objectives found in a typical curriculum for Grades 6 through 8: numeration, computation, proportional and algebraic reasoning, geometry, measurement, statistics and probability, all supporting NCTM Standards.

Contents

The Author xv

Notes to the Teacher xvii

Section 1: Number, Operation, and Quantitative Reasoning 1

Objectives

1. Compare and order fractions, decimals (including tenths
   and hundredths), and percents, and find their
   approximate locations on a number line 1
2. Multiply decimals to solve word problems 12
3. Divide decimals to solve word problems 26
4. Estimate solutions to multistepped word problems
   by rounding with decimals 44
5. Add fractions or mixed numbers to solve word problems 55
6. Subtract fractions or mixed numbers to solve word problems 69
7. Divide fractions or mixed numbers to solve word problems 82
8. Multiply fractions or mixed numbers to solve word problems 97
9. Develop and apply scientific notation to solve word problems 113

Practice Test 123

Section 2: Proportional and Algebraic Reasoning. 129

Objectives

1. Apply ratios in proportional relationships involving unit
   rates, scale factors, probabilities, or percents 129
2. Add integers to solve word problems 142
3. Subtract integers to solve word problems 151

4. Multiply and divide integers to solve word problems 161
5. Model situations with linear equations of the form:
   aX + b = c, where a, b, and c are integers or decimals
   and X is an integer 171
6. Identify linear and nonlinear functions and contrast
   their properties using tables, graphs, or equations 179

Practice Test **189**

Section 3: Geometry, Spatial Reasoning, and Measurement. 193

Objectives

1. Sketch side views (orthogonal views) of solids and identify
   different perspectives of solids that satisfy the side views 193
2. Identify or graph reflections (flips), rotations (turns),
   and translations (slides) on a coordinate plane 203
3. Use dilations to generate similar two-dimensional shapes,
   and compare their side lengths, angles, and perimeters;
   find missing measurements using proportional relationships . . . 214
4. Model and apply the Pythagorean theorem to solve
   real-life problems 222
5. Generate the formulas for the circumference and the area
   of a circle; apply the formulas to solve word problems 231
6. Generate and apply the area formula for a parallelogram
   (including rectangles); extend to the area of a triangle 240
7. Generate and apply the area formula for a trapezoid 249
8. Apply nets and concrete models to find total or partial
   surface areas of prisms and cylinders 258
9. Find the volume of a right rectangular prism, or find a
   missing dimension of the prism; find the new volume
   when the dimensions of a prism are changed proportionally 266

Practice Test **275**

Section 4: Graphing, Statistics, and Probability 281

Objectives

1. Locate and name points using ordered pairs of rational
   numbers or integers on a Cartesian coordinate plane 281
2. Construct and interpret circle graphs 290

3. Compare different numerical or graphical models for
the same data, including histograms, circle graphs,
stem-and-leaf plots, box plots, and scatter plots; compare
two sets of data by comparing their graphs of similar type 301
4. Find the mean of a given set of data, using different
representations such as tables or bar graphs 312
5. Find the probability of a simple event and its complement 321
6. Find the probability of a compound event (dependent
or independent) 327
Practice Test **336**

The Author

Frances McBroom Thompson has taught junior high and senior high mathematics in Anaheim, California, and Dallas, Texas. She has also served as an educational consultant for grades K–12 in both Georgia and Texas. Frances currently is professor of mathematics at Texas Woman's University in Denton, where she focuses on the preparation of elementary and secondary teachers in mathematics. She is also actively involved as a staff development trainer for in-service teachers throughout North Texas.

Her teaching methods, based on many years of research with classroom teachers and their students, incorporate both manipulatives and diagrams for the development of new concepts. These methods have been successful with all types of learners, including gifted and learning disabled students. Frances has written two other resource books that reflect these methods: *Hands-on Math! Ready-to-Use Games and Activities for Grades 4–8* (1994) and *Hands-on Algebra! Ready-to-Use Games and Activities for Grades 7–12* (1998). Her professional goal is to help students enjoy mathematics while they grow in their abilities to understand and reason with new mathematical ideas.

Notes to the Teacher

Math Essentials, Middle School Level: Lessons and Activities for Test Preparation consists of thirty key objectives arranged in four sections. These objectives have been selected from the standard mathematics curriculum for Grades 6–8 and from the middle school curriculum recommended by the National Council of Teachers of Mathematics. Because of the cumulative nature of mathematics, some objectives from previous grades and from algebra will also be covered. For each objective, there are three activities (two developmental lessons and one independent practice), along with a list of common errors that students make with respect to problems related to the objective. A worksheet and answer key are provided for most activities. Each of the four sections also contains a practice test with an answer key.

Description of Activities

Each objective has two developmental activities: the first at the manipulative stage and the second at the pictorial stage. Detailed steps guide the teacher through each of these two activities. Activity 1 usually requires objects of some kind. Materials are described in detail, and necessary building mats, pattern sheets, and worksheets with answer keys are provided. Activity 2 involves pictures or diagrams that closely relate to the actions performed in Activity 1. Worksheets and answer keys are also provided for this second activity. Activity 3 provides an opportunity for students to practice the objective independently and at the abstract level of thinking. Worksheet items for this third stage often have multiple-choice responses to provide students with further testing experience. The items have been kept to a minimum to allow time for student discussions about their answers and the methods they used to find those answers. The communication of mathematical ideas is an essential classroom experience.

These three activities may be presented as a connected set, with the manipulative activity leading naturally to the pictorial activity and then the independent practice, or each activity may be used separately, depending on the students' learning needs. All students, however, regardless of intellectual ability or diversity of background, need to experience each of the three stages of learning at some point. The natural learning progression that moves from hands-on action to paper-and-pencil drawing and finally to abstract notation is essential for all students to experience and should not be excluded from classroom instruction. Therefore, it is recommended that the three activities be used together.

Common Errors Made by Students

When studying any mathematical objective, students will have errors in their work. Test developers know this and usually select item response choices that reflect these errors. Hence, it is helpful if the classroom teacher also is aware of these common errors and can identify them when they occur in an individual student's work.

To assist teachers with this process, a list of typical errors is given with each objective in this text. Various studies have found that if students are made aware of their particular mistakes in mathematics, they are more likely to replace them with correct procedures or conceptual understanding. When such errors are not specifically addressed, students are likely to continue making them, no matter how many times the teacher demonstrates the correct steps to use.

Section Practice Tests

A practice test, with an answer key, is provided at the end of each of Sections One through Four. For each objective in a section, two multiple-choice test items are provided on the section's practice test. The format and level of difficulty of these items are similar to those found in state or national standardized tests for middle school students. Where appropriate, the activity worksheets for an objective will reflect the types of problems included in the practice test. Otherwise, the activities are designed to give students the conceptual foundation needed to understand the test items.

Instructional Accountability

Teachers must be accountable for what they are teaching to students. The alternative instructional methods and assessment techniques presented in this book will greatly assist teachers as they seek to align their classroom instruction with their district and state mathematics guidelines and to measure the progress their students make.

Math Essentials,
Middle School Level

NUMBER, OPERATION, AND QUANTITATIVE REASONING

Objective 1

Compare and order fractions, decimals (including tenths and hundredths), and percents, and find their approximate locations on a number line.

Students must be able to compare different real numbers. The comparing and ordering of several decimal numbers requires a strong understanding of place value. The skill to order signed decimal numbers, both positive and negative numbers within the same set, is also expected at the middle school level. Thus, students need experience with ordering a variety of real numbers. The following activities provide such experience with decimals, fractions, and percents. The relationship of positive numbers to negative numbers is emphasized, and mastery of basic equivalent decimals, fractions, and percents will be assumed.

Activity 1: Manipulative Stage

Materials

    Pattern 1–1a and Pattern 1–1b for number cards for each pair of students
    Worksheet 1–1a
    Scissors
    Regular pencil

Procedure

1. Give each pair of students a copy of Pattern 1–1a, Pattern 1–1b, and scissors. Each student should also receive a copy of Worksheet 1–1a.

2. Each pair should cut apart the number cards shown on the two pattern sheets. These cards will be used to determine the order of each set of numbers on the worksheet.

3. For each exercise, partners should select a tentatively lesser number in the set and build it with the appropriate number cards. Then they should add on other cards having positive values in order to change from the selected number's value

to a total card value equal to another number in the set. If this can be done, the selected number is less than the new number found. If this cannot be done, the selected number is greater than any of the other numbers in the set.

4. Other numbers from the set may need to be tested in this same manner before the final order of all numbers in the set can be determined. Once the order is found, students should record the numbers in the correct order below the exercise, using the appropriate < or > sign.

5. Guide students through Exercise 1 on Worksheet 1–1a before they proceed to the other exercises.

For the first exercise on Worksheet 1–1a, the set of numbers, +2.5, –3, –1.5, +0.75, must be ordered *from least to greatest.* Since the numbers in this exercise are all decimals, only the integer and decimal cards need to be used.

As an example, have students select –1.5 as the first number to build with the number cards. Students should place one (–1) card and one (–0.5) card on the desktop; these two cards have the total value of –1.5. Ask the students to place more cards beside these two cards but to use only positive cards. The process of adding only positive amounts to some given real number will produce new numbers greater than the given number. When appropriate, encourage them to use positive cards to form 0-pairs with any given negative cards. For example, if a (–0.5) card has been used, a (+0.5) card might be added to form a 0-pair with it.

Students should find the total value of the cards after each new card is added. If one (+1) card is added, the total value will be –0.5; if two (+0.5) cards are also added, the total value will be +0.5. Then if two more (+1) cards are added, the value will be +2.5, where +2.5 is a number in the original set. This result indicates that +2.5 is greater than –1.5 in the set. Here is a possible card arrangement for this process. Notice that negative amounts are placed to the left and positive amounts are added to the right, reflecting a general sense of direction. Also, positive amounts are placed below negative amounts in order to form 0-pairs easily. If no negative amount were present, there would just be a row of positive amounts being joined to the right.

Notice that when increasing from –1.5 to +2.5, the number –3 was not found as a total value. So –3 needs to be tested. After three (–1) cards are placed on the desktop, one (+1) card might be added to produce a value of –2. Then one (–1) card might be traded for two (–0.5) cards. One (+0.5) card may now be added, yielding a total card value of –1.5. The total card value has increased from –3 to –1.5, a member of the given set, so –1.5 is greater than –3. Here is a possible arrangement of the final cards used:

–1	–1	–0.5	–0.5
+1		+0.5	

Similarly, +0.75 can be built by adding one (+1) card, one (+0.5) card, and one (+0.75) card to the cards for –1.5; by adding to the (+0.75) card one (+0.25) card, one (+1) card, and one (+0.5) card, +0.75 can be increased to +2.5. These two tests confirm that –1.5 < +0.75 and +0.75 < +2.5. Applying some logical reasoning, students should now be able to write the four numbers in the required increasing order below Exercise 1 on Worksheet 1–1a:

$$-3 < -1.5 < +0.75 < +2.5$$

Answer Key for Worksheet 1–1a

1. $-3 < -1.5 < +0.75 < +2.5$

2. $+3.5 > 0 > 0.5 > -4$

3. $-3.5 < -2.5 < -1 < +3.0$

4. $+1.25 > +0.50 > -0.5 > -2.75$

5. $+\frac{3}{4} > 0 > -1 > -1\frac{1}{2}$

6. $-3\frac{1}{2} < -2 < +2\frac{1}{4} < +4$

7. $+1\frac{3}{4} > -\frac{1}{2} > -1\frac{3}{4} > -2$

8. $-3 < -\frac{3}{4} < +1\frac{1}{4} < +2$

4

WORKSHEET 1–1a   Name _____

Ordering Real Numbers by Building   Date _____

Find the required order of each set of real numbers by using the number cards from
Pattern 1–1a or Pattern 1–1b. Record the correct order below each set, using < or >.

1. Order from least to greatest: +2.5, –3, –1.5, +0.75

2. Order from greatest to least: –4, 0, +3.5, –0.5

3. Order from least to greatest: –2.5, –3.5, +3.0, –1

4. Order from greatest to least: +1.25, –0.5, –2.75, +0.50

5. Order from greatest to least: $-1\frac{1}{2}$, 0, $+\frac{3}{4}$, –1

6. Order from least to greatest: +4, –2, $+2\frac{1}{4}$, $-3\frac{1}{2}$

7. Order from greatest to least: –2, $+1\frac{3}{4}$, $-\frac{1}{2}$, $-1\frac{3}{4}$

8. Order from least to greatest: +2, $+1\frac{1}{4}$, –3, $-\frac{3}{4}$

Instructions: Cut the cards apart.

Pattern 1–1a. Decimal Cards

−1	−1	−1	−1
+1	+1	+1	+1
+1	+1	+1	+1
+0.5	+0.5	+0.25	+0.25
+0.75	+0.75	−0.5	−0.5
−0.25	−0.25	−0.75	−0.75

6

Instructions: Cut the cards apart.

Pattern 1–1b. Fraction Cards

-1	-1	-1	-1
$+1$	$+1$	$+1$	$+1$
$+1$	$+1$	$+1$	$+1$
$+\dfrac{1}{2}$	$+\dfrac{1}{2}$	$+\dfrac{1}{4}$	$+\dfrac{1}{4}$
$+\dfrac{3}{4}$	$+\dfrac{3}{4}$	$-\dfrac{1}{2}$	$-\dfrac{1}{2}$
$-\dfrac{1}{4}$	$-\dfrac{1}{4}$	$-\dfrac{3}{4}$	$-\dfrac{3}{4}$

Activity 2: Pictorial Stage

Materials

Worksheet 1–1b

Regular pencil

Procedure

1. Give each student a copy of Worksheet 1–1b. Have students work in pairs.

2. Review the methods for finding equivalent percents, decimals, and fractions. For example, students should recognize 25% as "25 per hundred" or "25-hundredths" by definition and then write it in decimal form as 0.25. They should also be able to write "25-hundredths" in fraction form as 25/100 and then reduce it to 1/4. This renaming process is a prerequisite for this activity.

3. Using the unit length from 0 to +1 marked off on the number line on the worksheet as the whole for comparison purposes, have students locate points on the number line whose distances from 0 represent specific portions of the unit bar length. These distances also order the numbers they represent. Portions in the positive direction will indicate increases, and portions in the negative direction will indicate decreases.

4. Guide students through Exercise 1 on Worksheet 1–1b before they proceed to the other exercise.

In Exercise 1, a situation concerning increases and decreases in profit is given. Students are asked to rank the three levels of performance and then represent their order on the number line. The total annual sales used to determine a store's profit may differ among the stores, but it is only their levels of performance (rates) that are being compared. Hence, students must think of the 75% increase as +0.75, the 0.3 increase as +0.3, and the 20% decrease as –0.20.

These three decimal numbers may now be easily compared and ordered, from least to greatest or from greatest to least. If ordered from least to greatest, the order will be –0.20, +0.3, +0.75. Then students should use the original numbers and record the following below Exercise 1: –20% < +0.3 < +75%. If they decide to order from greatest to least, they will record: +75% > +0.3 > –20%.

The ordered amounts should finally be marked on the number line. Percents, fractions, and decimals should be written in different horizontal lines for later ease of reading and comparing. Since markings are not shown on the number line for –20% or +0.3, students must estimate where their markings should be relative to the markings already shown. Here is the number line containing the numbers for Exercise 1:

Answer Key to Worksheet 1–1b

1.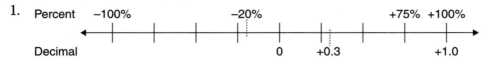

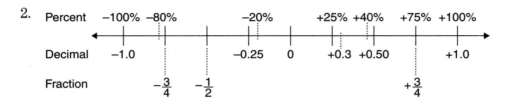

WORSHEET 1–1b

Name _____

Ordering Real Numbers
on a Number Line

Date _____

Order the real numbers in the list by marking and labeling a point on the number line for each number. Each fraction, decimal, or percent represents a certain portion of the indicated unit length from 0 to +1 or from 0 to –1 on the number line. The positive unit length represents a "100% increase," and the negative unit length represents a "100% decrease." A point marked on a unit length will represent a portion of either the increase or the decrease. Answer any additional questions given in the exercises.

1. This year, store 1 showed a 75% increase over last year's profits, store 2 showed a 0.3 increase, and store 3 showed a 20% decrease in profits. Use signed numbers with < or > to rank these three levels of performance. Estimate and label positions on the number line to represent the ranking.

2. Order the following numbers by estimating and labeling their positions on the number line:

$$+25\%, \ +0.50, \ -\frac{3}{4}, \ -0.25, \ -1.0, \ +40\%, \ +\frac{3}{4}, \ -80\%, \ -\frac{1}{2}$$

Activity 3: Independent Practice

Materials
Worksheet 1–1c
Regular pencil

Procedure
Give each student a copy of Worksheet 1–1c. Have students work independently. When all are finished, discuss their results.

Answer Key for Worksheet 1–1c
1. B

2. C

3. A

4. 0.2

Possible Testing Errors That May Occur for This Objective
- The numbers are sequenced by size but in reverse order; for example, they are arranged in decreasing order, but the test item requires them to be in increasing order. Students clearly understand how to order the numbers but did not read the test item carefully.

- The first and last numbers listed in the sequence are correct, but the other numbers are randomly ordered between those two numbers. Students focus on the "least" and the "greatest" numbers, but disregard any others given in the list.

- The positive and negative signs are ignored, and the numbers are ordered only by their absolute values. Hence, +2, –3.5, and –1.8 are ordered from least to greatest as 1.8, 2, and 3.5.

- Decimal points are ignored, so decimal numbers like 4.25, 10.8, and 0.586 are ordered from greatest to least as 586, 425, and 108. This results in the incorrect answer choice being selected (0.586, 4.25, 10.8).

WORSHEET 1–1c

Name _____

Ordering Real Numbers Involving
Percents, Decimals, and Fractions

Date _____

Solve the problems provided. Draw a number line, and use it to order numbers if helpful.

1. The Triangle Mall manager reviewed a report that showed the percent increase in sales at 4 stores.

Store 1	Store 2	Store 3	Store 4
3.5%	0.78%	2.75%	2.06%

   Which lists the percent increase in sales from greatest to least for all 4 stores?

   A. 3.5%, 0.78%, 2.75%, 2.06%

   B. 3.5%, 2.75%, 2.06%, 0.78%

   C. 0.78%, 2.06%, 2.75%, 3.5%

   D. 2.75%, 2.06%, 0.78%, 3.5%

2. The high temperatures in Anchorage, Alaska, for 5 consecutive days were –5 degrees, 0.6 degrees, –3.8 degrees, –1.9 degrees, and 4.2 degrees Fahrenheit. Which shows the temperatures in order from coldest to warmest?

   A. 4.2°F, 0.6°F, –1.9°F, –3.8°F, –5°F

   B. –5°F, 0.6°F, –1.9°F, –3.8°F, 4.2°F

   C. –5°F, –3.8°F, –1.9°F, 0.6°F, 4.2°F

   D. 4.2°F, –3.8°F, –1.9°F, 0.6°F, –5°F

3. A librarian arranged some books on the shelf using the Dewey decimal system. Which group of book numbers is listed in order from least to greatest?

   A. 724, 724.29, 724.3, 724.39

   B. 105.4, 105.04, 108.21, 110.0

   C. 391.5, 397.53, 399.62, 399.05

   D. 549.01, 549.10, 549.02, 549.4

4. Joe is offered sales commissions of 18%, 0.2, and 3/20 of every dollar sold by three different stores, respectively. Which rate is the highest?

Objective 2
Multiply decimals to solve word problems.

The algorithm for the multiplication of decimal numbers needs to be developed well before students are required to independently work story problems requiring decimal multiplication. The algorithm depends heavily on an understanding of multiplication as the repetition of all or part of a set. It is also very complex in terms of place value. Many students have difficulty with it because they do not understand how place value changes will cause partial products to be recorded in different columns.

Activities for the development of the algorithm are described next. It is assumed for this objective that the multiplication facts have already been fully developed with manipulative materials.

Activity 1: Manipulative Stage

Materials
Building Mat 1–2a
Set of base 10 blocks per pair of students (6 flats, 30 rods, 30 small cubes)
Worksheet 1–2a
Regular pencil

Procedure
1. Give each pair of students a set of base 10 blocks (6 flats, 30 rods, 30 small cubes) and a copy of Building Mat 1–2a. For the multiplicand or the set to be repeated, a flat will represent a one or a whole unit, a rod will represent a tenth of the one, and a small cube a hundredth of the one.

2. Give each student a copy of Worksheet 1–2a. Worksheet exercises will involve ones and tenths in one- or two-digit decimal numbers.

3. Have students model each exercise with their blocks. Then on Worksheet 1–2a below the exercise, have them record a word sentence that shows the results found on the building mat. They should count up their total blocks in the product region (that is, in the interior of the angle of the L-shape) of the mat in order to find their answers. Do not trade any blocks found in the product region. For example, if 10 hundredths are there, do not exchange them for 1 tenth. Always have students use proper place value language when verbally describing their steps to the class.

4. First discuss Exercise 1 on Worksheet 1–2a in detail with the students. Then allow them to work the other exercises with their partners.

Here is the story problem for Exercise 1: "Marian has several bags of candy in the store display case. Each bag holds 2.4 ounces of candy. A customer needs 1.3 bags for a cookie recipe. How many ounces of candy does the customer need?"

Have students place 1 flat and 3 rods along the vertical bar of the L-frame for the multiplier, and place 2 flats and 4 rods below the horizontal bar of the frame for the multiplicand (see the illustration for block placement). For both factor sets, the rods should be placed closest to the corner of the L-frame and the flats placed toward the ends.

Discuss the idea that the flat or one along the vertical bar means to build one complete copy of each block below the horizontal bar. Each rod or tenth along the vertical bar means to build one part of ten parts of each block below the horizontal bar. So 1-tenth of a flat (or 1-tenth of one whole) will be a rod or tenth block in the product region, and 1-tenth of a rod (or 1-tenth of a tenth of a whole) will be a small cube or hundredth block in the product region.

Guide students to apply the blocks in the multiplier one block at a time. This process will build blocks in the product region one row at a time. For Exercise 1, when applied to the blocks in the horizontal multiplicand, each tenth block in the vertical multiplier will produce a product row that contains two tenths (rods) and four hundredths (cubes). The ones block or flat will produce a product row of two ones (flats) and four tenths (rods). Each row in the product represents an application of the distributive property of multiplication over addition.

Here is the final block arrangement on Building Mat 1–2a that represents the product of 1.3 bags of 2.4 ounces each:

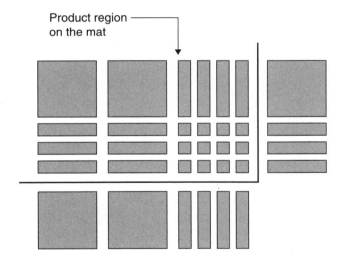

The product is found by counting the blocks in the product region according to their place value, which yields 2 ones, 10 tenths, and 12 hundredths. Students should simplify the product mentally without removing any blocks physically from the mat. Allow students with weak place value skills to trade the 10 tenths for a one and trade 10 hundredths for a tenth in order to find the final numerical answer—3 ones, 1 tenth, and 2 hundredths, or 3.12 ounces—but have them return the original blocks to the product region of the mat once the answer is found.

Students should write below Exercise 1 on Worksheet 1–2a the following sentence about their results: "1.3 bags of 2.4 ounces each of candy will be 3.12 ounces in all."

Answer Key for Worksheet 1–2a

Here are some possible sentences to write:

1. 1.3 bags of 2.4 ounces each of candy will be 3.12 ounces in all.

2. 2 cartons weighing 1.4 pounds each will weigh 2.8 pounds together. [Only 2 rows of blocks will be built in the product region.]

3. 0.4 of 1.2 yards equals 0.48 yard used for the tie. [Only 4 rows of blocks will be built in the product region.]

4. 1.2 of 1.5 liters of cream makes 1.8 liters of cream for the recipe.

5. 0.5 of 3 gallons makes 1.5 gallons of ice cream eaten at the party.

Building Mat 1–2a

16

WORKSHEET 1–2a   Name _____

Building Decimal Products   Date _____
with Base 10 Blocks

Build with base 10 blocks on Building Mat 1–2a to solve the word problems provided.
Below each exercise, write a word sentence about the result found for that word problem.

1. Marian has several bags of candy in the store display case. Each bag holds
    2.4 ounces of candy. A customer needs 1.3 bags for a cookie recipe. How many
    ounces of candy does the customer need?

2. There are 2 cartons. Each carton weighs 1.4 pounds. What is the total weight in
    pounds of the 2 cartons?

3. George, a tailor, has 1.2 yards of silk fabric. He will use 0.4 of that amount to
    make a silk tie for a customer. How many yards of the fabric will he use?

4. The chef has 1.5 liters of cream. A recipe requires 1.2 times that amount of
    cream. How much cream will he need for the recipe?

5. Lin bought 3 gallons of ice cream for her party. Her friends ate only 0.5 of the ice
    cream. How many gallons of ice cream were eaten at the party?

Activity 2: Pictorial Stage

Materials
> Worksheet 1–2b
> Red pencil and regular pencil

Procedure
1. Give each student a copy of Worksheet 1–2b and a red pencil. Students will draw short and long rectangles on L-frames on the worksheet to represent base 10 blocks on a building mat and to find products for the exercises.

2. For each exercise, after drawing the product on the L-frame students will write a number sentence about the product below the L-frame.

3. Students will then label different parts of the product region and transfer the labels and their descriptions to the vertical numerical format for the multiplication algorithm.

4. For each exercise, guide students to find a relationship between the digits of the two factors used and the arrangement of the rectangles in the L-frame.

5. Discuss Exercise 1 on Worksheet 1–2b in detail with students before having them work the other exercises on the worksheet. There will be three stages to apply to each exercise.

Here is a discussion for Exercise 1: "Luigi has 2.3 gallons of spaghetti sauce. He will need 1.4 times that amount to serve with spaghetti at a dinner. How many gallons of sauce will he need for the dinner?"

Drawing the Product Region
Following the repeated row method used in Activity 1 and drawing short and long rectangles to represent the ones, tenths, and hundredths, here is the final frame for Exercise 1 as drawn on Worksheet 1–2b:

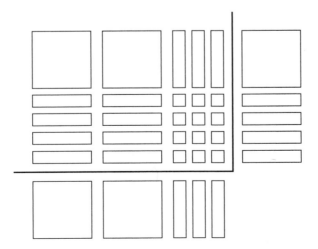

After all students have finished the drawing, have them count the shapes by their value to find the product; 2 ones, 11 tenths, and 12 hundredths make 3 ones, 2 tenths, and 2 hundredths, or 3.22. Do not show any trades on the drawing. Write an equation or number sentence below the frame to show the product found: "1.4 × 2.3 = 3.22 gallons of spaghetti sauce needed."

Labeling Parts of the Product Region

Next, discuss the four parts or smaller regions of shapes within the product region in Exercise 1. Separate the ones, tenths, and hundredths in the product region by drawing in red pencil a vertical bar between the left and right groups of shapes and a horizontal bar between the upper and lower levels of shapes. Also, label each of the four regions as shown (to stay in keeping with the order used in the traditional algorithm):

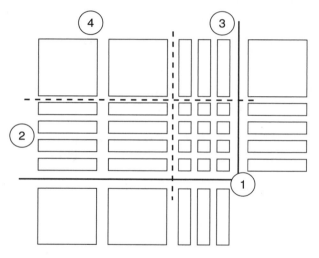

The arrangement of the shapes within each region of the example for Exercise 1 should be described in the following way: "Region 1 (lower right region) has four rows of 3 hundredths, or 12 hundredths; region 2 (lower left region) has four rows of 2 tenths, or 8 tenths; region 3 (upper right region) has one row of 3 tenths, or 3 tenths; and region 4 (upper left region) has one row of 2 ones, or 2 ones."

Note that in regions 3 and 4, there is only one row, which is determined by the 1 one to the right of the vertical bar of the L-frame (which is the 1 one in the multiplier). Some students will think there are three rows in region 3, but these are columns (vertical) and not rows (horizontal), as used in arrays in multiplication. Also notice that region 1 contains *hundredths* (as the product of tenths with tenths) and that region 3 (or the region above region 1) contains the next higher place value, *tenths*. In addition, each region on the left always contains the next-higher place value than that value found in the region immediately to the right. Students should now transfer the descriptions for the regions onto the vertical format to the right of the completed L-frame as shown. Notice where the decimal is placed in each partial product. The partial product for region 1 aligns at the right with the initial factors of the exercise, but the decimal for that first partial product is determined by that product's digits independent of the decimal positions in the factors above. The decimal position for region 1 then determines the place value alignment for the other partial products.

```
    2.3
  × 1.4      Regions:
  0.1  2   (1) 4 × 3 hundredths = 12 hundredths
  0.8      (2) 4 × 2 tenths = 8 tenths
  0.3      (3) 1 × 3 tenths = 3 tenths
  2.       (4) 1 × 2 ones = 2 ones
 ─────
  3.2  2
```

Pattern Search

After the regions of the finished frame for Exercise 1 have been transferred to the vertical format, ask students to compare the factors that were used to describe the shape arrangements in the four parts or smaller regions of the product region with the digits in the original two numbers (1.4 and 2.3) in Exercise 1. All digits in these two numbers must be unique so that the comparison will be easy for the students. They should notice that the factors in 4 × 3, 4 × 2, 1 × 3, and 1 × 2 use the same digits as those used in the original numbers, 1.4 and 2.3. Now have students draw red arrows on the original numbers to show the connection between these groups of numbers. The arrows should be drawn so that they do not cross each other and then labeled for the regions they represent.

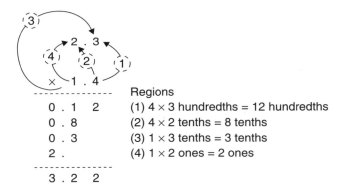

```
          Regions
  0 . 1  2   (1) 4 × 3 hundredths = 12 hundredths
  0 . 8      (2) 4 × 2 tenths = 8 tenths
  0 . 3      (3) 1 × 3 tenths = 3 tenths
  2 .        (4) 1 × 2 ones = 2 ones
  ─────
  3 . 2  2
```

Have students repeat these three stages with the other exercises on Worksheet 1–2b. Exercise 3 will need only two regions of blocks; otherwise, the procedure remains the same. Emphasize the pattern of the arrows.

It is recommended that the four rows of partial products not be collapsed into two rows at this time. (Regions 1 and 2 are typically written as one row, and regions 3 and 4 are written as a second row in the traditional algorithm.) There is no need to do so mathematically, because students are no longer expected to multiply extremely large numbers by hand. It will also postpone the regroupings students have to do until they add at the end. The traditional multiplication algorithm is quite complex. Students need to go through the stages described here slowly so they will understand the process clearly. This entire development normally requires several class periods in order for most students to comprehend all the steps well. Once students see the pattern in the arrows for multiplying two-digit numbers by two-digit numbers, they will be able to extend the pattern to three-digit numbers as well. The arrow-region procedure reflects the place value changes that occur during multiplication and accounts for the directions concerning "column shifting" that have been used by teachers in the past.

Answer Key for Worksheet 1–2b

1. $1.4 \times 2.3 = 3.22$ gallons of spaghetti sauce needed

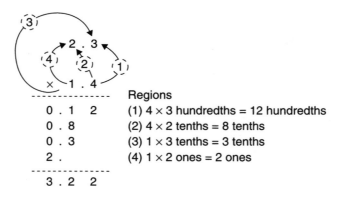

0 . 1	2
0 . 8	
0 . 3	
2 .	

3 . 2 2

Regions
(1) 4×3 hundredths = 12 hundredths
(2) 4×2 tenths = 8 tenths
(3) 1×3 tenths = 3 tenths
(4) 1×2 ones = 2 ones

2. $1.3 \times 2.1 = 2.73$ gallons of gas used

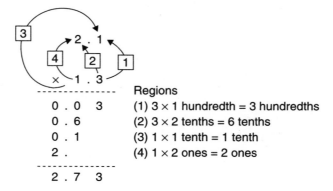

0 . 0 3
0 . 6
0 . 1
2 .

2 . 7 3

Regions
(1) 3×1 hundredth = 3 hundredths
(2) 3×2 tenths = 6 tenths
(3) 1×1 tenth = 1 tenth
(4) 1×2 ones = 2 ones

3. $3 \times 2.5 = 7.5$ liters of water in 3 buckets [only 2 regions of blocks needed]

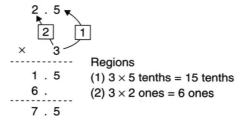

1 . 5
6 .

7 . 5

Regions
(1) 3×5 tenths = 15 tenths
(2) 3×2 ones = 6 ones

4. $2.4 \times 3.5 = 8.4$ meters of fabric used in all

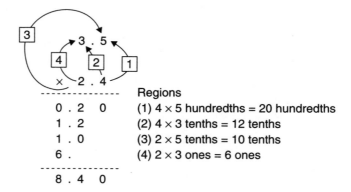

0 . 2 0
1 . 2
1 . 0
6 .

8 . 4 0

Regions
(1) 4×5 hundredths = 20 hundredths
(2) 4×3 tenths = 12 tenths
(3) 2×5 tenths = 10 tenths
(4) 2×3 ones = 6 ones

WORKSHEET 1–2b

Drawing Decimal Products
for Word Problems

Name _____

Date _____

Draw rectangles on each L-frame to find the product for each exercise. Below the frame, write a number sentence that shows the product. Follow your teacher's instructions to finish each exercise.

1. Luigi has 2.3 gallons of spaghetti sauce. He will need 1.4 times that amount to serve with spaghetti at a dinner. How many gallons of sauce will he need for the dinner?

2. Marsha's motorcycle tank holds 2.1 gallons of gas. If her weekend trip will use 1.3 tanks of the gas, how many gallons of gas will be used for the trip?

WORKSHEET 1–2b Continued

Name _____

Date _____

3. A bucket holds 2.5 liters of water. How many liters of water will 3 buckets hold?

4. There are 3.5 meters of fabric on 1 bolt. Lily needs 2.4 bolts of fabric to make some curtains. How many meters of fabric will be used in all?

Activity 3: Independent Practice

Materials

Worksheet 1–2c
Red pencil and regular pencil

Procedure

Give each student a copy of Worksheet 1–2c and a red pencil. On the worksheet, students will work several exercises without drawing on L-frames. To check for understanding initially, have them reverse the labeling process used in Activity 2: they should draw the arrows first in red pencil, then use the arrow information to identify and record the region equations needed to find the partial products of the vertical algorithm.

For the example of a one-digit multiplier in Exercise 1, to work 6×3.4, arrow 1 will connect the 6 to the 4, which indicates the partial product 6×4 tenths = 24 tenths found in region 1. Arrow 1 represents ones multiplied by tenths, or complete copies of tenths. Arrow 2 will connect the 6 to the 3, indicating the partial product 6×3 ones = 18 ones. Applying the place value pattern found in Activity 2, ones are used for region 2 since ones are the next higher place value to the left of the tenths in region 1. When the 24 tenths and 18 ones are recorded and combined, the final product will be 20.4.

For the example of a two-digit multiplier in Exercise 2, when working 0.17×3.2, arrow 1 will connect the 7 to the 2, which indicates the partial product 7×2 thousandths = 14 thousandths. The blocks in region 1 will be thousandths because we are finding a hundredth of a tenth, which will be a thousandth of a whole. Arrow 2 will connect the 7 to the 3, indicating the partial product 7×3 hundredths = 21 hundredths, the next higher place value from thousandths. Arrow 3 will connect the 1 to the 2 for 1×2 hundredths = 2 hundredths. In this example, arrow 3 represents the group *above* the thousandths in region 1 of the L-frame, so region 3 must be hundredths. Finally arrow 4 will connect the 1 to the 3 for 1×3 tenths = 3 tenths. Region 4 contains tenths since region 3 to the right contains hundredths. When the partial products (14 thousandths, 21 hundredths, 2 hundredths, and 3 tenths) are recorded and combined, the final product will be 0.544.

The remaining exercises are word problems to be worked using the vertical notation of the algorithm that was developed in Activity 2. Below each word problem, students should record an equation that states the product found. Encourage students to find the partial products mentally, but allow them to continue drawing arrows or writing equations for the partial products to the right of the vertical notation if they find that helpful. After they become proficient in finding the partial products, they will no longer need to draw the arrows or record the region equations for the partial products.

Answer Key for Worksheet 1–2c

1. 20.4 (arrows are discussed in the text)

2. 0.544 (arrows are discussed in the text)

Be sure to keep the multiplier as the first factor in each equation below.

3. 6×2.8 pounds = 16.8 pounds of cheese

4. 13×2.5 kilograms = 32.5 kilograms of birdseed

5. $9 \times \$1.45 = \$13.05$ total for gas

6. $2.8 \times 2.8 = 7.84$ square meters, closest to 8 square meters

Possible Testing Errors That May Occur for This Objective

- The correct algorithm for multiplication is applied, but an incorrect multiplication fact is used when finding one of the partial products. For example, in 6×3.4, 6×4 tenths is recorded as the partial product 27 tenths instead of 24 tenths.

- All partial products are right-justified. For example, in 2.3×4.5, when finding the partial product for 2×5, students record the amount as 10 hundredths instead of 10 tenths.

- The two original factors in the problem are added instead of multiplied. For example, 1.3×2.4 is incorrectly computed as $1.3 + 2.4$.

WORKSHEET 1–2c   Name _____

Finding Products with Decimals   Date _____

To work Exercises 1 and 2, draw arrows with a red pencil. Then write equations to the right for the partial products in order to find the partial products and their sum for each exercise.

1.
$$\begin{array}{r} 3\ .\ 4 \\ \times\qquad 6 \\ \hline \end{array}$$

2.
$$\begin{array}{r} 3\ .\ 2 \\ \times 0\ .\ 1\quad 7 \\ \hline \end{array}$$

Solve Exercises 3 through 6 by using the multiplication algorithm. Show your steps on the back of the worksheet. Below each word problem, write a number sentence that shows the answer.

3. There are 6 display trays at the deli counter. Each tray holds 2.8 pounds of cheese. How many pounds of cheese total are on display at the deli counter?

4. Luis has 13 bags of birdseed for his bird feeder. Each bag weighs 2.5 kilograms. What is the weight of all 13 bags together?

5. Kandi bought 9 gallons of gasoline for her car at $1.45 per gallon. How much did she pay for the gasoline?

6. The area of a square is 8 square meters. Which best represents the length of a side of the square: 2.8 meters or 3.1 meters?

Objective 3
Divide decimals to solve word problems.

The division algorithm for decimal numbers needs to be developed carefully for students. The estimation of quotient digits and the backward trading or regrouping between place values are quite difficult for them. The activities described next present a method for introducing two- and three-digit dividends (ones, tenths, hundredths) with one- and two-digit divisors (ones, tenths). The divisor will represent the set being removed or copied from the dividend several times. It will be assumed here that the multiplication algorithm of decimals has already been mastered.

Activity 1: Manipulative Stage

Materials
> Set of base 10 blocks per pair of students (6 flats, 40 rods, 40 small cubes)
> Building Mat 1–3a
> Worksheet 1–3a
> Regular pencil

Procedure
1. Give each pair of students a set of base 10 blocks (6 flats, 40 rods, 40 small cubes) and Building Mat 1–3a. The building mat should be positioned so that the short bar is vertical and at the left side of the mat and the long bar is horizontal and at the top of the mat.

2. Give each student a copy of Worksheet 1–3a.

3. Have students model each worksheet exercise with their blocks. Then they should record below the exercise a word sentence that shows the results found on the building mat.

4. Students should look at the blocks in each row of the dividend region of the building mat in order to determine the quotient. Always have students use proper place value language when verbally describing their steps to the class.

5. Discuss Exercise 1 on Worksheet 1–3a in detail with the class before allowing partners to work the other exercises on their own.

Consider Exercise 1 on Worksheet 1–3a: "Marge has 3.18 ounces of fudge in the store display case. A customer wants several bags of the fudge with 1.5 ounces in each bag. How many complete bags will Marge be able to prepare for the customer?"

Have students place 1 flat and 5 rods along the left side of the vertical bar of the L-frame for the divisor 1.5. The flat should be placed closest to the corner of the L-frame and the rods placed toward the end of the vertical bar. Then place 3 flats, 1 rod, and 8 small cubes below the horizontal bar of the frame near the bottom edge of the mat for the dividend 3.18 (see the illustration for initial block placement). The interior of the L-frame will contain the dividend each time. Eventually the quotient will be placed above the horizontal bar of the L-frame.

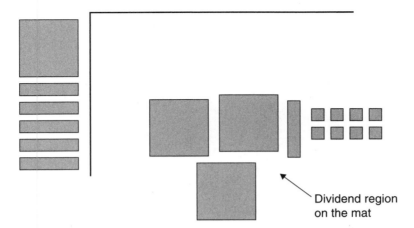

Dividend region
on the mat

The divisor represents the set of blocks to be made or copied, using the blocks from the dividend. Students should try to make complete copies of the entire divisor set first. Two complete copies of the one (flat) and the five tenths (rods) can be made inside the L-frame, but a one will need to be traded for 10 tenths first in order to have enough tenths for the copies. After the two complete copies are made, 1 tenth and the 8 hundredths will remain in the dividend but not yet used in the new arrangement.

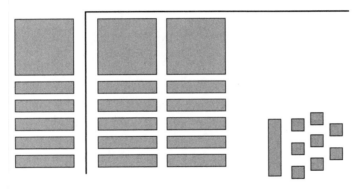

Students should now try to make a tenth of a copy of each block in the divisor. A tenth (rod) represents 1-tenth of the one (flat) in the divisor, and a hundredth (cube) represents 1-tenth of each tenth (rod) in the divisor. Hence, the remaining tenth should be placed beside the ones in the top row of the arrangement in the dividend, and each hundredth should be placed in a row of tenths in the dividend. So 1 tenth and 5 hundredths are 1-tenth of the divisor, which is 1 one and 5 tenths. Three hundredths will remain unused from the total dividend.

Now that all possible complete and partial (tenth) copies have been made, the quotient may be shown above the top bar of the L-frame. A flat or one should be placed above each column of blocks in the dividend that makes a complete copy of the divisor, and a rod or tenth should be placed above the column of blocks that shows 1-tenth of a copy of the divisor. Thus, the final quotient should have 2 ones and 1 tenth, or 2.1. Here is the final block arrangement on Building Mat 1–3a that represents 2.1 bags of 1.5 ounces each made from a total of 3.18 ounces with 0.03 ounce left unused:

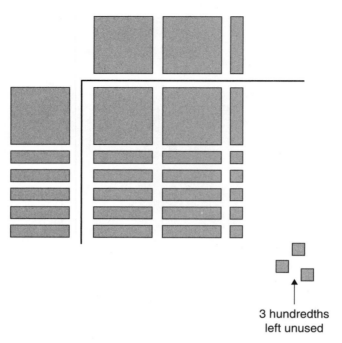

3 hundredths
left unused

Below Exercise 1 on Worksheet 1–3a, students should record a word sentence about their result, such as the following: "3.18 ounces of fudge will make 2.1 bags of 1.5 ounces per bag with 0.03 ounce left unused. So 2 complete bags can actually be made for the customer."

Answer Key for Worksheet 1–3a

1. 3.18 ounces of fudge will make 2.1 bags of 1.5 ounces per bag with 0.03 ounce left unused. So 2 complete bags can actually be made for the customer.

2. 3.0 pounds of salmon will make 1.5 packages at 2 pounds per package.

3. $1.15 will buy 2.3 pounds of carrots at $0.50 per pound.

4. 1.2 yards of fabric will make 3 ties, using 0.4 yard per tie.

5. 3.0 ounces of cream will make 1.2 servings of the dessert, using 2.5 ounces per dessert.

Building Mat 1–3a

30

WORKSHEET 1–3a

Building Decimal Quotients
with Base 10 Blocks

Name _____

Date _____

Build with base 10 blocks on Building Mat 1–3a to solve the word problems provided. Below each exercise, write a word sentence about the result found for that word problem.

1. Marge has 3.18 ounces of fudge in the store display case. A customer wants several bags of the fudge with 1.5 ounces in each bag. How many complete bags will Marge be able to prepare for the customer?

2. The fishmonger has 3.0 pounds of salmon to put in individual packages. He wants to cut and wrap 2 pounds of salmon in each package. How many packages will he be able to make, including a partial package?

3. Sally has $1.15 and wants to buy carrots that sell for $0.50 per pound. How many pounds will Sally be able to buy if she spends all her money?

4. George, a tailor, has 1.2 yards of silk fabric. He needs 0.4 yard to make a silk tie. How many ties can he make with the fabric?

5. The chef has 3.0 ounces of cream. She needs 2.5 ounces of cream to make a single serving of a dessert. How many servings, including tenths of a serving, can be made?

Activity 2: Pictorial Stage

Materials
Worksheet 1–3b
Red pencil and regular pencil

Procedure
1. Give each student a red pencil and a copy of Worksheet 1–3b.

2. Students will draw diagrams to find quotients for word problems. The drawings should look just like the finished mat in the example discussed for Activity 1.

3. After drawing the diagram for each exercise on Worksheet 1–3b, students will write a number sentence or equation below the diagram to record the results found.

4. Students will label the parts of the shared dividend and transfer the labels to the box format for the division algorithm. For each exercise, the box format will be recorded to the right of the diagram.

5. Students will look for patterns among the digits of the divisor and quotient that will help them identify the partial products involved in the division process.

6. Guide students through Exercise 1 before allowing them to proceed to others independently.

Exercise 1 on Worksheet 1–3b provides this example: "Pete has 3.14 pounds of bananas. He wants to bundle them into bags of 1.3 pounds each for his fresh produce display. How many bags, including tenths of a bag, will he be able to make?"

Drawing the Dividend Region
Following the copying method used in Activity 1 and drawing large squares for ones and long and short rectangles to represent the tenths and hundredths, respectively, here is the initial frame for the problem in Exercise 1:

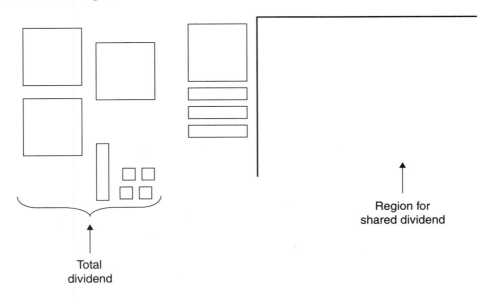

Total
dividend

Region for
shared dividend

Note that the dividend shapes are drawn to the left of the L-frame this time instead of below the L-frame, as was done in Activity 1. This minimizes the need to erase. The large square and three long rectangles drawn immediately to the left of the vertical bar of the L-frame represent the divisor, 1.3, or the set to be copied.

A row of shapes must eventually be drawn under the L-frame to correspond to each of the shapes in the divisor. Shapes in the dividend at the left are marked out (/) in regular pencil as they are redrawn under the L-frame. Trades are shown by marking out (×) shapes in red pencil and then drawing new, smaller shapes in regular pencil.

Students must copy the divisor under the L-frame. A complete copy cannot be made at first because there are not enough tenths available. So a one (large square) should be marked out in red pencil and traded for 10 new tenths (long rectangles) in the dividend. A complete copy (as a column) of 1 one and 3 tenths can then be drawn twice, so 2 ones and 6 tenths should be marked out in the dividend shapes at the left to show the transfer to the L-frame.

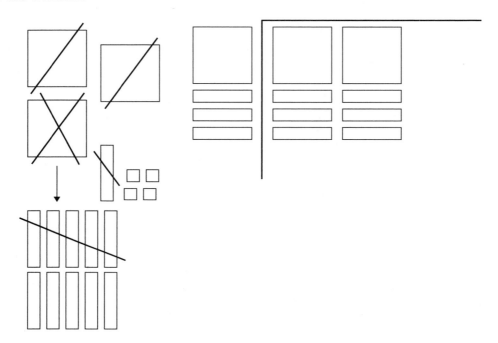

Since another complete copy of the divisor cannot be made, students should try to make partial copies. To do this, they need to compare the largest shape (long rectangle) remaining in the dividend to the largest shape (large square) in the divisor. Since the long rectangle represents 1 tenth of the large square, this indicates that a tenth of a copy of the divisor can probably be made. A tenth of a copy requires 1 tenth (long rectangle) and 3 hundredths (small squares), which equal a tenth of 1 one and 3 tenths, respectively. One partial copy can be drawn immediately, but a tenth in the dividend must be traded for 10 hundredths first before another three partial copies can be drawn under the L-frame. Two hundredths will remain in the dividend unused. These should be circled in the dividend and labeled.

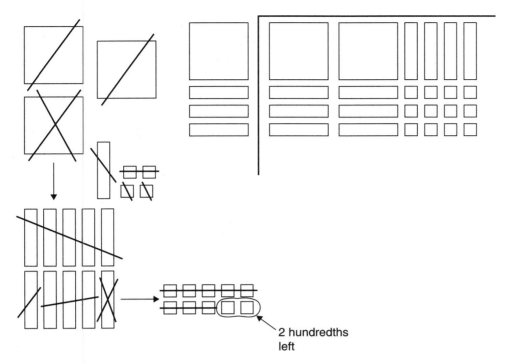

Now that the complete and partial copies of the divisor have been drawn under the L-frame, the quotient needs to be shown. A large square (one) should be drawn above the top bar of the L-frame over each complete copy, and a long rectangle (tenth) should be drawn over each tenth of a copy. The final quotient will contain 2 ones and 4 tenths, representing 2.4 copies of the divisor. This indicates that 2 complete bags and 0.4 of another bag of bananas could be made, excluding 0.02 of a pound of the original bananas. Here is the finished diagram for Exercise 1 on Worksheet 1–3b:

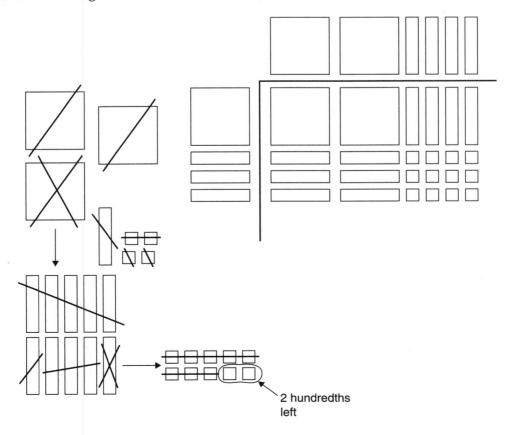

After all students have finished the drawing, they should write an equation below the frame to show the results: "3.14 ÷ 1.3 = 2.4 bags of bananas at 1.3 pounds each with 0.02 of a pound left unbagged." Draw frames for the other exercises on Worksheet 1–3b before continuing to the next step of this activity.

Labeling Parts of the Dividend Region

After drawing frames for all exercises on Worksheet 1–3b, return to the frame for Exercise 1. Label and discuss the four regions of shapes below the L-frame. Have students draw a vertical red bar to separate the complete copies from the partial copies. They should also draw a horizontal red bar between the upper level and lower level of shapes below the L-frame. Label the lower left region of tenths as region 1, the upper left region of ones as region 2, the lower right region of hundredths as region 3, and the upper right region of tenths as region 4. (There may not be four regions produced in every exercise, but the numbering always begins with the left or lower left region.)

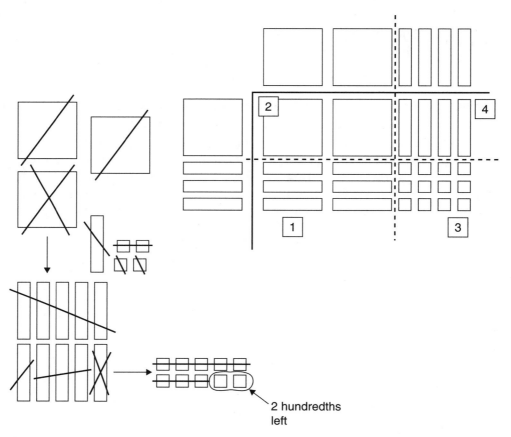

The arrangement of the shapes within each part under the L-frame of the example should be described in the following way: "Region 1 has 3 rows of 2 tenths, or 6 tenths; region 2 has 1 row of 2 ones, or 2 ones; region 3 has 3 rows of 4 hundredths, or 12 hundredths; and region 4 has 1 row of 4 tenths, or 4 tenths." Students should transfer these descriptions onto the box format to the right of the completed diagram of Exercise 1 as shown:

```
                    2 . 4        Regions
        1 . 3 ) 3 . 1  4        (1) 3 × 2 tenths = 6 tenths
             − 2 . 6            (2) 1 × 2 ones = 2 ones
             ──────
               0 . 5  4        (3) 3 × 4 hundredths = 12 hundredths
             − 0 . 5  2        (4) 1 × 4 tenths = 4 tenths
             ──────
               0 . 0  2        left unused
```

Because the 3 tenths in the divisor, along with the 1 one, must be copied in order to have a complete copy, the tenths in the divisor and the tenths in the dividend should be underlined in red pencil. This will indicate where the complete copies begin in the quotient and where the decimal point should be placed. Notice that regions directly above each other under the L-frame are recorded as one combined subtraction step in the box format. This follows the practice of our standard algorithm for division. If necessary for some students, each region might be subtracted from the dividend separately. Also note that the decimal point in the dividend continues down through the partial products being subtracted. Now repeat the labeling and transfer process for the other exercises on Worksheet 1–3b. Exercises 2 and 4 will involve only partial copies, and Exercise 4 will require a hundredth of a copy, as well as a tenth of a copy.

Pattern Search

After all finished frames have been transferred to the box format, return to Exercise 1. Ask students to compare the factors that were used to describe the shape arrangements in the four regions with the digits in the divisor and quotient (1.3 and 2.4) in the example. All digits in these two numbers are unique, so the comparison should be easy for the students. They should notice that the factors in 3 × 2, 1 × 2, 3 × 4, and 1 × 4 use the same digits as those used in the 1.3 and 2.4. Now have students draw arrows on the divisor and quotient to show the connection between these groups of numbers. The arrows should be drawn and labeled for the regions they represent.

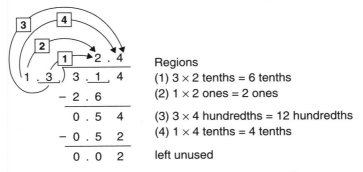

Have students examine all the other exercises on Worksheet 1–3b that they have worked at this stage of development, in order to see if their digits have the same relationship as shown in the example of Exercise 1. The pattern should hold for all the problems. Thus, students should draw and label arrows on the rest of the exercises as they have done for Exercise 1.

At this point, discuss how division is different from the other three operations in that students must *estimate* the first digit or left-most digit of the quotient, then compare the product of that digit and the divisor against the first left-most digits within the dividend. As in the case of Exercise 1, students have to look at the 3 ones and 1 tenth in the dividend to decide what factor is needed in the quotient to pair with the 1 one and 3 tenths in the divisor. The choice, 3, for the quotient digit would be too high since the arrow pattern would yield the product, 3 ones and 9 tenths, which is more than the 3 ones and 1 tenth found in the dividend. So the better estimate for the quotient's first digit would be 2.

The traditional division algorithm is quite complex. Students need to go slowly through the stages described here so they will understand the process clearly. When the division algorithm is taught for the first time, this entire development usually requires several class periods in order for most students to comprehend all the steps well.

Answer Key for Worksheet 1–3b

1. 3.14 ÷ 1.3 = 2.4 bags of bananas at 1.3 pounds each with 0.02 of a pound left unbagged. [The diagram and box format are shown in the text.]

2. 1.2 ÷ 2.3 = 0.5 bag of birdseed at 2.3 pounds per bag with 0.05 of a pound not included. [There were 0 complete copies made.]

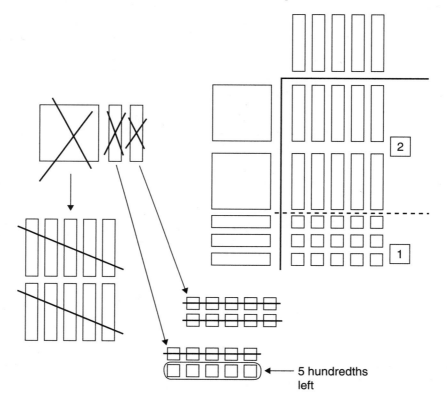

5 hundredths left

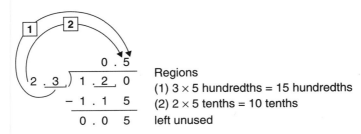

Regions
(1) 3 × 5 hundredths = 15 hundredths
(2) 2 × 5 tenths = 10 tenths
left unused

3. 1.2 ÷ 0.3 = 4 pencils bought at $0.30 per pencil. [Since no pennies were involved, no hundredths were drawn in the diagram.]

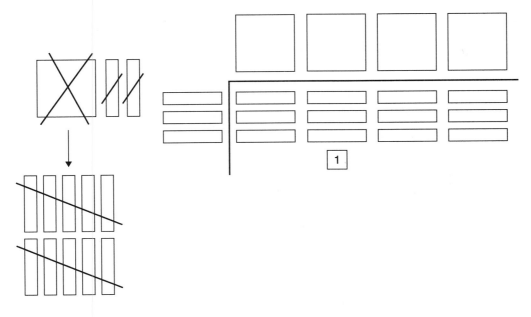

Region
(1) 3 × 4 tenths = 12 tenths

4. 1.26 ÷ 2 = 0.63 of a package of hamburger at 2 pounds per package.

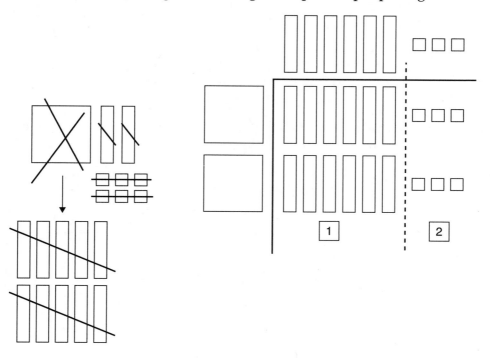

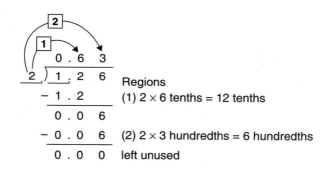

Regions

(1) 2 × 6 tenths = 12 tenths

(2) 2 × 3 hundredths = 6 hundredths

left unused

WORKSHEET 1–3b

Drawing Decimal Quotients

Name _____

Date _____

Draw rectangles on each L-frame to find the quotient for each exercise. Below the frame, write a number sentence that shows the results. Follow your teacher's instructions to finish each exercise.

1. Pete has 3.14 pounds of bananas. He wants to bundle them into bags of 1.3 pounds each for his fresh produce display. How many bags, including tenths of a bag, will he be able to make?

2. Juan has only 1.2 pounds of birdseed left. The original bag contained 2.3 pounds. What fractional part of the original bag does he have left?

40

Name _____

Date _____

3. Lucy has $1.20 and wants to buy pencils that sell for $0.30 per pencil (including tax). How many pencils will Lucy be able to buy if she spends all her money?

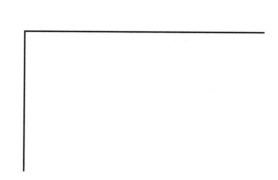

4. The butcher wants to make a 2-pound package of hamburger. She only has 1.26 pounds of hamburger. How much of a package will she be able to make?

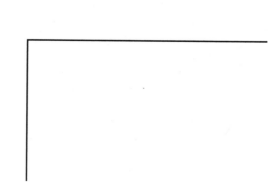

Activity 3: Independent Practice

Materials

    Worksheet 1–3c

    Red pencil and regular pencil

Procedure

Give each student a red pencil and a copy of Worksheet 1–3c. Students will work several problems without drawing on frames. Exercise 1 will show the quotient already written over the dividend but no partial products recorded below the dividend. Students should first draw and number the arrows. Then, using those arrows, they should write the region factor equations to the right of the problem and write the region products under the dividend to subtract. Exercises 2 through 4 are word problems to be worked with the box format. Encourage students to find the region factor equations mentally, but if necessary, allow them to continue drawing arrows and writing the equations beside the division box.

    In all exercises, have students underline in red pencil the right-most digit in the divisor, as well as the left-most digits in the dividend that represent the first amount to be used for copies of the divisor. For example, in $2.19 \div 0.7$, 2.1 and 0.7 should be underlined in red to show that 2 ones and 1 tenth in the dividend must first be used (through trading) to make copies of the 7 tenths in the divisor. Since three complete copies can be made, the left-most digit in the quotient should be marked as the ones place.

Answer Key for Worksheet 1–3c

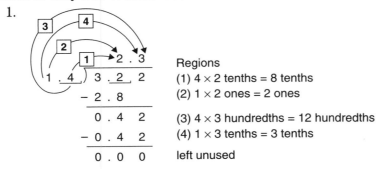

1.

    Regions

    (1) 4×2 tenths = 8 tenths

    (2) 1×2 ones = 2 ones

    (3) 4×3 hundredths = 12 hundredths

    (4) 1×3 tenths = 3 tenths

    left unused

2. $5.7 \div 1.5 = 3.8$ packages of cheese at 1.5 pounds per package

3. $3.2 \div 8 = 0.4$ of a carton of yogurt left

4. $\$32.10 \div \$5.35 = 6$ CDs at \$5.35 each

Possible Testing Errors That May Occur for This Objective

- Students do not apply the division or separation/copying process described in the story situation. Rather, they incorrectly choose multiplication to solve the problem.

- The dividend and divisor numbers are reversed in the box format. For example, instead of finding $4.5 \div 6.1$, students will compute $6.1 \div 4.5$, using the lesser number as the divisor.

- An incorrect multiplication fact is used to find a partial product during the division process.

- After subtracting the first partial product found and getting a remainder, students drop that initial remainder when finding the second partial product. For example, in $2.29 \div 7$, 1 tenth will remain; this tenth is ignored, and only the 9 hundredths are divided by 7 instead of the 19 hundredths.

WORKSHEET 1–3c   Name _____
Dividing with Decimal Numbers   Date _____

In Exercise 1, draw arrows with a red pencil. Then write factor equations to the right of the box in order to find the partial products to subtract during division. Be sure to number the arrows and the equations correctly.

1.
$$1.4 \overline{\smash{)}3.2\ 2}\ \ ^{2\ .\ 3}$$

Solve Exercises 2 through 4 by using the box method of the division algorithm. Show your steps on the back of the worksheet. Below each word problem, write a number sentence that shows the answer.

2. A block of cheese weighs 5.7 pounds. How many packages of sliced cheese can be made from this block if each package is to weigh 1.5 pounds?

3. If Rachel has 3.2 ounces left from an 8-ounce carton of yogurt, what fractional part of the original carton does she have left?

4. Bert bought some CDs for a total cost of $32.10. If each CD sells for $5.35, how many CDs did Bert buy?

Objective 4
Estimate solutions to multistepped word problems by rounding with decimals.

When using estimation, the general principle is to have students round numbers to levels
that will allow them to mentally apply the various facts of the four operations and not have
to regroup. Rounding each number to its highest place value is usually the best approach.
Any rounding that causes a number to round to zero should be avoided unless the context
of the situation allows it. In the following activities, students will be required to set up the
series of equations needed to solve each multistepped word problem or to find a single
equation that combines all the steps together. The original numbers in the equations will be
rounded so that students may mentally estimate the answer to each computation.

Activity 1: Manipulative Stage

Materials
    Building Mat 1–4a for each pair of students
    50 small counters for each pair of students (same color or same style)
    Worksheet 1–4a
    Regular pencil

Procedure
1. Provide each pair of students with a building mat, counters, and two copies of
   Worksheet 1–4a, which involves one- to four-digit decimal numbers or whole
   numbers in two-step problems.

2. The numbers needed for each problem should be shown on the mat and then
   rounded. The rows on the mat are only for rounding, not for computation. For
   convenience, if two numbers need to be added or subtracted, they should be
   shown on the top two rows of the mat. If a number will serve as a multiplier
   or a divisor, it should be shown on the bottom row.

3. Once the numbers are rounded, students will perform the required computations
   mentally, if possible, or with the appropriate written algorithms, if preferred.

4. Remind students that they may need to use "backward thinking" here; that is,
   they may have to think of the second or final step first before they can decide
   what the first step should be.

5. The two number sentences, which contain the rounded numbers and were used
   to solve a word problem, should be recorded below that exercise on Worksheet
   1–4a to show the estimated work. Also have students describe a numerical
   interval that contains the estimate they have found. (Intervals will vary.)

6. Guide students through the first exercise before they proceed to the others.

    Consider Exercise 1: "Kelly rode her bicycle for 7.8 kilometers on Friday and for 6.2 kilo-
meters on Saturday. Estimate how many kilometers she averaged per day for the two days."
    Have students place counters on the top two rows of Building Mat 1–4a to represent
7.8 kilometers and 6.2 kilometers. They should also place counters on the bottom row to
show the two days involved.

Tens	Ones	Tenths	Hundredths
	⦾ ⦾ ⦾ ⦾ ⦾ ⦾ ⦾	⦾ ⦾ ⦾ ⦾ ⦾ ⦾ ⦾ ⦾	
	⦾ ⦾ ⦾ ⦾ ⦾ ⦾	⦾ ⦾	
	⦾ ⦾		

Discuss the idea that the top two numbers need to be added together, then divided by the bottom number in order to find the average kilometers per day. Since the top two numbers have ones as their higher place value, both numbers should be rounded to the nearest one: 7.8 will round up to 8, and 6.2 will round down to 6. This should be shown on the building mat by removing the 8 tenths from the top row but bringing in a new ones counter on that same row. On the second row, only the 2 tenths need to be removed from the mat. Since the 2 in the bottom row will serve as a divisor and is already a 1-digit number in the ones place, it does not need to be rounded. Here is the final mat arrangement:

Tens	Ones	Tenths	Hundredths
	⦾ ⦾ ⦾ ⦾ ⦾ ⦾ ⦾ ⦾		
	⦾ ⦾ ⦾ ⦾ ⦾ ⦾		
	⦾ ⦾		

The rounded numbers are now ready to be computed mentally. It is possible to use facts for each step. The first step will be "8 + 6 = 14 kilometers total for 2 days," and the second step will be "14 ÷ 2 = 7 kilometers estimated per day." Students should record these two equations below Exercise 1 on Worksheet 1–4a. An interval for the estimated solution also needs to be written below the exercise. These will vary. One possibility might be, "Estimate is between 5 and 10 kilometers." Intervals should be reasonable. "Between 0 and 50 kilometers" would not be considered reasonable.

Answer Key for Worksheet 1–4a

1. 8 + 6 = 14 kilometers total for 2 days; 14 ÷ 2 = 7 kilometers estimated per day. Possible interval: Estimate is between 5 and 10 kilometers.

2. $10 + $10 = $20; $30 − $20 = $10 left in savings. Possible interval: Estimate is between $5 and $20.

3. 3 × $2 = $6; $6 + $3 = $9, estimated cost for both cheeses. Possible interval: Estimate is between $8 and $10.

4. 1 + 3 = 4 pounds; $4 ÷ 4 = $1, estimated cost per pound of apples. Possible interval: Estimate is between $0.50 and $1.50.

5. 80 ÷ 4 = 20 miles estimated per day; 20 ÷ 5 = 4 miles estimated per hour. Possible interval: Estimate is between 3 and 6 miles per hour.

Building Mat 1-4a

Tens	Ones	Tenths	Hundredths

WORSHEET 1–4a   Name _____

Estimating with Multistepped   Date _____
Problems

Use Building Mat 1–4a and counters to round the numbers in each exercise. Compute mentally with the rounded numbers to estimate a solution for the problem, and write the final equations below the exercise. Write an interval that contains the estimated solution.

1. Kelly rode her bicycle for 7.8 kilometers on Friday and for 6.2 kilometers on Saturday. Estimate how many kilometers she averaged per day for the two days.

2. Lanny has $32.75 saved up. He wants to buy a new CD for $12.50 and a cassette tape for $9.95, including tax. Estimate how much money he will have left after the two purchases.

3. Mario bought 2.6 pounds of cheddar cheese that cost $1.80 per pound. He also bought some swiss cheese for $2.59. About how much did he pay for all the cheese?

4. Susan bought 1.4 pounds of gala apples, then another 2.7 pounds of apples. The total cost of the apples was $3.65. About how much per pound did the apples cost?

5. The Johnsons hiked 79.5 miles over 4 days. If they hiked approximately 6 hours per day, estimate their hiking rate in miles per hour.

Activity 2: Pictorial Stage

Materials

Worksheet 1–4b
Worksheet 1–4c
Red pencil and regular pencil

Procedure

1. Give each student a copy of Worksheet 1–4b and a red pencil. The worksheet contains small frames that look like the earlier building mat. Above each frame is a blank writing space for writing the initial numbers needed to solve the problem.

2. Each student will solve problems by completing the frames on her or his own worksheet but might share results with a partner. Instead of placing counters on the mat to show numbers, students will now draw circles in the columns of the frames. If a number must round up to the next place value, students should mark out the extra circles in the columns to the right of the new place value column, and draw a new circle in the selected place value column. If a number must round down to a certain place value, then the extra circles in the columns to the right of that place value will just be marked out in red pencil.

3. Also give each student a copy of Worksheet 1–4c, which contains several word problems involving up to four-digit numbers. Below each word problem, students will record the two equations used to estimate the solution and then write a final equation that combines the two equations.

4. Guide students through Exercise 1 before allowing them to proceed to others independently.

Here is Exercise 1 from Worksheet 1–4c to discuss with students as an example: "George has 17.9 ounces of sunflower seeds in a bag. If he triples this amount, then adds 8.5 more ounces to the bag, about how many ounces will he have in all?"

Have students write the numbers 17.9, 3, and 8.5 in the blank above the first frame on Worksheet 1–4b. These are the numbers needed to solve the problem. Students should draw circles in the appropriate columns to represent the three numbers. Since 3 serves as a multiplier, draw it on the bottom row of the frame. The top two rows may be used for 17.9 and 8.5. Here is how the frame will look initially:

17.9, 3, 8.5

Tens	Ones	Tenths	Hundredths
○	○ ○ ○ ○ ○ ○ ○	○ ○ ○ ○ ○ ○ ○ ○ ○	
	○ ○ ○ ○ ○ ○ ○ ○	○ ○ ○ ○ ○	
	○ ○ ○		

Students should now decide how to round each number so that mental facts might be used to compute an estimate. They should round 17.9 to the nearest ten; this will be 2 tens, or 20, since there are 7 ones. With a red pencil, students should draw a new circle in the tens column and mark out all the circles in the ones and tenths columns.

They might round 8.5 to the nearest one or to the nearest ten. Since it will need to combine with the tens number for 17.9, it is better to round to the nearest ten, which will be 1 ten, or 10, since there are 8 ones. In red pencil, students should draw a new circle in the tens column and mark out all the circles in the ones and tenths columns. Since the number 3 is already a one-digit whole number, it will not be rounded. The final frame appears as follows:

17.9, 3, 8.5

Tens	Ones	Tenths	Hundredths
○ ◯	⊖⊖⊖⊖ ⊖⊖⊖	⊖⊖⊖⊖⊖ ⊖⊖⊖⊖	
◯	⊖⊖⊖⊖⊖ ⊖⊖⊖	⊖⊖⊖⊖⊖	
	○ ○ ○		

Once students have rounded their numbers, they should write the equations needed to solve the problem. These equations should be recorded below Exercise 1 on Worksheet 1–4c. The equations are as follows: "$3 \times 20 = 60$" and "$60 + 10 = 70$ ounces total of seed estimated in the bag." Write the factors in the first equation in correct order; 3×20 means 3 of 20. Discuss the facts used: $3 \times 2 = 6$ and $6 + 1 = 7$. Students should also combine the two equations into one equation and record it as well: "$(3 \times 20) + 10 = 70$ ounces estimated." This is excellent preparation for future studies in algebra.

Answer Key for Worksheet 1–4c

1. $3 \times 20 = 60$; $60 + 10 = 70$ ounces estimated for seed in bag; $(3 \times 20) + 10 = 70$ ounces estimated

2. $\$40 - \$10 = \$30$; $\$30 + \$20 = \$50$ estimated in savings; $(\$40 - \$10) + \$20 = \$50$ estimated

3. $4 \times \$30 = \$120$; $\$120 + \$60 = \$180$, estimate for two jobs; $(4 \times \$30) + \$60 = \$180$ estimated

4. $10 \div 2 = 5$ packages; $5 \times \$3 = \$15$, estimated earnings; $(10 \div 2) \times \$3 = \$15$ estimated

50

WORKSHEET 1–4b

Name _____

Drawing to Estimate with
Multistepped Problems

Date _____

Base 10 Drawing Frames

1. _____

Tens	Ones	Tenths	Hundredths

2. _____

Tens	Ones	Tenths	Hundredths

WORKSHEET 1–4b Continued

Name _____

Date _____

3. _____

Tens	Ones	Tenths	Hundredths

4. _____

Tens	Ones	Tenths	Hundredths

52

Drawing to Estimate with
Multistepped Problems

Name _____

Date _____

To solve each word problem, draw circles on a frame on Worksheet 1–4b to show each
number. Then round as needed in order to use facts when solving. Below the word problem on this worksheet, record the final estimating equations, as well as a combination
equation.

1. George has 17.9 ounces of sunflower seeds in a bag. If he triples this amount and
   then adds 8.5 more ounces to the bag, about how many ounces will he have in all?

2. Chui had $38.25 in her savings account. She took out $11.50 to go to a movie.
   A week later, she received $15.00 for a birthday gift and put it into her savings
   account. Estimate the new balance in the savings account.

3. Lana earned $27.50 each week for 4 weeks of baby-sitting. She also earned $63.95
   total working at her aunt's candy store that same month. About how much did
   Lana earn from both jobs?

4. The grocer has 9.8 pounds of hamburger to put into 2-pound packages. If each
   package sells for $3.45, estimate how much the grocer will earn.

Activity 3: Independent Practice

Materials
Worksheet 1–4d
Regular pencil

Procedure
Students work independently to complete Worksheet 1–4d. When all are finished, discuss the results.

Answer Key for Worksheet 1–4d
1. B

2. C

3. B

4. A

5. D

Possible Testing Errors That May Occur for This Objective
- One or more numbers are rounded incorrectly.

- A fact error is made for one of the operations involved in the problem.

- In a two-step problem, students use only two of the three given numbers; that is, they perform only one of the required steps.

- The wrong operations are applied. For example, if multiplication and subtraction are needed, students might use multiplication and addition. This is generally caused by a misunderstanding of the meanings of the operations.

54

Name _____
Estimating with Multistepped Problems   Date _____

Show your work on another sheet of paper. Circle the best answer choice for each problem on this worksheet. Be ready to discuss how you solved each problem with your classmates. Remember to try to round numbers so that facts may be used mentally.

1. A bakery had 12.6 pounds of fudge to sell. It sold 5 boxes containing 1.8 pounds each on Monday. Find the best estimate of the number of pounds of fudge remaining to be sold on Tuesday.

    A. 2   B. 3   C. 5   D. 7

2. Mr. Jeffers bought a digital camera on sale plus a flash attachment for $454.64 total. The discount off the original camera price was $194.30, and the flash attachment cost $89.99. Which is the best estimate of the original price of the camera?

    A. $400   B. $500   C. $600   D. $700

3. Amy sold $32.10 in candy, $14.80 in notebook paper, and $8.50 in pencils at the school store. What is the best interval for an estimate of her total sales?

    A. Less than $45

    B. Between $45 and $55

    C. Between $55 and $65

    D. More than $65

4. Eli has 8.25 yards of fabric for making some vests. Each vest requires 1.75 yards. He wants to sell each vest for $28.95. About how much should he expect to earn from selling the vests?

    A. $120   B. $180   C. $240   D. $300

5. Bill earned $18.50 each week for 2.5 weeks at one store, and then he earned $14.65 for one week at another store. Which expression is a reasonable estimate of his total earnings from the two stores?

    A. (2 × $20) + $10

    B. 3 × ($20 + $10)

    C. ($20 ÷ 2) + $10

    D. (3 × $20) + $10

Objective 5
Add fractions or mixed numbers to solve word problems.

Students have great difficulty transferring from their comfortable whole number world to the less familiar fraction world. They need many experiences involving fractional measurements. The use of manipulatives assists students in the adding or combining of different fractional part sizes by showing the need for a common denominator.

Activity 1: Manipulative Stage

Materials
> Set of fraction bars per pair of students (Pattern 1–5a)
> Building Mat 1–5a per pair of students
> Worksheet 1–5a
> Regular pencil

Procedure
1. For each set of fraction bars, prepare and cut out five copies of Pattern 1–5a. The whole bar on Building Mat 1–5a should be congruent to the whole bar on Pattern 1–5a. If preferred, each type of fraction might be colored to match the corresponding type in the teacher's set of fraction bars.

2. Give each pair of students a set of fraction bars, one copy of Building Mat 1–5a, and two copies of Worksheet 1–5a.

3. It is assumed for this activity that students have had experience with equivalent fractions. The trading action for finding common denominators will reinforce their understanding of the concept.

4. Students should build with the fraction bars on Building Mat 1–5a to solve each word problem on Worksheet 1–5a. Then they should write a word sentence below the exercise to describe the results.

5. Discuss Exercise 1 on Worksheet 1–5a before allowing students to solve the other exercises independently.

Consider the word problem in Exercise 1 on Worksheet 1–5a: "Carl jogged 1 and 1-half miles before he stopped to rest. Then he jogged another 3-fourths of a mile. How many miles in all did he jog?"

Have students place one whole fraction bar on the top bar of Building Mat 1–5a and then place a half bar on the second bar of the mat. To show the 3-fourths of a mile, they should place 3 of the fourth bars on the third bar of the mat. Here are the initial fraction bars on the building mat:

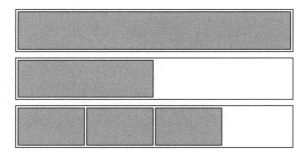

Ask students if all the fraction bars on the building mat are the same size. Since they are not, students must trade the bars for smaller fraction bars until they find a common bar size. Allow students to explore to find what size is needed. It is not necessary for them to find the largest common bar size (the "least common denominator"). Smaller bar sizes will also work as long as the size is common to all numbers shown on the mat.

A possible trade is to trade or replace the whole bar on the mat with 4 fourths and to trade or replace the half bar with 2 fourths. The third bar on the mat already contains 3 fourths. Once the trading is complete and all fraction bars on the mat are the same size, students should recount all the parts or fraction bars to find their total, which will be 9 fourths of a whole.

Discuss the idea that the total of 9 fourths of a whole can be grouped as 4 fourths, 4 fourths, and 1 fourth. So another way of thinking about the total might be 1 whole, 1 whole, and 1 fourth of a whole, which can be named as 2 and 1-fourth of a whole. Do not exchange each 4 fourths for 1 whole on the mat; only make the trade mentally at this time. The phrase "of a whole" needs to be used regularly so that students realize the significance of the whole to any of its fractional parts. In Exercise 1, the whole corresponds to the mile so that 1-fourth of a whole is equivalent to 1-fourth of a mile.

Because of the algorithm being developed in this objective, the improper fraction name needs to be recorded along with the mixed number name. Thus, students should write the following word sentence below Exercise 1: "Carl jogged 9-fourths of a mile or 2 and 1-fourth miles in all."

Answer Key for Worksheet 1–5a

1. Carl jogged 9-fourths of a mile or 2 and 1-fourth miles in all.

2. Kate ate 17-sixths of an ounce or 2 and 5-sixths ounces of candy.

3. Maria did homework for 19-twelfths of an hour or 1 and 7-twelfths hours.

4. 5-sixths of the whole class ate during lunch A or lunch B.

5. Sam cut lawns for 23-eighths of an hour or 2 and 7-eighths hours.

Building Mat 1-5a. Fraction Addition

58

WORKSHEET 1–5a

Adding with Fractions
and Mixed Numbers

Name _____

Date _____

Use fraction bars on Building Mat 1–5a to solve the word problems provided. Write a word sentence below each exercise to record the result found.

1. Carl jogged 1 and 1-half miles before he stopped to rest. Then he jogged another 3-fourths of a mile. How many miles in all did he jog?

2. Kate ate 1 and 2-thirds ounces of rocky road fudge and 1 and 1-sixth ounces of peanut brittle. How many ounces total did Kate eat of both candies?

3. Maria worked on her math homework for 3-fourths of an hour and on her science homework for 5-sixths of an hour. How much time did she spend on homework?

4. One-third of the class ate during lunch A and 1-half of the class ate during lunch B. The rest ate during lunch C. What fractional part of the whole class ate during lunch A or lunch B?

5. Sam took 1 and 2-fourths hours to cut his lawn and another 1 and 3-eighths hours to cut a neighbor's lawn. How many hours did Sam take to cut both lawns?

Pattern 1–5a. Fraction Bars

WHOLE											
HALF						HALF					
THIRD				THIRD				THIRD			
FOURTH			FOURTH			FOURTH			FOURTH		
SIXTH		SIXTH		SIXTH		SIXTH		SIXTH		SIXTH	
EIGHTH	EIGHTH	EIGHTH	EIGHTH	EIGHTH	EIGHTH	EIGHTH	EIGHTH				
TWELFTH	TWELFTH	TWELFTH	TWELFTH	TWELFTH	TWELFTH	TWELFTH	TWELFTH	TWELFTH	TWELFTH	TWELFTH	TWELFTH

Activity 2: Pictorial Stage

Materials
Worksheet 1–5b
Worksheet 1–5c
Red pencil and regular pencil

Procedure

1. Give each student a copy of Worksheet 1–5b, a copy of Worksheet 1–5c, and a red pencil. Now that students are comfortable adding with fraction bars on the building mat, they will work similar word problems with diagrams.

2. Each student should complete the frames on her or his own Worksheet 1–5b, but might share results with a partner.

3. For each exercise, students will subdivide whole bars on a frame to show different fractional amounts of a whole. They will shade the initial amounts, using diagonal stripes for easy recognition.

4. Students will then determine how each initial part must be traded in order to have only one common part size appearing on the frame. Trades will be shown by marking new subdivisions with red pencil.

5. The total shaded parts will be counted to find the answer to the word problem. An equation for this sum should be written below the exercise on Worksheet 1–5c. The equation should indicate the trades that were made in order to find the sum.

6. Exercise 1 on Worksheet 1–5c should be discussed with the class in detail before students are allowed to work the additional problems on the worksheet on their own.

Here is Exercise 1 from Worksheet 1–5c to consider: "Dave bought 1 and 1-eighth pounds of taffy at the fair, and Robin bought 3-fourths of a pound of taffy. How much taffy did they buy in all?"

To show the 1 and 1-eighth pounds, students should shade (use diagonal stripes) with regular pencil the top whole bar on the first frame of Worksheet 1–5b, then subdivide the second whole bar into 8 equal parts and shade one of the 8 parts. To show the 3-fourths of a pound, students should subdivide the third whole bar into four equal parts, then shade three of the four parts. Reverse the direction of the diagonal shading in adjacent parts for easy viewing. The initial shading should appear as follows:

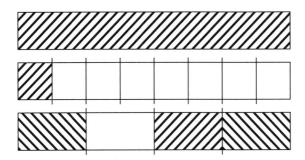

Since a total is needed for all the shaded parts together, students must find a part size common to all three whole bars being used. They no longer have the advantage of actual fraction bars to test, so they must begin to count the total parts marked off on each whole bar in order to know the part size involved. For example, if a whole bar is divided into eight equal parts, the part size will be an eighth. The total number of parts on a bar might be written at the left or right end of the bar for easy reference. Thus, the top bar might have the number 1 written at the left end, the second bar might have 8 written at the left, and the third bar might have 4 written at the left.

Encourage students to think in terms of possible trades. In other words, can each fourth (the largest part size except for the whole bar on top) on the third bar be traded for two new parts, three new parts, and so forth? If each fourth trades for two new parts, there will be eight new parts forming the whole bar, yielding a new part size of an eighth. Since the second bar also has eight equal parts and the top whole bar can easily be changed to eighths, students should now use the red pencil to subdivide the top whole bar into eight equal parts and to subdivide each original part of the third bar into two new equal parts for a total of eight parts on the third bar. The numbers at the ends of the bars may also be changed to show the new total parts per bar. Here is the final diagram:

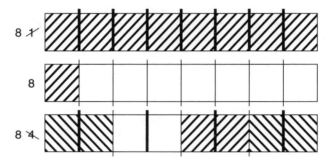

Since all part sizes are now the same (in this case, eighths), students should count to find the total shaded parts, which is 15 eighths from the three bars. Discuss how this total might be viewed as 8-eighths and 7-eighths of a whole, or as 1 whole and 7-eighths of another whole.

At this stage, students need to record their result with a notation that reflects the trades that were used. The top 1 whole bar was traded for 8 new parts, and the 4 fourths on the third whole bar were each traded for 2 new parts. The second bar remained unchanged. The notation that shows the trades over the entire bar, as well as for the shaded parts, is given below and should also be recorded below Exercise 1 on Worksheet 1–5c:

$$1 + \frac{1}{8} + \frac{3}{4} = \frac{8}{8} + \frac{1}{8} + \frac{3 \times 2}{4 \times 2} = \frac{8}{8} + \frac{1}{8} + \frac{6}{8} = \frac{15}{8} \text{ pounds}$$

$$\text{or } 1 \text{ and } \frac{7}{8} \text{ pounds of taffy}$$

If the first amount had been 2 and $\frac{1}{8}$, the 2 would require 2 whole bars and $2\frac{1}{8}$ would be recorded as $1 + 1 + \frac{1}{8} = \frac{8}{8} + \frac{8}{8} + \frac{1}{8}$.

Answer Key for Worksheet 1–5c

1. $1 + \dfrac{1}{8} + \dfrac{3}{4} = \dfrac{8}{8} + \dfrac{1}{8} + \dfrac{3 \times 2}{4 \times 2} = \dfrac{8}{8} + \dfrac{1}{8} + \dfrac{6}{8} = \dfrac{15}{8}$ pounds,

   or 1 and $\dfrac{7}{8}$ pounds of taffy

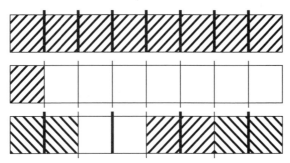

2. $\dfrac{1}{2} + \dfrac{2}{3} = \dfrac{1 \times 3}{2 \times 3} + \dfrac{2 \times 2}{3 \times 2} = \dfrac{3}{6} + \dfrac{4}{6} = \dfrac{7}{6}$ hrs., or 1 and $\dfrac{1}{6}$ hrs.

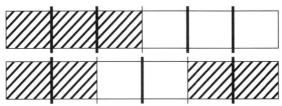

3. $1 + \dfrac{5}{6} + 1 + \dfrac{1}{3} = \dfrac{6}{6} + \dfrac{5}{6} + \dfrac{6}{6} + \dfrac{1 \times 2}{3 \times 2} = \dfrac{6}{6} + \dfrac{5}{6} + \dfrac{6}{6} + \dfrac{2}{6} = \dfrac{19}{6}$ lbs., or 3 and $\dfrac{1}{6}$ lbs.

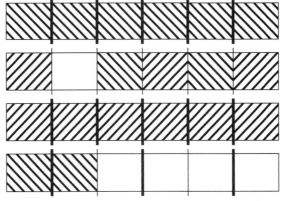

4. $\dfrac{7}{8} + \dfrac{3}{4} + 1 + \dfrac{1}{2} = \dfrac{7}{8} + \dfrac{3 \times 2}{4 \times 2} + \dfrac{8}{8} + \dfrac{1 \times 4}{2 \times 4} = \dfrac{7}{8} + \dfrac{6}{8} + \dfrac{8}{8} + \dfrac{4}{8} = \dfrac{25}{8}$ miles, or 3 and $\dfrac{1}{8}$ miles

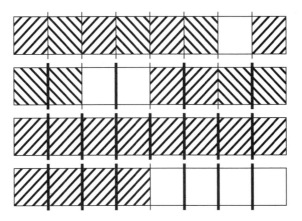

64

WORKSHEET 1–5b
Drawing Frames

Name _____

Date _____

1.

2.

WORKSHEET 1–5b Continued

Name _____

Date _____

3.

4.

WORKSHEET 1–5c   Name _____

**Drawing to Add Fractions
and Mixed Numbers**   Date _____

Use a red pencil and Worksheet 1–5b (the frames) to solve the word problems provided. Write an equation below each exercise to record the result found. Record any trades made in the equation.

1. Dave bought 1 and 1-eighth pounds of taffy at the fair, and Robin bought 3-fourths of a pound of taffy. How much taffy did they buy in all?

2. Lynda's kite flew in the air for 1-half of an hour, then later flew for another 2-thirds of an hour. What was the total time the kite flew in the air?

3. Juan bought 1 and 5-sixths pounds of birdseed in July. In August, he had to buy another 1 and 1-third pounds of seed. How much birdseed did he buy total for both months?

4. Caron walked 7-eighths of a mile on Monday, 3-fourths of a mile on Tuesday, 1 mile on Wednesday, and 1-half mile on Thursday. How many miles did she walk over the four days?

Activity 3: Independent Practice

Materials

   Worksheet 1–5d

   Regular pencil

Procedure

Give each student a copy of Worksheet 1–5d. Have students solve each exercise by using the addition algorithm, which was developed as the final notation in Activity 2. Discuss the alternative method that allows whole amounts, especially larger numbers, to be added separately from fractional amounts. For example, the addend 15 and $\frac{1}{2}$ may be viewed several ways: $1 + 1 + \ldots + 1 + \frac{1}{2} = \frac{2}{2} + \frac{2}{2} + \ldots + \frac{2}{2} + \frac{1}{2}$; $\frac{30}{2} + \frac{1}{2}$; or just $15 + \frac{1}{2}$. So in order to add 15 and $\frac{1}{2}$ to 24 and $\frac{3}{4}$, students might choose to add 15 to 24 to get 39 wholes, then add $\frac{1}{2}$ to $\frac{3}{4}$ to get $\frac{5}{4}$, or 1 whole and $\frac{1}{4}$ of a whole. The final answer would be 40 wholes and $\frac{1}{4}$ of a whole.

   Encourage students to use the trading language for finding equivalent fractions as needed. The cup-quart conversion will be needed for Exercise 3. When all students have finished the worksheet, have several students share their answers with the rest of the class.

Answer Key for Worksheet 1–5d

   1. A

   2. C

   3. B

   4. C

   5. D

Possible Testing Errors That May Occur for This Objective

   - To add fractions with unlike denominators, students do not find a common denominator. Instead, they find the new numerator by adding the original numerators, and they find the new denominator by adding the original denominators.

   - If the sum of several fractions produces an improper fraction (for example, 14-tenths), students will change the improper fraction to an incorrect mixed number. A subtraction fact error may be the cause.

   - The computation yields a fractional sum that is not in lowest terms, and students do not recognize the reduced fraction in the response choices.

WORKSHEET 1–5d   Name _____

Adding Fractions and Mixed Numbers   Date _____
to Solve Word Problems

Solve the word problems provided. Write an equation on the back of the worksheet to show the steps used for each exercise.

1. A jeweler used $\frac{3}{5}$ meter of silver chain to make a bracelet and $\frac{7}{10}$ meter to make a necklace. How many meters of silver chain were used in all to make the 2 pieces of jewelry?

   A. $1\frac{3}{10}$ m   B. $\frac{10}{15}$ m   C. $\frac{1}{10}$ m   D. $1\frac{1}{5}$ m

2. Over a 3-month period, Dave's Market donated $12\frac{3}{4}$ pounds, $25\frac{3}{8}$ pounds, and $15\frac{1}{2}$ pounds of food, respectively, to the local shelter for abused children. How many pounds of food total were donated over the 3 months?

   A. $52\frac{3}{4}$ lbs.   B. $53\frac{1}{2}$ lbs.   C. $53\frac{5}{8}$ lbs.   D. $53\frac{3}{4}$ lbs.

3. A recipe for apple sparkle punch requires the following ingredients: $4\frac{1}{2}$ cups of apple juice, $\frac{1}{4}$ cup of lime juice, 3 quarts of water, $3\frac{1}{2}$ cups of pineapple juice, and $2\frac{3}{4}$ cups of lime soda. What is the smallest-sized pitcher that will hold all the ingredients?

   A. 7-qt.   B. 6-qt.   C. 5-qt.   D. 4-qt.

4. Julio hiked $16\frac{3}{5}$ kilometers on Monday, $11\frac{1}{2}$ kilometers on Tuesday, and 10 kilometers on Wednesday. What is the total number of kilometers Julio hiked during these 3 days?

   A. $37\frac{4}{7}$ km   B. 38 km   C. $38\frac{1}{10}$ km   D. Not shown here

5. Marjorie has a casserole recipe that serves 4 people and requires $2\frac{7}{8}$ pounds of chicken. If she wants to serve 12 people, how many pounds of chicken will she need?

   A. $5\frac{3}{4}$ lbs.   B. 6 lbs.   C. $6\frac{7}{8}$ lbs.   D. $8\frac{5}{8}$ lbs.

Objective 6
Subtract fractions or mixed numbers to solve word problems.

Students need many experiences involving fractional measurements. They have great difficulty transferring the four operations from their comfortable whole number world to the less familiar fraction world. Manipulatives assist students in applying the subtraction or removal process to different fractional part sizes by showing the need for a common denominator.

Activity 1: Manipulative Stage

Materials
        Set of fraction bars per pair of students (use Pattern 1–5a)
        Building Mat 1–6a per pair of students
        Worksheet 1–6a
        Regular pencil

Procedure
1. Use the sets of fraction bars prepared for addition in Objective 5. Each set of fraction bars should contain cut-out bars from five copies of Pattern 1–5a. The whole bar on Building Mat 1–6a should be congruent to the whole bar on Pattern 1–5a. An alternative is to have each type of fraction colored to match the corresponding type in the teacher's set of fraction bars.

2. Give each pair of students a set of fraction bars, one copy of Building Mat 1–6a, and two copies of Worksheet 1–6a.

3. It is assumed for this activity that students have had experience with equivalent fractions. The trading action for finding common denominators, however, will reinforce their understanding of the concept.

4. Students should build with the fraction bars on Building Mat 1–6a to solve each word problem on Worksheet 1–6a. Then they should write a word sentence below the exercise to describe the results.

5. Discuss Exercise 1 on Worksheet 1–6a before allowing students to solve the other exercises independently.

       Consider the word problem in Exercise 1 on Worksheet 1–6a: "Sandy jogged 2 and 1-half miles in all on Saturday. She jogged 1 and 5-eighths miles of that distance before stopping to rest. How many more miles did she jog after she rested?"
       Have students place one whole bar on each of the top two bars of Building Mat 1–6a and place a half bar on the third bar of the mat. This represents 2 and 1-half miles, the total distance in the problem. Students should then place 1 whole bar on the fourth bar of the mat below the phrase "Take away," and place five of the eighth bars on the bottom bar of the mat. This will show 1 and 5-eighths miles, the first distance Sandy jogged. The fraction bars placed above the broken line segment on the mat represent the *minuend*, and the bars placed below the broken line segment represent the *subtrahend*. Here are the fraction bars on the building mat as they appear initially:

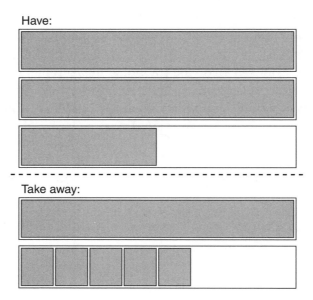

Ask students if all the fraction bars on the building mat are the same size. Since they are not, students must trade the bars for smaller fraction bars until they find a common bar size. Allow students to explore to find what size is needed. Any smaller bar size will work as long as the size is common to all numbers shown on the mat.

A possible trade is to trade or replace each whole bar on the mat with 8 eighths and to trade or replace the half bar with 4 eighths. The bottom bar on the mat already contains 5 eighths. Once the trading is complete and all fraction bars on the mat are the same size, there will be 20 eighths in the upper minuend region of the mat and 13 eighths in the lower subtrahend region of the mat. Students should begin to match each fraction bar in the lower region of the mat with a fraction bar in the upper region. Each matched pair should be removed from the mat as it is made. This action shows the removal process for subtraction. Here is the appearance of the mat before the matching begins:

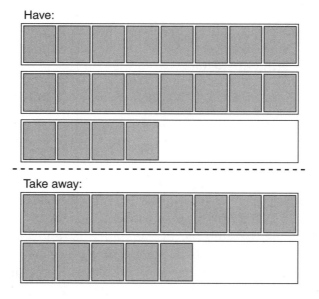

The 13 eighths in the lower region will match to 13 eighths in the upper region, so 13 pairs of eighths will be removed from the building mat. As a result, 13 eighths have been taken away from 20 eighths, leaving 7 eighths as the difference in the upper region.

These 7 eighths may now be moved to the same bar on the mat if they are not already. They may be placed on either of the top three bars. Below Exercise 1 on Worksheet 1–6a, students should record their answer as a word sentence: "Sandy jogged 7-eighths of a mile after resting." The final fraction bars remaining on the building mat after the removal will appear as follows:

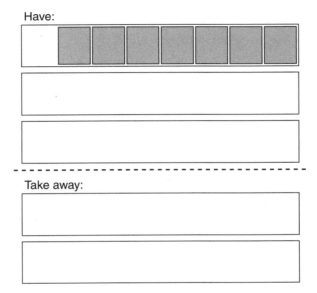

Discuss the idea that if there had been more than 8 eighths of a whole left after the removal, the fraction bars could have been grouped in sets of 8. For example, if the difference had been 17 eighths of a whole, each 8 eighths could be exchanged for 1 whole, yielding 2 wholes and 1 eighth of another whole for the answer. Students should not exchange each 8 eighths for 1 whole on the mat; they should make the trade mentally. The phrase "of a whole" needs to be used regularly so that students realize the significance of the *whole* to any of its fractional *parts*. In Exercise 1, the whole corresponds to the mile, so that 1-eighth of a whole is equivalent to 1-eighth of a mile.

Because of the algorithm being developed in this objective, when the difference occurs as an improper fraction, the improper fraction name needs to be recorded along with the mixed number name in the final word sentence. As an example, students might include the following phrase in the word sentence for an exercise: "17-eighths of a mile, or 2 and 1-eighth miles left."

Answer Key for Worksheet 1–6a

1. Sandy jogged 7-eighths of a mile after resting.

2. Allen had 1 and 1-sixth ounces of fudge left.

3. Sonja spent 5-sixths of an hour on science homework.

4. One-half of the eighth-grade class ate hot dogs on Monday.

5. Sam took 1 and 5-eighths hours to cut his own lawn.

Building Mat 1–6a. Fraction Subtraction

Have:

Take away:

WORSHEET 1–6a   Name _____

Subtracting with Fractions   Date _____
and Mixed Numbers

Use fraction bars on Building Mat 1–6a to solve the word problems provided. Write a word sentence below each exercise to record the result found.

1. Sandy jogged 2 and 1-half miles in all on Saturday. She jogged 1 and 5-eighths miles of that distance before stopping to rest. How many more miles did she jog after she rested?

2. Allen bought 2 and 5-sixths ounces of marshmallow fudge. He ate 1 and 2-thirds ounces of the fudge. How many ounces of the fudge did he have left?

3. Sonja spent 1 and 7-twelfths hours total on her math and science homework. If she studied for 3-fourths of an hour on her math homework, how much time did she spend on science homework?

4. Five-sixths of the eighth-grade class ate in the school cafeteria on Monday. Only pizzas and hot dogs were served that day. If 1-third of the class ate pizzas, what fractional part of the class ate hot dogs?

5. Sam took 3 hours to cut his lawn and a neighbor's lawn. If he took 1 and 3-eighths hours to cut the neighbor's lawn, how many hours did Sam take to cut his own lawn?

Activity 2: Pictorial Stage

Materials
>   Worksheet 1–6b
>   Worksheet 1–6c
>   Red pencil and regular pencil

Procedure

1. Give each student a copy of Worksheet 1–6b, a copy of Worksheet 1–6c, and a red pencil. Now that students are comfortable subtracting with fraction bars on the building mat, they will work similar word problems with diagrams.

2. Each student should complete the frames on her or his own Worksheet 1–6b, but might share results with a partner.

3. For each exercise, students will subdivide whole bars on a frame to show different fractional amounts of a whole. The initial amounts will be shaded, using diagonal stripes for easy recognition.

4. Students will determine how each initial part must be traded in order to have only one common part size appearing on the frame. Trades will be shown by marking new subdivisions with red pencil.

5. Each part in the lower region will be matched to a unique part in the upper region, and both parts will be marked out. This process continues until all parts in the lower region of the frame are marked out. The shaded parts remaining in the upper region will then be counted to find the answer to the word problem. An equation for this difference should be written below the exercise on Worksheet 1–6c. The equation should indicate the trades that were made in order to find the difference.

6. Exercise 1 on Worksheet 1–6c should be discussed with the class in detail before students are allowed to work the additional problems on the worksheet on their own.

Here is Exercise 1 from Worksheet 1–6c to consider: "Marion bought 1 and 2-thirds pounds of taffy at the state fair. He ate 3-fourths of a pound of the taffy while at the fair. How many pounds of taffy did he have left?"

On the first frame of Worksheet 1–6b, have students shade the top bar completely (using diagonal stripes) to show 1 whole, and then subdivide the second bar into 3 equal parts and shade 2 of the parts to show 2-thirds of another whole. In the lower region below the broken line segment, have them subdivide the first bar into 4 equal parts and shade 3 of the parts; the shaded parts will represent the subtrahend, 3-fourths of a whole. The initial appearance of the diagram is shown here:

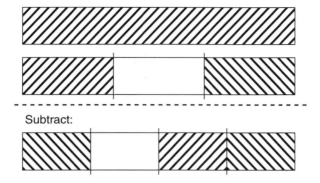

Subtract:

Have students count the total parts in each whole bar and write the number at the left end of the bar. The top bar contains only 1 part, the second bar has 3 parts, and the third bar has 4 parts. Students must decide how to trade or subdivide the parts of each whole bar so that all the whole bars contain the same total number of equal parts; hence, all parts will be the same size. Guide students through the thinking process.

For example, if each of the three parts in the second bar is traded for 2 new parts, there will be 6 new parts for the whole bar. Similarly, if each of the 4 parts in the third bar is traded for 2 new parts, there will be 8 new parts for the whole bar. Now consider the second bar again with 3 new parts for each original part; there will be 9 new parts total for the whole bar. Continue this process until 12 parts per whole bar are discovered as the best choice. Then a 4-for-1 trade will be needed for the thirds on the second whole bar and a 3-for-1 trade will be needed for the fourths on the third whole bar. The number 12 should be recorded at the left end of each whole bar. With a red pencil, students should subdivide each whole bar in order to show 12 equal parts on each. The changed diagram will appear as follows:

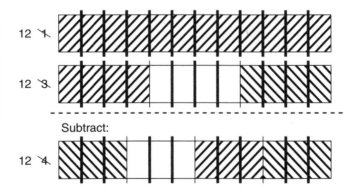

Subtract:

The diagram is now ready for students to begin the subtraction or removal process. This is done by marking out 1 part in the subtrahend (the third bar in this case) and matching it to 1 part in the upper region (minuend) and marking out that part as well. This marking-out process continues one pair at a time until all parts in the lower region have been marked out. The parts that remain unmarked in the upper region will be the *difference* sought. Since there are 12-twelfths + 8-twelfths, or 20-twelfths, in the upper region and 9-twelfths must be removed, the difference will be 11-twelfths of a whole. Here is the completed diagram for this exercise:

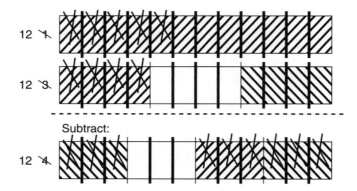

Students should record equations or number sentences below Exercise 1 on Worksheet 1–6c to show their results. Because the upper region initially contained a mixed number, one number sentence will be needed to show the change of the mixed number to an improper fraction. Then another number sentence will be needed to show the subtraction. The number sentences should also reflect the trades that were used on each whole bar. Here is an example of a recording for Exercise 1:

$$1 + \frac{2}{3} = \frac{12}{12} + \frac{2 \times 4}{3 \times 4} = \frac{12}{12} + \frac{8}{12} = \frac{20}{12}$$

$$\frac{3 \times 3}{4 \times 3} = \frac{9}{12} \quad \text{So } \frac{20}{12} - \frac{9}{12} = \frac{11}{12} \text{ lbs. of taffy left}$$

Answer Key for Worksheet 1–6c

The answer key provides possible number sentences to use.

1. The number sentences are given in the text (see above).

2. $\frac{7}{8} - \frac{2}{4} = \frac{7}{8} - \frac{2 \times 2}{4 \times 2} = \frac{7}{8} - \frac{4}{8} = \frac{3}{8}$ of a yard of fabric left

3. $1 + \frac{1}{2} = \frac{2}{2} + \frac{1}{2} = \frac{3}{2}$ and $1 + \frac{1}{3} = \frac{3}{3} + \frac{1}{3} = \frac{4}{3}$

   $\frac{3}{2} - \frac{4}{3} = \frac{3 \times 3}{2 \times 3} - \frac{4 \times 2}{3 \times 2} = \frac{9}{6} - \frac{8}{6} = \frac{1}{6}$ of a pound of seed left

   Alternative with whole numbers:

   wholes: 1 − 1 = 0 wholes left

   parts: $\frac{1}{2} - \frac{1}{3} = \frac{1 \times 3}{2 \times 3} - \frac{1 \times 2}{3 \times 2} = \frac{3}{6} - \frac{2}{6} = \frac{1}{6}$ of a pound left

4. $2 = 1 + 1 = \frac{5}{5} + \frac{5}{5} = \frac{10}{5}$ and $1 + \frac{3}{5} = \frac{5}{5} + \frac{3}{5} = \frac{8}{5}$

   So $\frac{10}{5} - \frac{8}{5} = \frac{2}{5}$ of a mile more on Monday

   Alternative with whole numbers:

   wholes: 2 − 1 = 1 whole left

   parts: $1 - \frac{3}{5} = \frac{5}{5} - \frac{3}{5} = \frac{2}{5}$ of a mile more on Monday

WORKSHEET 1–6b   Name _____
Drawing Frames   Date _____

1.

Subtract:

2.

Subtract:

78

Name _____

Date _____

3.

```
┌─────────────────────────────┐
│                             │
│                             │
│                             │
└─────────────────────────────┘

┌─────────────────────────────┐
│                             │
│                             │
│                             │
└─────────────────────────────┘
```

Subtract:
```
┌─────────────────────────────┐
│                             │
│                             │
│                             │
└─────────────────────────────┘

┌─────────────────────────────┐
│                             │
│                             │
│                             │
└─────────────────────────────┘
```

4.
```
┌─────────────────────────────┐
│                             │
│                             │
│                             │
└─────────────────────────────┘

┌─────────────────────────────┐
│                             │
│                             │
│                             │
└─────────────────────────────┘
```

Subtract:
```
┌─────────────────────────────┐
│                             │
│                             │
│                             │
└─────────────────────────────┘

┌─────────────────────────────┐
│                             │
│                             │
│                             │
└─────────────────────────────┘
```

79

WORKSHEET 1–6c

Name _____

Drawing to Subtract Fractions
and Mixed Numbers

Date _____

Use a red pencil and Worksheet 1–6b (frames) to solve the word problems provided. Write one or more equations below each exercise to record the result found. Record any trades made in the equations.

1. Marion bought 1 and 2-thirds pounds of taffy at the state fair. He ate 3-fourths of a pound of the taffy while at the fair. How many pounds of taffy did he have left?

2. Harriet had 7-eighths of a yard of fabric. She used 2-fourths of a yard of the fabric to make a chair cushion. How much fabric did Harriet have left?

3. Juan had 1 and 1-half pounds of birdseed. He gave 1 and 1-third pounds of the seed to his sister. How much birdseed did he have left?

4. Leslie walked 2 miles on Monday, then walked 1 and 3-fifths miles on Tuesday. How many more miles did she walk on Monday than on Tuesday?

Activity 3: Independent Practice

Materials
 Worksheet 1–6d
 Regular pencil

Procedure

Give each student a copy of Worksheet 1–6d. Have students solve each exercise by using the subtraction algorithm for fractions, which was developed as the final notation in Activity 2. Mastery of fraction addition is assumed. Discuss the alternative method that allows whole amounts, especially larger numbers, to be subtracted separately before fractional amounts are subtracted. For example, the subtrahend 18 and 1/2 may be viewed several ways: $1 + 1 + \ldots + 1 + \frac{1}{2} = \frac{2}{2} + \frac{2}{2} + \ldots + \frac{2}{2} + \frac{1}{2}$; $\frac{36}{2} + \frac{1}{2}$; or just $18 + \frac{1}{2}$. So in order to subtract 18 and $\frac{1}{2}$ from 23 and $\frac{1}{3}$, students might choose to subtract 18 from 23 to get 5 wholes left, then subtract $\frac{1}{2}$ from the remaining 5 wholes and the $\frac{1}{3}$. Then this becomes $\frac{32}{6}$ take away $\frac{3}{6}$, which equals $\frac{29}{6}$ or 4 wholes and $\frac{5}{6}$ of another whole as the final answer. Encourage students to use the trading language for finding equivalent fractions as needed. When all students have finished the worksheet, have several students share their answers with the rest of the class.

Answer Key for Worksheet 1–6d
 1. C

 2. A

 3. D

 4. A

 5. B

Possible Testing Errors That May Occur for This Objective
- Students apply subtraction correctly but use incorrect equivalent fractions.
- Students make errors when changing a mixed number to an improper fraction; otherwise, the subtraction process is correct.
- Students subtract the numerators and subtract the denominators separately as though there are two different problems. No common denominator is found.
- Students add the fractions instead of subtracting them.

WORSHEET 1–6d

**Subtraction with Fractions
and Mixed Numbers**

Name _____

Date _____

Solve the word problems provided. Write an equation on the back of the worksheet to show the steps used for each exercise.

1. In a trip across a lake, Boat A had an average speed of $41\frac{1}{5}$ miles per hour, and Boat B had an average speed of $27\frac{1}{2}$ miles per hour. What was the difference between the two speeds?

    A. $14\frac{3}{10}$ mph
    B. $14\frac{1}{5}$ mph
    C. $13\frac{7}{10}$ mph
    D. $12\frac{1}{2}$ mph

2. Luis bought 5 gallons of gasoline in a large container. He poured $1\frac{3}{8}$ gallons of the gasoline into his lawn mower. How many gallons remain in the container?

    A. $3\frac{5}{8}$ gal.
    B. 4 gal.
    C. $4\frac{3}{8}$ gal.
    D. $6\frac{3}{8}$ gal.

3. A box contained $\frac{3}{4}$ of a pound of peanut brittle candy. George ate $\frac{3}{5}$ of a pound of the candy. How many pounds of candy were left in the box?

    A. $\frac{6}{9}$ lb.
    B. $\frac{1}{4}$ lb.
    C. $\frac{2}{5}$ lb.
    D. $\frac{3}{20}$ lb.

4. Katy spent $\frac{1}{6}$ of Saturday at the Heard Museum. Then she spent $\frac{1}{4}$ of the day baby-sitting. What fraction of Saturday was Katy not baby-sitting or visiting the museum?

    A. $\frac{7}{12}$
    B. $\frac{5}{12}$
    C. $\frac{2}{10}$
    D. $\frac{1}{12}$

5. During spring break, Ann traveled $185\frac{3}{4}$ miles, and Carl traveled $256\frac{2}{3}$ miles. How many miles longer was Carl's trip than Ann's trip?

    A. $71\frac{2}{3}$ mi.
    B. $70\frac{11}{12}$ mi.
    C. $70\frac{1}{2}$ mi.
    D. $69\frac{3}{4}$ mi.

Objective 7
Divide fractions or mixed numbers to solve word problems.

The "common denominator" model will be used to develop the division algorithm for fractions. This approach seems to be easier for students to understand than the more traditional approach that depends on multiplication by the reciprocal of the divisor. In the exercises, the divisor will represent the set to be reproduced or copied, and the quotient will count the number of copies made. It is assumed for this activity that students have had experience with equivalent fractions. The trading action for finding common denominators, however, will reinforce their understanding of the concept.

Activity 1: Manipulative Stage

Materials
Set of fraction bars per pair of students (use Pattern 1–5a)
Building Mat 1–7a per pair of students
Worksheet 1–7a
Regular pencil

Procedure
1. Use the sets of fraction bars prepared for addition in Objective 5. Each set of fraction bars should contain cut-out bars from five copies of Pattern 1–5a. If preferred, each type of fraction might be colored to match the corresponding type in the teacher's set of fraction bars.

2. Give each pair of students a set of fraction bars, one copy of Building Mat 1–7a, and two copies of Worksheet 1–7a.

3. Students should build with the fraction bars on Building Mat 1–7a to solve each word problem on Worksheet 1–7a. Then they should write a word sentence below the exercise to describe the results.

4. With the common denominator method, students will trade all fraction bars on the building mat to a common bar size. Then they will compare the new fraction bars in the upper region of the building mat (dividend) to those in the lower region (divisor) to find how many copies the dividend amount will make of the divisor amount. The quotient will be the number of complete or partial copies made.

5. Discuss Exercise 1 on Worksheet 1–7a before allowing students to solve the other exercises independently.

Consider the word problem in Exercise 1 on Worksheet 1–7a: "Carrie has 2 and 1-half kilograms of fudge in the store display case. She wants to package the fudge in bags with 3-fourths of a kilogram per bag. How many bags, including a partial bag, will Carrie be able to prepare?"

Have students place 2 whole bars and 1 half bar in the upper region of Building Mat 1–7a. This represents the dividend. They should then place 3 fourths bars in the lower region of the mat to represent the divisor. The 3 fourths bars should be touching end to end and will be viewed as a connected group. Here is a possible initial arrangement of the fraction bars on the building mat:

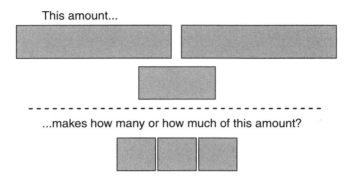

Students should determine a common fraction bar size for all bars on the mat. Since wholes, halves, and fourths are involved, all bars should be traded for fourths. The upper region will contain 4 fourths, 4 fourths, and 2 fourths, or 10 fourths total. The lower region will contain the original 3 fourths. Students should now slide the *group* of 3 fourths (the divisor) from the lower region to the upper region and try to match the *group* with similar groups from the 10 fourths (the dividend). Each new group of 3 fourths formed should be moved away from the other bars so that the groups are easily seen. Three such groups of 3 fourths each should be formed, leaving 1 fourth bar isolated in the upper region.

The divisor *group* should now be slid over and aligned with this single fourth. Discuss the idea that a complete group contains 3 fourths, so this single fourth represents one out of three parts needed for a complete group. Therefore, the single fourth is only a partial group and will be called *1-third of a complete group*. Once the partial group has been named, the original divisor group should be moved back down into the lower region so it will not be counted as part of the answer.

The dividend has been separated into three complete groups and 1 third of another complete group. That means 3 and 1-third bags of fudge can be prepared, using 3-fourths of a kilogram per bag. Students should write the following word sentence below Exercise 1 on Worksheet 1–7a: "Carrie can prepare 3 and 1-third bags of fudge." Here is the final appearance of the fraction bars on the mat. The dashed shapes indicate where the divisor group had been placed earlier in order to determine the partial group's name:

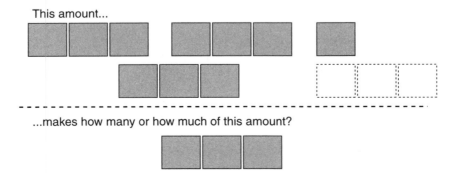

Answer Key for Worksheet 1–7a

1. Carrie can prepare 3 and 1-third bags of fudge. [Trade all bars to fourths.]

2. The tailor can make 5 scarves. [Trade all bars to thirds.]

3. The fishmonger can make 6 and 2-thirds packages of salmon. [Trade all bars to twelfths.]

4. Rita can fill 2-thirds of a container. [Do not trade; use three whole bars as group to form.]

5. The chef can make 4 and 4-fifths servings. [Trade all bars to eighths.]

Building Mat 1–7a. Fraction Division

This amount...

...makes how many or how much of this amount?

86

WORSHEET 1–7a   Name _____

Dividing with Fractions   Date _____
and Mixed Numbers

Use fraction bars on Building Mat 1–7a to solve the word problems provided. Write a word sentence below each exercise to record the result found.

1. Carrie has 2 and 1-half kilograms of fudge in the store display case. She wants to package the fudge in bags with 3-fourths of a kilogram per bag. How many bags, including a partial bag, will Carrie be able to prepare?

2. The tailor has 1 and 2-thirds yards of silk fabric. He needs 1-third of a yard to make a silk scarf. How many scarves can he make with the fabric?

3. The fishmonger has 1 and 2-thirds pounds of salmon to put in individual packages. He wants to cut and wrap 1-fourth of a pound of salmon in each package. How many packages will he be able to make, including a partial package?

4. Rita's recipe makes 2 liters of punch. How many 3-liter containers can be filled using all the punch from one recipe?

5. The chef has 3 cups of whipped cream and needs 5-eighths of a cup of cream for a single serving of a dessert. How many servings, including a partial serving, can be made?

Activity 2: Pictorial Stage

Materials

> Worksheet 1–7b
> Worksheet 1–7c
> Red pencil and regular pencil

Procedure

1. Give each student a copy of Worksheet 1–7b, a copy of Worksheet 1–7c, and a red pencil. Now that students are comfortable dividing with fraction bars on the building mat, they will work similar word problems with diagrams.

2. Each student should complete the frames on her or his own Worksheet 1–7b, but might share results with a partner.

3. For each exercise, students will subdivide whole bars on a frame to show different fractional amounts of a whole. The initial amounts will be shaded, using diagonal stripes for easy recognition. The upper region of the frame will be for the dividend, and the lower region will be for the divisor. For ease of grouping, any fractional parts on the same whole bar in the divisor should be drawn adjacent to each other.

4. Students will determine how each initial part must be traded in order to have only one common part size appearing on the frame; that is, a common denominator is needed. Trades will be shown by marking new subdivisions with red pencil.

5. A ring will be drawn in red pencil around all the parts in the lower region (divisor) to signify the group to be formed. Then a matching group will be located in the upper region (dividend) and a red ring drawn around that new group. This process continues until all parts in the upper region of the frame have been ringed as a complete group or a partial group. The ringed groups in the upper region will then be labeled and counted to find the quotient or answer to the word problem. An equation for this process should be written below the exercise on Worksheet 1–7c. The equation should indicate the trades that were made in order to find the quotient.

6. Exercise 1 on Worksheet 1–7c should be discussed with the class in detail before students are allowed to work the additional problems on the worksheet independently.

Here is Exercise 1 from Worksheet 1–7c to consider: "Jerry has 1 and 7-eighths kilograms of bananas. He wants to bundle them into bags weighing 3-fourths of a kilogram each. How many bags, including a partial bag, will he be able to make?"

On the first frame of Worksheet 1–7b, students should shade (with diagonal stripes) the top whole bar, then subdivide the second whole bar into 8 equal parts and shade 7 of those parts. Together, these two bars will represent the dividend, 1 and 7-eighths kilograms. On the third whole bar of the frame, which is the first whole bar in the lower region, students should subdivide the bar into 4 equal parts and shade 3 of those parts. This will represent the divisor, 3-fourths of a kilogram. Here is the appearance of the frame with the initial shadings:

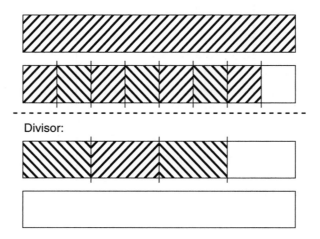

Have students count the total parts in each whole bar, and write the number at the left end of the bar. The top bar contains only 1 part, the second bar has 8 parts, and the third bar has 4 parts. Students must decide how to trade or subdivide the parts of each whole bar so that all the whole bars contain the same total number of equal parts; hence, all parts will be the same size. Guide students through the thinking process.

For example, if each of the 4 parts in the third bar is traded for 2 new parts, there will be 8 new parts for the whole bar. The second bar already has 8 original parts. Therefore, the top bar should also be traded for 8 new parts. So an 8-for-1 trade will be needed for the top whole bar and a 2-for-1 trade will be needed for the fourths on the third whole bar. The number 8 should be recorded at the left end of each whole bar that is changed. With a red pencil, students should subdivide each whole bar in order to show 8 equal parts on each. The changed diagram will appear as follows:

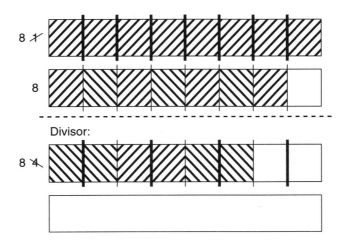

The diagram is now ready for students to begin the separation or grouping process. This is done by drawing a red ring around all the shaded parts in the divisor (the third bar in this case); this indicates how many parts will be in a *group*. Students should find and ring similar complete groups (similar by having the same number of parts in each group) in the upper region (dividend). This ringing process continues one group at a time until all parts in the upper region have been ringed. Finally, if some parts are left in the upper region, which are too few to form a complete group, additional parts should be drawn in red pencil adjacent to those parts to complete a group. Then a red ring should be drawn around that final partial group, including both the shaded parts and the newly drawn red parts. The shaded parts in the partial group compared to the total parts that should be in a complete group will identify the fractional name for the partial group formed.

In Exercise 1, the partial group will contain 3 shaded parts out of 6 total parts needed, so the partial group will represent 3-sixths of a complete group. Since after trading there are 8-eighths + 7-eighths, or 15-eighths, in the upper region and 6-eighths in the lower region (as the *group* to form), 2 complete groups and 3-sixths of another complete group should be ringed in the upper region. Here is the completed diagram for this exercise:

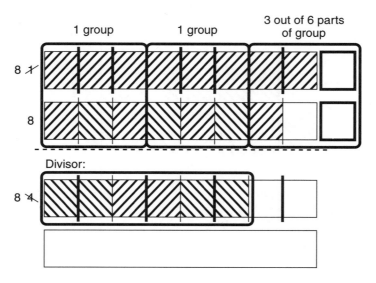

Students should record an equation or a number sentence below Exercise 1 on Worksheet 1–7c to show their results. It will be assumed that students are able to change the mixed number in the dividend directly to an improper fraction. Discuss the idea that the top bar showing 1 whole might be temporarily traded to eighths since its included common fraction is already eighths. Then both bars of eighths can be tested for possible trading, along with the third bar that contains fourths. The number sentence should also reflect the trades that were used on each whole bar of the diagram. Here is an example of a recording for Exercise 1:

$$1\frac{7}{8} \div \frac{3}{4} = \frac{15}{8} \div \frac{3\times 2}{4\times 2} = \frac{15}{8} \div \frac{6}{8} = 2 \text{ and } \frac{3}{6} \text{ bags of bananas,}$$

$$\text{or } 2 \text{ and } \frac{1}{2} \text{ bags of bananas}$$

Observe that after a common denominator or part size is found, only the new numerators contribute to the final answer or the quotient. In Exercise 1, it is 15 divided by 6 (the group size), which yields 2 complete groups and 3-sixths of another complete group. Encourage students to find other names for their answers when possible, but the initial quotient should be recorded first before a reduced form is given.

Answer Key for Worksheet 1–7c

Here are possible number sentences to use.

1. $1\frac{7}{8} \div \frac{3}{4} = \frac{15}{8} \div \frac{3 \times 2}{4 \times 2} = \frac{15}{8} \div \frac{6}{8} = 2$ and $\frac{3}{6}$ bags of bananas,

    or 2 and $\frac{1}{2}$ bags of bananas

2. $\frac{2}{3} \div 1\frac{1}{2} = \frac{2}{3} \div \frac{3}{2} = \frac{2 \times 2}{3 \times 2} \div \frac{3 \times 3}{2 \times 3} = \frac{4}{6} \div \frac{9}{6} = \frac{4}{9}$ of the original bag left

3. $2 \div \frac{1}{2} = \frac{4}{2} \div \frac{1}{2} = 4$ half-dollars in 2 whole dollars

4. $1\frac{1}{3} \div \frac{2}{5} = \frac{4}{3} \div \frac{2}{5} = \frac{4 \times 5}{3 \times 5} \div \frac{2 \times 3}{5 \times 3} = \frac{20}{15} \div \frac{6}{15} = 3$ and $\frac{2}{6}$ sections of cable, or 3 and $\frac{1}{3}$ sections of cable

92

WORKSHEET 1–7b
Drawing Frames

Name _____

Date _____

1.

Divisor:

2.

Divisor:

WORKSHEET 1–7b Continued

Name _____

Date _____

3.

(blank box)

(blank box)

- -

Divisor:

(blank box)

(blank box)

4.

(blank box)

(blank box)

- -

Divisor:

(blank box)

(blank box)

94

WORKSHEET 1–7c   Name _____

Drawing to Divide with Fractions   Date _____
and Mixed Numbers

Draw on a frame on Worksheet 1–7b to find the quotient for each exercise on this worksheet. Below each exercise, write a number sentence or equation that shows the results.
Show the trades used by recording them within the number sentences.

1. Jerry has 1 and 7-eighths kilograms of bananas. He wants to bundle them into
   bags weighing 3-fourths of a kilogram each. How many bags, including a partial
   bag, will he be able to make?

2. Cindy has only 2-thirds of a pound of birdseed left. The original bag contained
   1 and 1-half pounds. What fractional part of the original bag does she have left?

3. How many half-dollars are in 2 whole dollars?

4. The city utility company has 1 and 1-third kilometers of cable on a large spool.
   The company needs sections cut from this cable so that each section is 2-fifths of
   a kilometer long. How many sections, including a partial section, can be cut from
   the cable?

Activity 3: Independent Practice

Materials
Worksheet 1–7d
Regular pencil

Procedure

Give each student a copy of Worksheet 1–7d. Have students solve each exercise by using the common denominator algorithm for dividing fractions, which was developed as the final notation in Activity 2. Encourage students to use the trading language for finding equivalent fractions as needed. It is assumed that students have already mastered changing mixed numbers to improper fractions. Be careful to avoid shortcuts when explaining these changes. For example, students should understand that for 12 and $\frac{1}{3}$, each of the 12 wholes trades for 3 thirds to agree with the given $\frac{1}{3}$. After trading, there will be 12 of the $\frac{3}{3}$, which combine with the given $\frac{1}{3}$. So we have $\frac{36}{3} + \frac{1}{3}$, or $\frac{37}{3}$ as the improper fraction equivalent to the mixed number, 12 and $\frac{1}{3}$. When all students have finished the worksheet, have several students share their answers with the rest of the class.

Answer Key for Worksheet 1–7d
1. C

2. D

3. B

4. B

5. D [The correct answer is $1\frac{5}{6}$ packages.]

Possible Testing Errors That May Occur for This Objective

- Students apply division correctly but use incorrect equivalent fractions. An incorrect multiplication fact may have been used when finding an equivalent fraction.

- Students make errors when changing a mixed number to an improper fraction; otherwise, the division process is correct.

- Students divide the original numerators and divide the original denominators separately as though there are two different division problems.

- Students multiply the fractions instead of dividing them. They do not apply the division or separation/copying process described in the story situation.

- The order of the dividend and the divisor is reversed before the division algorithm is applied.

WORSHEET 1–7d

Name _____

**Dividing with Fractions
and Mixed Numbers**

Date _____

Solve the word problems provided. Write an equation on the back of the worksheet to show the steps used for each exercise. Reduce fractions in answers to the lowest terms.

1. Sheryl rode her bike for $27\frac{1}{2}$ miles total over several days. If she averaged $5\frac{1}{2}$ miles per day, how many days did she ride her bike?

   A. 7 days   B. 6 days   C. 5 days   D. 4 days

2. A block of cheese weighs $5\frac{7}{8}$ pounds. How many packages of sliced cheese can be made from this block if each package is to weigh $1\frac{1}{2}$ pounds?

   A. $7\frac{3}{8}$ pkg.   B. $5\frac{1}{2}$ pkg.   C. $4\frac{3}{8}$ pkg.   D. $3\frac{11}{12}$ pkg.

3. If José has $3\frac{1}{5}$ ounces left from an 8-ounce carton of yogurt, what fractional part of the original carton does he have left?

   A. $\frac{1}{5}$ carton   B. $\frac{2}{5}$ carton   C. $\frac{3}{4}$ carton   D. Not shown here

4. The farmer has $15\frac{3}{4}$ kilograms of carrots. He plans to sell them in bunches at $2\frac{1}{4}$ kilograms per bunch. How many bunches will he be able to make?

   A. $7\frac{1}{2}$ bunches   B. 7 bunches   C. $6\frac{3}{4}$ bunches   D. $5\frac{1}{2}$ bunches

5. The fishmonger has $3\frac{2}{3}$ pounds of tuna to put in individual packages. He wants to cut and wrap 2 pounds of tuna in each package. How many packages will he be able to make, including a partial package?

   A. $1\frac{1}{6}$ pkg.   B. $1\frac{2}{3}$ pkg.   C. 2 pkg.   D. Not shown here

Objective 8

Multiply fractions or mixed numbers to solve word problems.

Often multiplication of fractions is viewed as a simple concept to teach. This is because students seem to quickly recognize the pattern of "numerator times numerator" and "denominator times denominator." Unfortunately, many do not truly understand the process. When interviewed, students have revealed that they see fraction multiplication as two separate problems: a multiplication problem with whole numbers above the bars, and another similar problem below the bars. To avoid the phenomenon of getting the right answer for the wrong reason, students need to experience whole number multipliers with fraction multiplicands before they are introduced to fraction multipliers. The lessons that follow use such a sequence. It is assumed for this activity that students have had experience with equivalent fractions. They will often be trading given fraction bars for several copies of smaller fraction bars. They should also be comfortable with changing improper fractions to mixed numbers or mixed numbers to improper fractions.

Activity 1: Manipulative Stage

Materials

> Set of fraction bars per pair of students (use Pattern 1–5a)
> Building Mat 1–8a per pair of students
> Worksheet 1–8a
> Regular pencil

Procedure

1. Use the sets of fraction bars prepared for addition in Objective 5. Each set should contain cut-out bars from five copies of Pattern 1–5a. The whole bars in the student sets must be congruent to the whole bars drawn on Building Mat 1–8a. If preferred, each type of fraction might be colored to match the corresponding type in the teacher's set of fraction bars.

2. Give each pair of students a set of fraction bars, one copy of Building Mat 1–8a, and two copies of Worksheet 1–8a.

3. Students should build with the fraction bars on Building Mat 1–8a to solve each word problem on Worksheet 1–8a. Then they should write a word sentence below the exercise to describe the results.

4. Students will first work with exercises that use a whole number as the multiplier (Exercises 1 and 2). Then they will be introduced to fractions as multipliers in Exercises 3 through 5. Do not require students to write the whole number 1 as the *missing denominator* for a whole number factor. This step is unnecessary, and a denominator of 1 seems to have little meaning to students. One pattern will be identified when a whole number factor is present, and another pattern will be identified when both factors are fractions. These patterns are discussed in Activity 3.

5. Discuss Exercises 1 and 3 on Worksheet 1–8a before allowing students to solve the other exercises independently.

Here is Exercise 1 on Worksheet 1–8a to discuss with the students: "Kerry sells candy in bags of 1 and 5-sixths ounces each. A customer wants 2 of the bags. How many ounces will Kerry sell to the customer?"

Students should place 1 whole bar on the top bar of Building Mat 1–8a and 5 sixths bars on the second bar of the mat. These fraction bars are in the Given Set region of the mat and represent the multiplicand, 1 and 5-sixths ounces. To help with the development of the algorithm, have students trade the 1 whole bar for 6 sixths bars on the mat. The Given Set region will then contain 11 sixths bars total. The initial fraction bars are shown here before the whole bar is traded for sixths:

Given set:

Product:

The multiplier tells how many *complete* or *partial* copies of the multiplicand are needed. Since Exercise 1 involves a whole number 2 as the multiplier, this indicates that complete copies are needed. Thus, students should build 2 complete copies of the multiplicand, 11-sixths, on the whole bars in the Product region of the building mat. The sixths bars placed on the whole bars in the lower region should be grouped like those in the upper region, so that they reflect the repetition involved. When all bars have been placed on the building mat, the building mat will appear as follows:

Given set:

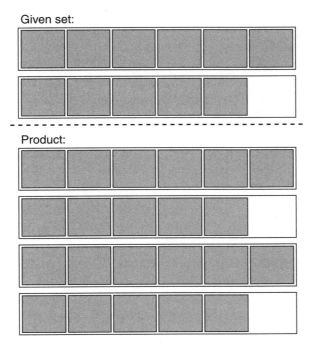

Product:

Now 6-sixths + 5-sixths + 6-sixths + 5-sixths, or 22-sixths total, appear in the Product region as the final product. On Worksheet 1–8a below Exercise 1, students should record a word sentence about their result. A possible sentence might be the following: "Kerry will sell 22-sixths ounces of candy, which is also 3 and 4-sixths ounces or 3 and 2-thirds ounces." Be sure to record 22-sixths as the first answer in the sentence. The numerator-denominator format will be needed to show the numerical pattern in the algorithm.

Now discuss Exercise 3 of Worksheet 1–8a with students. This exercise introduces a common fraction as the multiplier: "Jana has 1 and 1-half yards of felt. She will use 3-fourths of that amount to make a small table cover. How many yards of the felt will she use?"

Since the multiplier is 3-fourths, guide students to use the language "Copy 3 out of every 4 equal parts of 1 and 1-half" rather than "3-fourths of 1 and 1-half." Three out of every 4 equal parts indicates the action to be taken on the multiplicand. In other words, a partial copy of the multiplicand must be built, not a complete copy. Students should first place the multiplicand, 1 whole bar and 1 half bar, on the top two bars of Building Mat 1–8a as shown:

Given set:

Product:

All the fraction bars in the Given Set region should now be traded to the same bar size. This procedure preserves the traditional algorithm being developed in this activity. Since a half bar is already present, the whole bar should be traded for 2 halves, making 3 halves total on the top 2 bars of the mat.

The multiplier 3-fourths now requires that students trade *each* half bar on the upper region of the mat for 4 equal parts, which will be eighths in this case, and then copy 3 of those 4 parts on a whole bar in the Product region of the mat. This trading-copying process will be done three times because there are 3 halves in the Given Set region of the mat. Each half bar should be traded for 4 new parts (eighths), and then 3 of those parts copied and placed in the Product region, before the next half bar is traded. This helps students to focus on the process indicated by the multiplier. Here is the final mat arrangement after all trading and copying have been completed:

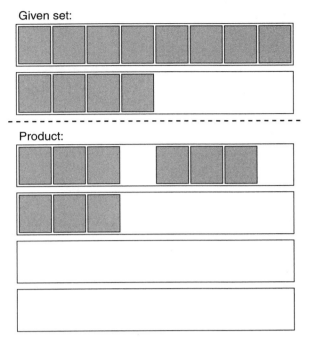

The Product region of the mat now contains 9 eighths bars, so the answer is 9-eighths yards. Notice how the 9 eighths have been grouped into 3 sets in the lower region of the mat. This is to show how each 3-eighths corresponds to the 1-half in the upper region from which it was copied. Students should record a word sentence below Exercise 3 on Worksheet 1–8a that is similar to the following: "Jana will use 9-eighths yards of the felt, which is 1 and 1-eighth yards." Be sure to record "9-eighths" first in the answer.

Answer Key for Worksheet 1–8a

The answer key provides possible sentences to use.

1. Kerry will sell 22-sixths ounces of candy, which is also 3 and 4-sixths ounces or 3 and 2-thirds ounces.

2. Three cartons weigh 21-eighths kilograms, or 2 and 5-eighths kilograms.

3. Jana will use 9-eighths yards of the felt, which is 1 and 1-eighth yards.

4. A one-way trip will be 3-eighths of a kilometer.

5. Josh will serve 10-twelfths of a gallon of ice cream, which is also 5-sixths of a gallon.

Building Mat 1–8a. Fraction Multiplication

Given set:

Product:

WORSHEET 1–8a
Building Products with Fraction Bars

Name _____

Date _____

Build with fraction bars on Building Mat 1–8a to solve the word problems provided. Below each exercise, write a word sentence about the result found for that word problem. When appropriate, state both the improper fraction and the equivalent mixed number.

1. Kerry sells candy in bags of 1 and 5-sixths ounces each. A customer wants 2 of the bags. How many ounces will Kerry sell to the customer?

2. There are 3 cartons. Each carton weighs 7-eighths of a kilogram. What is the total weight in kilograms of the 3 cartons?

3. Jana has 1 and 1-half yards of felt. She will use 3-fourths of that amount to make a small table cover. How many yards of the felt will she use?

4. The round trip between home and school is 3-fourths of a kilometer. How many kilometers equal 1-half of the round trip, or a 1-way trip?

5. Josh has 1 and 1-fourth gallons of ice cream. He plans to serve 2-thirds of the ice cream for dinner. How many gallons of ice cream will be served for dinner?

Activity 2: Pictorial Stage

Materials
 Worksheet 1–8b
 Worksheet 1–8c
 Red pencil and regular pencil

Procedure
1. Give each student a copy of Worksheet 1–8b, a copy of Worksheet 1–8c, and a red pencil. Now that students are comfortable multiplying with fraction bars on the building mat, they will work similar word problems with diagrams.

2. Each student should complete the frames on her or his own Worksheet 1–8b, but might share results with a partner.

3. For each exercise, students will subdivide whole bars in the upper region of a frame to show different fractional amounts of a whole for the multiplicand. The initial amounts will be shaded, using diagonal stripes for easy recognition.

4. If the multiplicand is a mixed number, the shaded whole bars must be traded to the smaller part size in order to have only one common part size appearing on the frame. These initial trades will be shown by marking new subdivisions with regular pencil.

5. The multiplier will then be applied to each individual part in the upper region of the frame. The denominator of the multiplier indicates how to subdivide each part of the multiplicand into new parts, and the numerator tells how many of the new parts to copy in the lower region of the frame. The subdividing into new parts should be shown with red pencil.

6. In order to copy parts of the correct size on the whole bars in the lower region of the frame, students must first subdivide those whole bars into the same number of parts shown on the whole bars in the upper region after subdivisions have been made with red pencil. Thus, the same final part size will be used on all whole bars of the frame. This allows a fractional name to be given to the copies drawn for the product.

7. Students must count the new parts drawn in the lower region to find the answer to the word problem. An equation for this product should be written below the exercise on Worksheet 1–8c.

8. Exercise 1 on Worksheet 1–8c should be discussed with the class in detail before students are allowed to work the additional problems on the worksheet on their own.

 Here is Exercise 1 from Worksheet 1–8c to consider: "Harold has 1 and 2-fourths gallons of spaghetti sauce. He will need 2-thirds of that amount to serve with spaghetti at a dinner. How many gallons of sauce will he need for the dinner?"

On the first frame of Worksheet 1–8b, have students shade (with diagonal stripes) the top whole bar and 2-fourths of the second whole bar to represent the multiplicand, 1 and 2-fourths. With their regular pencil, they should subdivide the top whole bar into 4 equal parts to show fourths, so that both whole bars in the upper region of the frame contain fourths. There will be 4-fourths and 2-fourths, or 6-fourths total, in the upper region. Here is the frame after this first trade on the top bar:

Since the multiplier is 2-thirds, remind students that this means that *each* fourth in the upper region must be subdivided into 3 equal parts. Then 2 of those 3 parts should be copied on a whole bar in the lower region of the frame. Discuss the idea that if each fourth of a whole bar in the upper region is subdivided into 3 new parts, the whole bar will be subdivided into 12 new parts total. Thus, the new parts being formed will be called twelfths of the whole bar.

Have students use regular pencil to divide the first two whole bars in the Product region of the frame into 12 equal parts per bar. They should then draw vertical segments in red pencil to subdivide each fourth in the upper region into 3 equal parts. Here is the frame after the subdividing is completed:

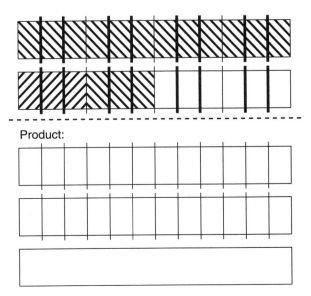

For every 3 shaded parts in the upper region students should mark 2 of the new parts with a red arrow. These 2 parts should be copied on one of the whole bars in the lower region by shading with regular pencil 2 of the twelfths already shown there. This process should continue until all shaded fourths have been considered. Encourage students to copy these parts in positions on the Product whole bars that are similar to their original locations in the upper region. This spacing will help students focus on the process being used. Here is how the final frame should appear:

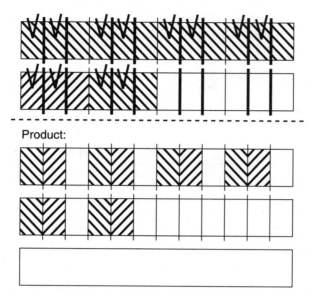

The total shaded parts in the Product region show the final answer to be 12-twelfths of a whole. Students should write a multiplication equation below Exercise 1 on Worksheet 1–8c that represents the change of the original mixed number to an improper fraction, as well as the final product. The other subdividing of the shaded parts will be reflected only in the final answer. Do not show any other changes, such as canceling, within the equation. This is necessary in order to see the numerical patterns for the algorithms, which will be discussed in Activity 3. Be sure to record the multiplier as the first factor and the multiplicand as the second factor. Here is a possible equation to use for Exercise 1:

$$\frac{2}{3} \times 1\frac{2}{4} = \frac{2}{3} \times \frac{6}{4} = \frac{12}{12} \text{ gallons, or 1 gallon of sauce used}$$

Answer Key for Worksheet 1–8c
This answer key provides possible equations to use.

1. $\frac{2}{3} \times 1\frac{2}{4} = \frac{2}{3} \times \frac{6}{4} = \frac{12}{12}$ gallons, or 1 gallon of sauce used

2. $\frac{1}{4} \times \frac{2}{3} = \frac{2}{12}$ of a gallon of gas, or $\frac{1}{6}$ of a gallon used

3. $3 \times \frac{5}{8} = \frac{15}{8}$ liters of water, or $1\frac{7}{8}$ liters

   [Do not write a 1 below the 3; it is not necessary, as will be discussed in Activity 3.]

4. $\frac{5}{6} \times 1\frac{1}{2} = \frac{5}{6} \times \frac{3}{2} = \frac{15}{12}$ meters of fabric, or $1\frac{3}{12}$ m or $1\frac{1}{4}$ m

WORKSHEET 1–8b

Drawing Products on
Fraction Bar Frames

Name _____

Date _____

1.

Product:

2.

Product:

WORKSHEET 1–8b Continued

Name _____

Date _____

3.

┌─────────────────────────────┐
│   │
│   │
└─────────────────────────────┘

┌─────────────────────────────┐
│   │
│   │
└─────────────────────────────┘

- -

Product:

┌─────────────────────────────┐
│   │
│   │
└─────────────────────────────┘

┌─────────────────────────────┐
│   │
│   │
└─────────────────────────────┘

┌─────────────────────────────┐
│   │
│   │
└─────────────────────────────┘

4.

┌─────────────────────────────┐
│   │
│   │
└─────────────────────────────┘

┌─────────────────────────────┐
│   │
│   │
└─────────────────────────────┘

- -

Product:

┌─────────────────────────────┐
│   │
│   │
└─────────────────────────────┘

┌─────────────────────────────┐
│   │
│   │
└─────────────────────────────┘

┌─────────────────────────────┐
│   │
│   │
└─────────────────────────────┘

WORSHEET 1–8c

Drawing Products Using
Fractions as Factors

Name _____

Date _____

Draw on a frame of Worksheet 1–8b to find the product for each exercise provided. Below the exercise on this worksheet, write number sentences that show the product.

1. Harold has 1 and 2-fourths gallons of spaghetti sauce. He will need 2-thirds of that amount to serve with spaghetti at a dinner. How many gallons of sauce will he need for the dinner?

2. Jody's motorcycle has 2-thirds of a gallon of gas. A trip to her aunt's house will use 1-fourth of the gas. How many gallons of gas will be used for the trip?

3. A bucket holds 5-eighths of a liter of water. How many liters of water will 3 buckets hold?

4. There are 1 and 1-half meters of fabric left on a bolt. Dana will use 5-sixths of the fabric to make some scarves. How many meters of fabric will be used in all for the scarves?

Activity 3: Independent Practice

Materials

Worksheet 1–8d
Regular pencil

Procedure

Give each student a copy of Worksheet 1–8d. Before students begin to work, discuss several exercises from Activities 1 and 2. On the board, write four or five equations from previous exercises where one factor was a whole number. For example, consider Exercise 1 from Activity 1, even though students did not record equations at that stage. The abstract equation would be $2 \times 1\frac{5}{6} = 2 \times \frac{11}{6} = \frac{22}{6}$. Do not change the answer to a mixed number at this point, and do not cancel among factors since a pattern is being sought. Have students compare the numbers used within each equation, beginning after a mixed number has been changed to an improper fraction. Guide students to discover that *the numerator of the answer equals the whole number factor multiplied by the numerator of the fraction factor, and the denominator of the answer just equals the denominator of the fraction factor.* This is a very easy pattern for students to see as long as it is developed *before* the pattern for fraction × fraction. No denominator of 1 needs to be created for the whole number factor. Students should write the italicized description in their notebooks.

Next, write four or five equations on the board that have fractions for both factors. For example, consider Exercise 5 from Activity 1: $\frac{2}{3} \times 1\frac{1}{4} = \frac{2}{3} \times \frac{5}{4} = \frac{10}{12}$. Do not reduce the final fraction, and do not cancel among the factors since a pattern is being sought. Again, have students compare the numbers used within each equation, beginning after a mixed number has been changed to an improper fraction. Guide students to discover that *the numerator of the answer equals the product of the numerators of the two fraction factors, and the denominator of the answer equals the product of the denominators of the two fraction factors.* Students should now write this second description in their notebooks.

Now have students solve each exercise on Worksheet 1–8d by writing an equation below the exercise similar to those equations recorded on Worksheet 1–8c. Encourage students to use the trading language for changing mixed numbers to improper fractions when needed and to apply the two multiplication algorithms they have discovered through their pattern searches. When all students have finished the worksheet, have several students share their answers with the rest of the class.

Answer Key for Worksheet 1–8d

1. $4 \times 2\frac{3}{10} = 4 \times \frac{23}{10} = \frac{92}{10}$ lbs., or $9\frac{2}{10}$ lbs. or $9\frac{1}{5}$ lbs.

2. $9 \times \frac{7}{12} = \frac{63}{12}$ kg, or $5\frac{3}{12}$ kg or $5\frac{1}{4}$ kg

3. $5 \times 3\frac{5}{8} = 5 \times \frac{29}{8} = \frac{145}{8}$ gal., or $18\frac{1}{8}$ gal.

4. $\frac{3}{4} \times 8\frac{4}{5} = \frac{3}{4} \times \frac{44}{5} = \frac{132}{20}$ sq m, or $6\frac{12}{20}$ sq m or $6\frac{3}{5}$ sq m

5. $\frac{1}{8} \times 35\frac{2}{3} = \frac{1}{8} \times \frac{107}{3} = \frac{107}{24}$ mi., or $4\frac{11}{24}$ mi.

6. $\frac{2}{3} \times \frac{15}{16} = \frac{30}{48}$ km, or $\frac{5}{8}$ km

Possible Testing Errors That May Occur for This Objective

- When one factor is a whole number, some students multiply the whole number by both the numerator and the denominator of the fraction factor. For example, $3 \times \frac{2}{5}$ incorrectly becomes $\frac{6}{15}$ instead of $\frac{6}{5}$.

- Students who have been taught to cancel among the factors may cancel incorrectly, producing incorrect new factors to use for the final product.

- If the product produces an improper fraction (for example, 14-tenths), students may change the improper fraction to an incorrect mixed number. A division or subtraction fact error may be the cause.

- The computation yields a fractional sum that is not in lowest terms, and students do not recognize the reduced fraction in the response choices.

112

WORKSHEET 1–8d

Multiplying Fractions and Mixed Numbers to Solve Word Problems

Name _____

Date _____

Solve the word problems provided. Write an equation below each exercise to show the multiplication steps used.

1. There are 4 display trays at the deli counter. Each tray holds $2\frac{3}{10}$ pounds of cheese. How many pounds of cheese total are on display at the deli counter?

2. Roy has 9 bags of birdseed for his bird feeder. Each bag weighs $\frac{7}{12}$ of a kilogram. What is the weight of all 9 bags together?

3. Candace filled each of 5 large containers with $3\frac{5}{8}$ gallons of gasoline. How many gallons total were in the 5 containers together?

4. The area of a garden is $8\frac{4}{5}$ square meters, and 3-fourths of the garden is planted with grass. How many square meters of grass are in the garden?

5. Juan drove $35\frac{2}{3}$ miles on business. He did 7-eighths of his driving during daylight. How many miles did he drive after dark?

6. Brooks jogged $\frac{15}{16}$ of a kilometer on Saturday, and his brother jogged 2-thirds of that distance. How far did his brother jog in kilometers?

Objective 9
Develop and apply scientific notation to solve word problems.

Students who are being introduced to scientific notation need activities that will help them focus on the meanings of the terms within the notation. The following lessons provide that experience. It is assumed that students have already mastered multiplication facts and the multiplication of more than two factors (for example, $3 \times 2 \times 2$). They should also understand the relationship between an exponent and its base. Thus, the focus here is on the grouping of certain factors of a number and the notation that shows such groupings.

Activity 1: Manipulative Stage

Materials
Packet of 15 paper squares, 2 inches by 2 inches, per pair of students (see packet details in step 1 of the procedure)
One flat coffee stirrer per pair of students
Worksheet 1–9a
Regular pencil

Procedure
1. Give each pair of students two copies of Worksheet 1–9a, a packet of 15 paper squares that are 2 inches by 2 inches, and one flat coffee stirrer. Five of the paper squares should have the numbers 1 through 5 written on them, with a different number on each square. Ten more squares should contain the number 10 on each square.

2. For each number on Worksheet 1–9a, write the number on the board. Some numbers will be in standard form, and others will be in scientific notation. Have students represent the number on their desktops with their paper squares.

3. Guide students to rearrange the paper squares and find a new name for the number in either scientific notation or standard form. The new name should be recorded beside the exercise on Worksheet 1–9a.

4. Discussion of Exercises 1–3 is provided. After the discussion, allow students to work the other exercises independently.

Consider Exercise 1: "Change 2,000,000 to scientific notation."
Write the number on the board: 2,000,000. Ask students to locate the left-most digit that is not zero, which will be 2, and to identify its place value position (1,000,000). Tell students to first think of the number as $2 \times 1,000,000$, then as the product of the 2 and several 10s. Have them show this last product by placing paper squares on their desktop to represent the *factors*. From left to right, the row of paper squares should show one 2 and six 10s:

| 2 | 10 | 10 | 10 | 10 | 10 | 10 |

Now have students place each set of similar factors in its own stack. The 2 will be alone, and the 10s will be in another stack. Tell them that the *exponent*, a number written higher on the writing line than the factor itself, will indicate how high the factor's stack is, and that the factors are still being multiplied, even though they are arranged in stacks. Since we are developing scientific notation, we will omit the exponent 1 when there is only one paper square in a stack:

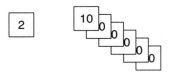

Students should now record the following beside Exercise 1 on Worksheet 1–9a: "2,000,000 = 2 × (10 × 10 × 10 × 10 × 10 × 10) = 2×10^6." Parentheses should be used to show each factor's own grouping or stack.

Now consider Exercise 2: "Change 0.0005 to standard form."

Write the number on the board: 0.0005. Have students state the word name for the number: 5 ten-thousandths. The 5 is the left-most digit that is not zero, and it is in the ten-thousandths position.

Since this is a fraction less than 1, tell students to think of 5 over 10,000. To show this fraction with paper squares, students should place the paper square for the number 5 on the desktop and place the flat coffee stirrer below the 5. Then below the coffee stirrer (the denominator position), they should place four paper squares containing 10s to show the product equal to 10,000:

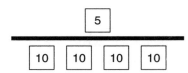

The 10s should now be placed in a stack together. Since the stack of four 10s is below the 5, or in the denominator, the stack must be expressed with a negative exponent when shown as a factor in the numerator. Thus, students should record the following beside Exercise 2 on Worksheet 1–9a:

$$0.0005 = \frac{5}{10 \times 10 \times 10 \times 10} = \frac{5}{10^4} = 5 \times 10^{-4}$$

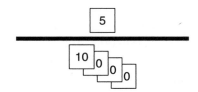

Now discuss Exercise 3: "Change 4×10^{-3} to standard form."

To work this exercise, students merely need to reverse the procedure of Exercise 2. That is, since a negative exponent is on the 10 factor, three 10s should be placed in a stack below the coffee stirrer, and one 4 should be placed above the coffee stirrer. Then the 10s should be unstacked to form a row of three 10s, representing $10 \times 10 \times 10$, or 1,000. The squares now show the fraction: 4-thousandths, whose number name is 0.004. Students should record the following beside Exercise 3:

$$4 \times 10^{-3} = \frac{4}{10^3} = \frac{4}{10 \times 10 \times 10} = 0.004$$

Answer Key for Worksheet 1–9a

1. $2{,}000{,}000 = 2 \times (10 \times 10 \times 10 \times 10 \times 10 \times 10) = 2 \times 10^6$

2. $0.0005 = \dfrac{5}{10 \times 10 \times 10 \times 10} = \dfrac{5}{10^4} = 5 \times 10^{-4}$

3. $4 \times 10^{-3} = \dfrac{4}{10^3} = \dfrac{4}{10 \times 10 \times 10} = 0.004$

4. $5{,}000{,}000{,}000 = 5 \times (10 \times 10 \times 10 \times 10 \times 10 \times 10 \times 10 \times 10 \times 10) = 5 \times 10^9$

5. $0.00002 = \dfrac{2}{10 \times 10 \times 10 \times 10 \times 10} = \dfrac{2}{10^5} = 2 \times 10^{-5}$

6. $3 \times 10^6 = 3 \times (10 \times 10 \times 10 \times 10 \times 10 \times 10) = 3{,}000{,}000$

116

WORKSHEET 1–9a   Name _____

Building with Scientific Notation   Date _____

Build with paper squares to work each exercise provided. Write an equation below each exercise to show how the given number is changed to its new form.

1. Change 2,000,000 to scientific notation.

2. Change 0.0005 to scientific notation.

3. Change 4×10^{-3} to standard form.

4. Change 5,000,000,000 to scientific notation.

5. Change 0.00002 to scientific notation.

6. Change 3×10^{6} to standard form.

Activity 2: Pictorial Stage

Materials

  Worksheet 1–9b
  Red pencil and regular pencil

Procedure

1. Give each student a copy of Worksheet 1–9b and a red pencil.

2. Have students change each number on Worksheet 1–9b according to the instructions. Have them express each number as the product of a decimal number less than 10 and several factors of 10. Then have students draw rings in red pencil around the groups of similar factors in the written notation. The red pencil will be used to identify factors to be represented by an exponent.

3. For each exercise, the resulting equation will reflect a notation similar to that used in Activity 1 and should be recorded below the exercise on the worksheet.

4. Discuss Exercises 1 and 2 with the class before allowing students to work the other exercises independently.

Consider Exercise 1 on Worksheet 1–9b: "Change 8,500 to scientific notation."

For the number 8,500, which is greater than 1, have students identify the place value of the left-most nonzero digit. The digit 8 is the left-most digit and is in the thousands place. The number 8,500 equals 8 thousands plus a little more; that is, $8{,}500 > (8 \times 1{,}000)$. So $\underline{8}{,}500$ is equivalent to $\underline{8}.5 \times 1{,}000$. Students should then write the equation below Exercise 1 on Worksheet 1–9b as follows: "$8{,}500 = \underline{8}.5 \times 1{,}000 = \underline{8}.5 \times 10 \times 10 \times 10$," underlining the digit 8 in each expression.

Have students draw a ring in red pencil around the group of 10s (equivalent to forming a stack of paper squares at the manipulative stage). Tell them that the number of factors inside a red ring indicates the "exponent," while the factor itself is the "base." Also remind students that a single factor, like 8.5 in this example, will be written without the exponent, 1. Students should then record the final exponential form below Exercise 1. The completed equation is shown below:

$$\underline{8}{,}500 = \underline{8}.5 \times 1{,}000 = \underline{8}.5 \times \boxed{10 \times 10 \times 10} = \underline{8}.5 \times 10^3$$

Now discuss Exercise 2: "Change 0.000034 to scientific notation."

The number 0.000034 is less than 1. Have students identify and underline the left-most digit that is not zero. They should also identify the digit's place value. The digit is 3, and it is in the hundred thousandths position. Since $0.000034 > 0.00003$, we also know $\dfrac{3.4}{100{,}000} > \dfrac{3}{100{,}000}$, which preserves the original place value (here shown by the denominator).

   The 100,000 should be factored into a product of 10s, and a ring drawn with red pencil around the product. Since the group of 10s is in the denominator, it must be shown with a negative exponent in the numerator. Students should write the following equation below Exercise 2 on Worksheet 1–9b, with the digit 3 underlined in each expression:

$$0.00003\underline{4} = \frac{3.4}{100,000} = \frac{3.4}{(10 \times 10 \times 10 \times 10 \times 10)} = 3.4 \times 10^{-5}$$

Answer Key for Worksheet 1–9b

1. $\underline{8},500 = \underline{8}.5 \times 1,000 = \underline{8}.5 \times (10 \times 10 \times 10) = \underline{8}.5 \times 10^{3}$

2. $0.00003\underline{4} = \dfrac{3.4}{100,000} = \dfrac{3.4}{(10 \times 10 \times 10 \times 10 \times 10)} = 3.4 \times 10^{-5}$

3. $\underline{4}.6 \times 10^{-2} = \dfrac{4.6}{10 \times 10} = \dfrac{4.6}{100} = 0.0\underline{4}6$

4. $\underline{5}30,000,000 = \underline{5}.3 \times 100,000,000 = \underline{5}.3 \times 10 \times 10 \times 10 \times 10 \times 10 \times 10 \times 10 \times 10 = \underline{5}.3 \times 10^{8}$

5. $0.000\underline{1}7 = \dfrac{1.7}{10,000} = \dfrac{1.7}{10 \times 10 \times 10 \times 10} = \underline{1}.7 \times 10^{-4}$

6. $\underline{6}.25 \times 10^{5} = \underline{6}.25 \times 10 \times 10 \times 10 \times 10 \times 10 = \underline{6}.25 \times 100,000 = \underline{6}25,000$

WORKSHEET 1–9b
Factoring with Scientific Notation

Name _____

Date _____

Ring in red pencil the factors of 10 needed to work each exercise provided. Write an equation below each exercise to show how the given number is changed to its new form.

1. Change 8,500 to scientific notation.

2. Change 0.000034 to scientific notation.

3. Change 4.6×10^{-2} to standard form.

4. Change 530,000,000 to scientific notation.

5. Change 0.00017 to scientific notation.

6. Change 6.25×10^{5} to standard form.

Activity 3: Independent Practice

Materials
Worksheet 1–9c
Regular pencil

Procedure
Give each student a copy of Worksheet 1–9c. After all have completed the worksheet, ask several students to share their answers with the rest of the class.

Answer Key for Worksheet 1–9c
1. C

2. A

3. B

4. A

5. D

6. D

Possible Testing Errors That May Occur for This Objective
- Students count the digits in the single factor along with the exponent on the 10 and ignore the decimal point. For example, in 3.5×10^4, they count the two digits in 3.5 and the exponent 4 for a total of 6 digits, which causes them to select 350,000 as the final number instead of 35,000.

- Students ignore the negative sign on the exponent and select a number greater than one. That is, the decimal is always moved to the right based on the absolute value of the exponent.

- Students use the exponent to determine the correct number of places to move the decimal, but they count in the wrong direction. For example, if they need to change 2.7 by 3 places to the left to get 0.0027, they will instead go 3 places to the right to get 2,700.

WORKSHEET 1–9c

Solving Word Problems with
Scientific Notation

Name _____

Date _____

Use scientific notation to work each exercise provided.

1. The average nitrogen gas molecule has a diameter of 3.7×10^{-10} meters. Which length is equivalent to the diameter's measure?

   A. 370,000,000,000 m

   B. 3,700,000,000 m

   C. 0.00000000037 m

   D. 0.0000000037 m

2. A certain radio signal travels at 3.4×10^{8} meters per second. Which is another way to express this measure?

   A. 340,000,000 m/sec

   B. 34,000,000 m/sec

   C. 0.000000034 m/sec

   D. 0.00000034 m/sec

3. Three large cities have a total population of 9,000,000 people. This amount may also be expressed with an exponent as:

   A. 9×10^{7}

   B. 9×10^{6}

   C. 9×10^{-6}

   D. 9×10^{-7}

WORKSHEET 1–9c Continued

Name _____

Date _____

4. An average nitrogen gas molecule travels 0.000000066 meter before smashing into another gas molecule. Express this distance as a decimal number.

   A. 6.6×10^{-8} m

   B. 6.6×10^{-7} m

   C. 6.6×10^{9} m

   D. 6.6×10^{8} m

5. Hydrofluoric acid is considered a weak acid in water because it has a low K_a value of 6.8×10^{-4}. This is equivalent to which decimal number?

   A. 68,000

   B. 680,000

   C. 0.000068

   D. 0.00068

6. At certain points in its orbit, the planet Mars is about 248,000,000 miles from earth. What is this distance in scientific notation?

   A. 2.48×10^{-8} mi

   B. 2.48×10^{-9} mi

   C. 2.48×10^{7} mi

   D. 2.48×10^{8} mi

Section 1

Name _____

Date _____

NUMBER, OPERATION, AND QUANTITATIVE REASONING: PRACTICE TEST ANSWER SHEET

Directions: Use the Answer Sheet to darken the letter of the choice that best answers each question.

1.	○ A	○ B	○ C	○ D	10.	○ A	○ B	○ C	○ D
2.	○ A	○ B	○ C	○ D	11.	○ A	○ B	○ C	○ D
3.	○ A	○ B	○ C	○ D	12.	○ A	○ B	○ C	○ D
4.	○ A	○ B	○ C	○ D	13.	○ A	○ B	○ C	○ D
5.	○ A	○ B	○ C	○ D	14.	○ A	○ B	○ C	○ D
6.	○ A	○ B	○ C	○ D	15.	○ A	○ B	○ C	○ D
7.	○ A	○ B	○ C	○ D	16.	○ A	○ B	○ C	○ D
8.	○ A	○ B	○ C	○ D	17.	○ A	○ B	○ C	○ D
9.	○ A	○ B	○ C	○ D	18.	○ A	○ B	○ C	○ D

SECTION 1: NUMBER, OPERATION, AND QUANTITATIVE REASONING: PRACTICE TEST

1. A librarian arranged some books on the shelf using the Dewey decimal system. Which group of book numbers is listed in order from least to greatest?

   A. 715, 715.29, 715.3, 715.39

   B. 108.4, 108.04, 110.21, 112.0

   C. 390.5, 396.53, 398.62, 398.05

   D. 529.01, 529.10, 529.02, 529.4

2. Joe is offered sales commissions of 18%, 0.2, $\frac{1}{4}$, and $\frac{3}{20}$ of every dollar sold by four different stores, respectively. Which rate is the highest?

   A. 18%   B. 0.2   C. $\frac{1}{4}$ D. $\frac{3}{20}$

3. Michelle has 12 bags of birdseed for her bird feeder. Each bag weighs 3.6 kilograms. What is the weight of all 12 bags together?

   A. 33.2 kg   B. 41.2 kg   C. 42.2 kg   D. 43.2 kg

4. Larry bought 8 gallons of gasoline for his car at $1.39 per gallon. How much did he pay for the gasoline?

   A. $11.42   B. $11.12   C. $11.04   D. $11.03

5. A block of cheese weighs 4.8 pounds. How many full packages of sliced cheese can be made from this block if each package is to weigh 1.5 pounds?

   A. 5 pkg.   B. 4 pkg.   C. 3 pkg.   D. 2 pkg.

6. Chui bought some CDs for a total cost of $43.75. If each CD sells for $6.25, how many CDs did Chui buy?

   A. 7 CDs   B. 6 CDs   C. 5 CDs   D. 4 CDs

SECTION 1: NUMBER, OPERATION, AND QUANTITATIVE REASONING: PRACTICE TEST (Continued)

7. A tailor has 8.75 yards of fabric for making some vests. Each vest requires 2.6 yards. He wants to sell each vest for $8.99. Which is a reasonable estimate of how much he should expect to earn from selling the vests?

   A. $50   B. $43   C. $35   D. $27

8. Jorge earned $89.50 each week for 2.5 weeks at one store, then earned $62.95 for one week at another store. Which expression is a reasonable estimate of his total earnings from the two stores?

   A. $(2 \times \$90) + \$60$ C. $(\$90 \div 3) + \$60$

   B. $(3 \times \$90) + \$60$ D. $2 \times (\$90 + \$60)$

9. Sharon hiked $11\frac{2}{5}$ miles on Monday, $10\frac{1}{2}$ miles on Tuesday, and 8 miles on Wednesday. What is the total number of miles Sharon hiked during these 3 days?

   A. 29 mi.   B. $29\frac{3}{7}$ mi.   C. $29\frac{9}{10}$ mi.   D. Not shown here

10. A jeweler used $\frac{3}{4}$ of a meter of silver chain to make a bracelet and $\frac{7}{8}$ of a meter to make a necklace. How many meters of silver chain were used in all to make the 2 pieces of jewelry?

    A. $1\frac{5}{8}$ m   B. $1\frac{1}{2}$ m   C. $\frac{5}{6}$ m   D. $\frac{13}{16}$ m

11. Bill bought 8 gallons of gasoline in a large container. He used $3\frac{5}{8}$ gallons of the gasoline for his boat motor. How many gallons remain in the container?

    A. $5\frac{5}{8}$ gal.   B. $4\frac{5}{8}$ gal.   C. $4\frac{1}{2}$ gal.   D. $4\frac{3}{8}$ gal.

12. During spring break, Maria traveled $147\frac{2}{3}$ miles, and Carlos traveled $195\frac{3}{4}$ miles. How many miles shorter was Maria's trip than Carlos's trip?

    A. $52\frac{1}{12}$ mi.   B. $48\frac{5}{7}$ mi.   C. $48\frac{1}{2}$ mi.   D. $47\frac{1}{2}$ mi.

13. If Dan has $2\frac{4}{5}$ ounces left from an 8-ounce carton of yogurt, what fractional part of the original carton does he have left?

    A. $\frac{1}{4}$ carton   B. $\frac{7}{20}$ carton   C. $2\frac{6}{7}$ carton   D. Not shown here

SECTION 1: NUMBER, OPERATION, AND QUANTITATIVE REASONING:
PRACTICE TEST (Continued)

14. Kristen rode her bike for $32\frac{1}{4}$ miles total over several days. If she averaged $5\frac{3}{8}$ miles per day, how many days did she ride her bike?

    A. 7 days   B. 6 days   C. 5 days   D. 4 days

15. Landon jogged $2\frac{7}{10}$ kilometers on Saturday, but his brother Harry jogged only two-thirds of that distance. How far did Harry jog in kilometers?

    A. $1\frac{4}{5}$ km   B. $1\frac{1}{3}$ km   C. $\frac{14}{15}$ km   D. Not shown here

16. Kendra filled each of 8 containers with $1\frac{5}{6}$ liters of punch for a party. How many liters of punch total were in the 8 containers together?

    A. $7\frac{2}{3}$ L   B. $8\frac{5}{6}$ L   C. $12\frac{1}{2}$ L   D. $14\frac{2}{3}$ L

17. Four large cities have a total population of 13,000,000 people. This amount may also be expressed in scientific notation as:

    A. 1.3×10^7 B. 1.3×10^6 C. 1.3×10^{-6} D. 1.3×10^{-7}

18. A gas molecule has an average diameter of 2.5×10^{-10} meters. Which length is equivalent to the diameter's measure?

    A. 250,000,000,000 m   C. 0.00000000025 m

    B. 2,500,000,000 m   D. 0.0000000025 m

Section 1: Number, Operation, and Quantitative Reasoning: Answer Key for Practice Test

The objective being tested is shown in brackets beside the answer.

1. A [1]	10. A [5]
2. C [1]	11. D [6]
3. D [2]	12. C [6]
4. B [2]	13. B [7]
5. C [3]	14. B [7]
6. A [3]	15. A [8]
7. D [4]	16. D [8]
8. B [4]	17. A [9]
9. C [5]	18. C [9]

PROPORTIONAL AND ALGEBRAIC REASONING

Objective 1
Apply ratios in proportional relationships involving unit rates, scale factors, probabilities, or percents.

Proportional thinking allows several major ideas to be placed into a larger family of concepts. These ideas include probability, percents, and rates. For example, given the rate of 30 mph, students are typically taught to multiply the given rate by a new time to find a new corresponding distance in miles. Using the *proportion* approach, however, students may equate the ratio of 30 miles to 1 hour to the ratio of the new distance to the new time. Similarly, probability and percent problems may be set up as proportions. The concept of proportions and its applications are developed in the following activities.

Activity 1: Manipulative Stage

Materials
> Building Mat 2–1a per pair of students
> Bag of small counters (2 colors, 20 counters per color) per pair of students
> Worksheet 2–1a
> Regular pencil

Procedure
1. Give each pair of students two copies of Worksheet 2–1a, a copy of Building Mat 2–1a, and a bag of small counters (2 colors, 20 counters per color). The top level on the mat will be for the *basic ratio* (a ratio that uses the smallest whole numbers possible), and the bottom level on the mat will be for the *secondary ratio* (the larger amounts formed by multiple amounts of the basic ratio's numbers, each amount being arranged as an array). One color of counter will be used to show the first amount in each ratio, and the second color of counter will show the second amount in each ratio.

2. Have students build basic ratios and their corresponding secondary ratios on Building Mat 2–1a with the counters, using the exercises in Worksheet 2–1a.

3. After students complete each exercise, have them write a word sentence below the exercise, describing their results.

4. Discuss Exercise 1 on Worksheet 2–1a before allowing students to work independently.

Consider Exercise 1 from Worksheet 2–1a: "At the store, 3 mechanical pencils cost $2. What will 12 pencils cost?"

Have students place three color 1 counters (the three pencils) in a row in the left empty region of the top level of Building Mat 2–1a and two color 2 counters (the $2 price for the 3 pencils) in the right empty region of the top level. The pencils will be represented in the left region since they were mentioned first before the cost in the exercise. Now have the students randomly place 12 color 1 counters in the left empty region of the lower level of the mat.

Students must find how many color 2 counters go in the lower right region of Building Mat 2–1a. Since the secondary ratio consists of repeats of the basic ratio, the color 1 counters in the lower left region must be rearranged into an array having three counters per row to match the row of color 1 counters in the top left region; four rows will be formed. The four rows indicate that four of the basic ratio have been used to make the secondary ratio. Thus, four rows of color 2 counters must be used in the lower right region of the mat.

Since two color 2 counters have been used in the basic ratio, two color 2 counters must be used in each of the four rows in the secondary ratio. The final mat arrangement yields eight color 2 counters in the right region of the secondary ratio. This indicates that twelve pencils will cost $8. Have students record the results on Worksheet 2–1a below Exercise 1 as follows: "Three pencils compare to $2 as 12 pencils compare to $8. So 12 pencils cost $8." The initial and final stages of mat work are shown below. The final completed building mat represents a proportion (that is, two equivalent ratios):

Initial Mat

Basic ratio	◌ ◌ ◌	● ●
Secondary ratio	◌ ◌ ◌ ◌ ◌ ◌ ◌ ◌ ◌ ◌ ◌ ◌	

Final Mat

Basic ratio	◌ ◌ ◌	● ●
Secondary ratio	◌ ◌ ◌ ◌ ◌ ◌ ◌ ◌ ◌ ◌ ◌ ◌	● ● ● ● ● ● ● ●

There are four regions to fill on Building Mat 2–1a. The word problems in the exercises of Worksheet 2–1a vary so that different regions need to be filled. In Exercise 1, the lower right region was needed. Whenever one region is needed, the numbers for the other three regions must be given in the word problem. The placement in the left and right regions of the building mat should follow the initial order given for the ratios in each exercise. For example, if the exercise states "3 girls for every 5 boys," then "3 girls" should be shown in the upper left region and "5 boys" should be shown in the upper right region.

Answer Key for Worksheet 2–1a
The answer key provides possible sentences to use.

1. 3 pencils compare to $2 as 12 pencils compare to $8. So 12 pencils cost $8.

2. 4 people compare to 3 dogs as 16 people compare to 12 dogs. So 16 people attended the dog show.

3. 12 girls compare to 15 boys as 4 girls compare to 5 boys. There are 5 boys in the class for every 4 girls.

4. 1 red marble compares to 3 blue marbles as 3 red marbles compare to 9 blue marbles. So there are 3 red and 9 blue marbles in 12 marbles total.

5. 12 cans compare to $16 as 3 cans compare to $4. The basic ratio is 3 cans for $4.

6. 5 miles compare to 1 hour as 15 miles compare to 3 hours. It will take 3 hours to ride 15 miles on the bike.

Building Mat 2–1a

Basic ratio	
Secondary ratio	

WORKSHEET 2–1a   Name _____
Building Ratios   Date _____

Solve the word problems provided by placing counters on Building Mat 2–1a. Below each exercise, write a word sentence that states as a proportion the results found for that exercise.

1. At the store, 3 mechanical pencils cost $2. What will 12 pencils cost?

2. At the dog show, there are 4 people for every 3 dogs. If there are 12 dogs in the show, how many people are present at the show?

3. Mr. Jordan's eighth-grade class has 12 girls and 15 boys. How many boys are in the class for every 4 girls?

4. There is 1 red marble for every 3 blue marbles in a box. If there are 12 marbles total in the box and each marble is either red or blue, how many marbles are red and how many are blue?

5. Jan bought 12 cans of stew for $16. What is the basic ratio of cans to dollars?

6. If George rides his bike at 5 mph, how many hours will it take him to ride 15 miles if his speed remains constant?

Activity 2: Pictorial Stage

Materials
> Worksheet 2–1b
> Red pencil and regular pencil

Procedure
1. Give each student a copy of Worksheet 2–1b and a red pencil.

2. Students should complete Exercises 1 through 3 by drawing small shapes in the ratio frames. The finished ratio frames should look much like the completed building mat illustrated in the manipulative stage.

3. Beside each completed ratio frame, have students record two equations that describe the proportion represented. The discussion of Exercise 1 will include the two types of equations to use.

4. For each exercise in Exercises 4 and 5, students will graph on a grid several ratio pairs that come from the same situation. On the grid, the points for the ratio pairs will then be connected in red pencil. In each case, a red line should be formed, which indicates that the proportional situations are linear relationships.

5. Discuss Exercise 1 on Worksheet 2–1b with the class before allowing students to finish the worksheet independently. Also review graphing techniques before having them work Exercises 4 and 5.

Consider Exercise 1: "There are 15 cats and 9 dogs at the pet shop. How many cats are there for every 3 dogs?"

Students should draw circles on the ratio frame to represent the cats and triangles to represent the dogs. At first, 3 triangles will be drawn in the upper right region of the ratio frame to represent the 3 dogs. The upper right region is used since "dogs" was stated second in the initial ratio of *cats* to *dogs*. Having "3 triangles in one row" then determines the number per row in the lower right region. This requires 3 rows of triangles to be drawn in order to show the 9 dogs total. Remind students that rows in an array are left to right, not up and down.

Students should now be aware that 3 *rows* of circles will have to be drawn in the lower left region of the frame when representing all the cats. Since 15 circles must be drawn to represent the 15 cats total and these circles must be drawn in 3 rows, this forces 5 circles to be in each row. In turn, this causes 5 circles to be drawn in the upper left region of the ratio frame. The initial and final stages of the ratio frame are shown here:

Initial Frame

Basic ratio		△△△
Secondary ratio		△△△ △△△ △△△

Final Frame

Basic ratio	○○○○○	△△△
Secondary ratio	○○○○○ ○○○○○ ○○○○○	△△△ △△△ △△△

Have students record their results beside the ratio frame that is now completed. Be sure that the two ratios keep the same order, that is, "cats to dogs." Have them use the following two formats:

$$15 \text{ cats to } 9 \text{ dogs} = 5 \text{ cats to } 3 \text{ dogs}$$
$$\frac{15}{9} = \frac{3 \times 5}{3 \times 3} = \frac{5}{3}$$

Notice that the left factor in the numerator and in the denominator of the middle expression, $\frac{(3 \times 5)}{(3 \times 3)}$, indicates the number of *rows* drawn in each region of the secondary ratio. The expression $\frac{15}{9}$ represents the secondary ratio, and $\frac{5}{3}$ represents the basic ratio (read as "15 to 9" and "5 to 3"). Discuss the idea that finding equivalent ratios in a proportion is similar to finding equivalent fractions. Interpret "3 × 5" to be "3 rows of 5 per row" in order to be consistent with the language of multiplication.

In preparation for Exercises 4 and 5 on Worksheet 2–1b, review the graphing of ordered pairs. Also discuss how to determine the step or interval sizes for the horizontal and vertical scales of a grid. In each of the two exercises, the three ordered pairs plotted will have collinear points. The red path connecting the three points will be straight. Equivalent ratios have a linear relationship. After students have completed Exercises 4 and 5, help them make these observations.

Answer Key for Worksheet 2–1b

1. 15 cats to 9 dogs = 5 cats to 3 dogs

   $$\frac{15}{9} = \frac{3 \times 5}{3 \times 3} = \frac{5 \text{ cats}}{3 \text{ dogs}}$$

2. $4 to 1 hr. = $20 to 5 hrs.

   $$\frac{\$4}{1} = \frac{5 \times \$4}{5 \times 1} = \frac{\$20}{5 \text{ hrs}}$$

3. 2 blue to 5 total marbles = 8 blue to 20 total marbles

   $$\frac{2}{5} = \frac{4 \times 2}{4 \times 5} = \frac{8 \text{ blue marbles}}{20 \text{ total marbles}}$$

4. Ordered pairs graphed: (1 hr., $4), (5 hrs., $20), (7 hrs., $28); connecting red path is straight

5. Ordered pairs graphed: (5 total, 2 blue), (15 total, 6 blue), (20 total, 8 blue); connecting red path is straight

WORKSHEET 2–1b
Drawing and Graphing Ratios

Name _____

Date _____

Solve the word problems provided by drawing circles and triangles on a ratio frame provided. Beside Exercises 1 through 3, write two equations that state as a proportion the results found for each exercise. For Exercises 4 and 5, graph ordered pairs for ratios on the grids as directed.

1. There are 15 cats and 9 dogs at the pet shop. How many cats are there for every 3 dogs?

Basic ratio		
Secondary ratio		

2. Lynn earns $4 per hour at her weekend job. How many hours must she work to earn $20?

Basic ratio		
Secondary ratio		

3. There are 2 blue marbles for every 5 marbles in a jar. If there are 20 marbles total, how many marbles are blue?

Basic ratio		
Secondary ratio		

138

WORKSHEET 2–1b Continued   Name _____

                                Date _____

On each grid for Exercises 4 and 5, plot points for the three ratios found, and draw a path in red pencil to connect the three points. What do you notice about the red path drawn on each grid?

4. Find another secondary ratio for Exercise 2, using 7 hours for the time. Then plot points for the 3 ratios found, using (hours worked, amount earned) as the ordered pair. Number the grid axes as needed.

Amount
earned

Hours
worked

5. Find another secondary ratio for Exercise 3, using 15 marbles total. Then plot points for the 3 ratios found, using (total number of marbles, number of blue marbles) as the ordered pair. Number the grid axes as needed.

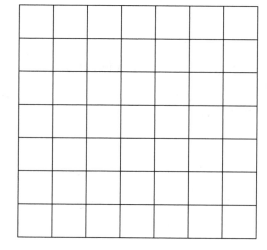

Number of
blue
marbles

Number of
total
marbles

Activity 3: Independent Practice

Materials
> Worksheet 2–1c
> Regular pencil

Procedure

Give each student a copy of Worksheet 2–1c. Encourage students to set up proportions similar to those equations used in Exercises 1 through 3 on Worksheet 2–1b of Activity 2. For example, in Exercise 3 of Worksheet 2–1c, they might write the following:

$$\frac{13}{20} = \frac{5 \times 13}{5 \times 20} = \frac{N}{100}, \text{ where N equals 65 shots made.}$$

Since N is compared to 100, finding N as 65 is equivalent to finding that 65% of the attempted shots were successful. Although Exercises 3 and 7 involve percents, students should focus on the proportion method to solve the problems and not on an alternative method often used for percents.

Also, in problems like Exercise 7, students may have difficulty finding the correct factor to use to form the new or equivalent ratio. In such cases, simple integral factors do not work. Show students how to construct the factor in the following way. The proportion needed is $\frac{\$24}{N} = \frac{40}{100}$, where the numerators are the dollars and the percent is the amount for the discount. The denominators N and 100 represent the dollars and percent amount for the total cost or regular price. The numerator and denominator of one ratio should multiply by the same factor to produce the numerator and denominator of the other ratio. To construct the factor, consider the two numerators with known values. How can 40 be changed to $24? A factor can be constructed so that 40 is divided out and $24 is brought in; that is, $\left(\frac{\$24}{40}\right)$ becomes the chosen factor. Then $40 \times \left(\frac{\$24}{40}\right)$ will equal $24. Then the denominators must use the same factor: $100 \times \left(\frac{\$24}{40}\right)$ must equal N. Students should not compute $\frac{\$24}{40}$ until this last equation is set up. So they will have $100 \times \left(\frac{\$24}{40}\right) = \$60$ for N, which is the regular price (total cost) of the jacket.

Answer Key for Worksheet 2–1c

1. B

2. D

3. A

4. B

5. C

6. D

7. B

Possible Testing Errors That May Occur for This Objective

- Students multiply the numerator of the initial ratio by one factor and the denominator by another factor when changing the initial ratio to an equivalent ratio.

- The initial ratio's numerator and denominator are changed to the new ratio's numerator and denominator by adding a constant instead of multiplying by a constant. For example, to compare $\frac{3}{8}$ to $\frac{N}{12}$ to find N, students incorrectly use $\frac{(3+4)}{(8+4)} = \frac{7}{12}$, instead of $\frac{(1.5 \times 3)}{(1.5 \times 8)} = \frac{4.5}{12}$.

- Students do not maintain the same order in the two ratios being compared in a proportion. For example, they will equate $\frac{cats}{dogs}$ to $\frac{dogs}{cats}$, instead of using $\frac{cats}{dogs} = \frac{cats}{dogs}$.

WORKSHEET 2–1c   Name _____

Using Ratios to Solve Word Problems   Date _____

Solve the word problems using proportions.

1. On the first day of his vacation, Thomas counted the car license plates he saw from different states. Of the 80 plates he counted, 45 were from Ohio, 23 from Illinois, and 12 from other states. If he sees 160 license plates on his return trip home, how many of these could he expect to be from Illinois?

   A. 24   B. 46   C. 80   D. 90

2. The Disco Shop is selling CDs at $7.50 per package of 3 CDs. What will it cost to purchase 12 CDs?

   A. $7.50   B.$15   C. $22.50   D. $30

3. Carrie made 13 out of 20 shot attempts during a recent basketball game. To find the percent of shots that Carrie made, how many successful shots out of 100 attempts would be equivalent to her score?

   A. 65   B. 72   C. 78   D. 85

4. A car is traveling at an average speed of 62 miles per hour. At this rate of speed, which is the best estimate for how long it will take the car to travel 356 miles?

   A. 5 hrs.   B. 6 hrs.   C. 7 hrs.   D. 8 hrs.

5. A box contains 24 colored cubes. There are 6 blue cubes, 3 red cubes, and 7 yellow cubes. The rest of the cubes are green. The ratio of green cubes to total cubes is equivalent to which probability for drawing out a green cube at random?

   A. $\frac{1}{8}$ B. $\frac{1}{4}$ C. $\frac{1}{3}$ D. $\frac{7}{24}$

6. Leo reported the following data on his time sheet at work: (2 hrs., $10), (5 hrs., $25), (8 hrs., $40), (7 hrs., $30), and (4 hrs., $20). If his hourly rate was constant, which data pair was incorrect?

   A. (2,10)   B. (5, 25)   C. (8, 40)   D. (7, 30)

7. Myshondi saved $24 when she bought a jacket on sale. If the discount was 40% of the regular price, what was the regular price of the jacket?

   A. $52   B. $60   C. $75   D. $80

Objective 2
Add integers to solve word problems.

Our everyday lives are filled with situations involving opposite actions, such as opening-closing, filling-emptying, raising-lowering, and increasing-decreasing. These actions can be represented with signed numbers: positive and negative numbers. The overall effect of two such actions may be found by adding two signed numbers. In many simple story situations involving opposite actions, however, students are able to avoid signed numbers by finding totals with unsigned numbers, then subtracting the totals to find the overall effect. As situations become more difficult or complex, this use of unsigned numbers loses its efficiency. Students need experience with activities that help them describe physical situations with signed numbers.

Activity 1: Manipulative Stage

Materials
> Packets of positive and negative tiles (30 tiles per packet)
> Worksheet 2–2a
> Regular pencil

Procedure
1. Give each student a copy of Worksheet 2–2a and a packet of 30 positive and negative tiles. Each tile will be an integral unit. Two-color tiles are commercially available, where one color represents positive values and the other color represents negative values. One-color tiles may also be used by marking a large X on one side to represent a negative unit; the plain side would be for a positive unit. One-inch paper squares with an X on one side also make effective manipulatives for this objective.

2. Students will use their tiles to model the actions in each exercise on Worksheet 2–2a. When tiles are combined, opposite tiles will be matched to form zero pairs, and the unmatched tiles that remain will represent the overall effect of the actions on the initial situation.

3. Below each exercise on the worksheet, students should write a word sentence stating the overall effect of the combined actions involved in the problem.

4. Discuss Exercise 1 on Worksheet 2–2a with the class before allowing students to work the other exercises on their own.

Consider Exercise 1: "A water tank has water added or taken out each day, but water always exists in the tank. A gallon added to the tank is considered a positive action (+1); a gallon removed from the tank is considered a negative action (–1). If 3 gallons are added and then 8 gallons are removed, how will the initial amount of water in the tank change overall as the result of these two actions?"

Have students place 3 positive unit tiles to the left on the desktop in order to show the first action: the 3 gallons added. Then have students place 8 negative unit tiles to the right on the desktop to show the second action: the 8 gallons removed. Students should form zero-pairs by matching a positive unit tile to a negative unit tile whenever possible. Five negative unit tiles will remain unmatched. The final arrangement of the tiles might have this appearance where the plain tile is the positive tile and the shaded tile is the negative tile:

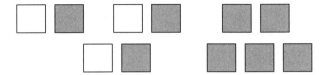

The matching indicates that for each 1 gallon added, 1 gallon is removed. Thus, a match has no effect on the original amount of water in the tank. The amount is unchanged. The five negative unit tiles left unmatched, however, show that 5 gallons of water will be removed with no gallons added in their place. Therefore, the final or overall effect on the water will be the decreasing of the initial amount by 5 gallons.

Have students write a word sentence below Exercise 1 on Worksheet 2–2a that states the overall effect. A possible sentence to use is the following: "3 gallons added and 8 gallons removed cause the initial amount of water to decrease by 5 gallons."

Answer Key for Worksheet 2–2a

1. 3 gallons added and 8 gallons removed cause the initial amount of water to decrease by 5 gallons.

2. 2 gallons removed and 5 more gallons removed cause the initial amount of water to decrease by 7 gallons.

3. 4 gallons removed and 7 gallons added cause the initial amount of water to increase by 3 gallons.

4. 6 positive units of force A and 4 negative units of force B cause the log to move in the positive (A) direction under 2 units of force. [Note: When a B horse matches an A horse with equal but opposite force on the log, the log is neutralized or does not move as a result of that pair's action.]

5. 0 units of force A and 3 negative units of force B cause the log to move in the negative (B) direction under 3 units of force.

6. 3 positive units of force A and 7 negative units of force B cause the log to move in the negative (B) direction under 4 units of force.

144

WORKSHEET 2–2a   Name _____
Building with Tiles to Model   Date _____
Signed Numbers

Build with tiles to model the actions occurring in each word problem. Write a word sentence below each exercise to represent the overall effect of the actions in the exercise.

For Exercises 1 through 3: A water tank has water added or taken out each day, but water always exists in the tank. A gallon of water added to the tank is considered a positive action (+1); a gallon removed from the tank is considered a negative action (–1).

1. If 3 gallons are added and then 8 gallons are removed, how will the initial amount of water in the tank change overall as the result of these two actions?

2. If 2 gallons are removed and then 5 more gallons removed, how will the initial amount of water change overall?

3. If 4 gallons are removed and then 7 gallons added to the tank, how will these two actions affect the initial amount of water?

For Exercises 4 through 6: In a contest, two teams of horses are hooked up to the same log but will pull in opposite directions. All horses have equal individual pulling strength: each horse will pull with 1 unit of force on the log. Consider team A to pull in the positive direction and team B to pull in the negative direction.

4. If team A has 6 horses and team B has 4 horses, what overall effect in terms of pulling force will the teams have on the log's initial position when the horses begin to pull on the log?

5. What is the overall effect on the log in terms of force and direction if team A has 0 horses and team B has 3 horses?

6. What is the overall effect on the log if team A has 3 horses and team B has 7 horses?

Activity 2: Pictorial Stage

Materials
   Worksheet 2–2b
   Regular pencil

Procedure
   1. Give each student a copy of Worksheet 2–2b.

   2. Students will draw small squares to model the actions in each exercise on
       Worksheet 2–2b. Plain squares will represent positive integral units, and squares
       with large X's will represent negative integral units. When sets of squares are
       combined, opposite squares will be matched or connected to form zero-pairs, and
       the unmatched squares that remain will represent the overall effect of the actions
       on the initial situation.

   3. Below each exercise on the worksheet, students should write a word sentence
       showing the overall effect of the combined actions involved in the problem. They
       should also write an equation with integers to show their results.

   4. Discuss Exercise 1 on Worksheet 2–2b with the class before allowing students to
       work the other exercises on their own.

       Consider Exercise 1: "Put 5 gallons of water into the tub (+), then take 3 gallons out
of the tub (–). How will the initial water in the tub be changed?"
       Since the worksheet already shows small squares for the 5 gallons (5 plain squares)
and the 3 gallons (3 X-squares), students only need to connect opposite squares in order
to form zero-pairs. This may be done by drawing a path to connect each pair of opposites. A possible drawing is shown here:

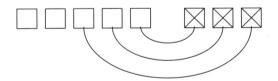

       Discuss how the two different actions affect the amount of water in the tub. Then
have students write a word sentence below the exercise to describe the result. A possible sentence might be the following: "The initial amount of water increases by 2 gallons."
Students should also write the following equation below the exercise: "(+5) + (–3) = +2."
       Now have students work the other exercises on Worksheet 2–2b. They will need to
draw the necessary squares on their worksheets for the remaining exercises, along with
writing the word sentences and equations.

Answer Key for Worksheet 2–2b

The answer key provides possible sentences. Drawings are not shown.

1. The initial amount of water increases by 2 gallons: $(+5) + (-3) = +2$.

2. Leon is 4 blocks east of home: $(-6) + (+2) = -4$

3. The door is opened 1 more time than it is closed, so it ends up open:
    $(+4) + (-3) = +1$

4. The final temperature is 3 degrees below the initial temperature: $(+5) + (-8) = -3$

WORKSHEET 2–2b

Drawing with Squares to Model Signed Numbers

Name _____

Date _____

Draw with squares to model the actions occurring in each problem. Write a word sentence and an equation below each exercise to represent the overall effect of the actions in the exercise. Signs have been assigned to opposite actions.

1. Put 5 gallons of water into the tub (+), and then take 3 gallons out of the tub (–). How will the initial water in the tub be changed?

2. From home Leon rides his bike 6 blocks east (–), then goes back 2 blocks west (+). Where is his destination with respect to his home?

3. A door is initially closed. It is opened 4 times (+) and closed 3 times (–). After all the opening and closing actions are completed, will the door be open or closed?

4. The initial room temperature increases 5 degrees (+), then decreases 8 degrees (–). What is the overall effect on the initial temperature?

Activity 3: Independent Practice

Materials

Worksheet 2–2c

Regular pencil

Procedure

Students work independently to complete Worksheet 2–2c. Encourage them to write integral equations to solve the word problems. Guide the students to look for patterns in the signs of addends to help them predict the sign of the sum. Avoid language like "the sign of the larger number" when referring to a negative addend. Rather, use language like "There are more negative units than positive units being added, so the sum will be negative." For example, in $(-12) + (+5)$, there are more negative units than positive units, so the sum will be negative based on the seven remaining negative units after five zeropairs are formed, but (-12) is not greater than $(+5)$ in value. When all students are finished, have them share their answers with the class.

Answer Key for Worksheet 2–2c

1. D

2. B

3. A

4. B

5. C

6. C

7. D

Possible Testing Errors That May Occur for This Objective

- Students fail to see the two actions in the story situation as opposites of each other. They treat the quantities involved as whole numbers rather than signed changes in the initial amount, and they either add or subtract the two numbers to get a result. Hence, they are unable to relate their answer to a change in the initial condition.

- Students make fact errors when adding two or more integers. For example, $(-8) + (-9)$ is considered to equal (-18) instead of (-17).

- Students ignore the signs of the integers being added and merely add together the absolute values of the integers.

WORSKHEET 2–2c   Name _____

Solving Problems with Signed Numbers   Date _____

In Exercises 1 through 4, solve the given equations.

1. $(+18) + (-25) =$

   A. +43   B. +7   C. –43   D. –7

2. $(-35) + (+35) =$

   A. +70   B. 0   C. –70   D. None of these

3. $(-28) + (-9) =$

   A. –37   B. –18   C. +37   D. +18

4. $(+23) + (-10) =$

   A. +33   B. +13   C. –33   D. –13

In Exercises 5 through 7, assign positive and negative signs to opposite actions, and identify the overall effect of the combined actions, either as an equation or as a statement.

5. The initial room temperature increases by 8 degrees, then decreases by 12 degrees. What equation best expresses the overall change to the initial room temperature?

   A. $(+8) + (+12) = +20$

   B. $(-8) + (-12) = -20$

   C. $(+8) + (-12) = -4$

   D. $(+8) + (+4) = +12$

150

WORKSHEET 2–2c Continued   Name _____

Date _____

6. On Monday, George drives 50 miles east from his factory to make his first delivery. Then from that stop, he drives 86 miles west on the same road to make his second delivery. At his second stop, where is George with respect to his factory?

   A. 136 miles east of the factory

   B. 36 miles east of the factory

   C. 36 miles west of the factory

   D. 136 miles west of the factory

7. On Saturday, 5 gallons of water were drained from the large aquarium at the museum. Then 8 gallons of fresh water were released into the aquarium. What overall change was produced in the initial amount of water in the aquarium?

   A. Decreased 3 gal.

   B. Decreased 13 gal.

   C. Increased 13 gal.

   D. Increased 3 gal.

Objective 3
Subtract integers to solve word problems.

Many actions in our everyday lives involve opposite actions, such as opening-closing, filling-emptying, raising-lowering, and increasing-decreasing. These actions can be represented with signed numbers, that is, positive and negative numbers. Several such actions may work together to have an initial overall effect, but this effect may later be adjusted by modifying one of the actions through subtraction (removal). The process of subtracting a signed or directed quantity is often difficult for students to understand. Students need experience with activities that help them describe physical situations that involve subtraction of signed numbers.

Activity 1: Manipulative Stage

Materials
   Packets of positive and negative tiles (30 tiles per packet)
   Flat coffee stirrers (1 per person)
   Worksheet 2–3a
   Regular pencil

Procedure
1. Give each student a copy of Worksheet 2–3a, 1 flat coffee stirrer, and a packet of 30 positive and negative tiles. Each tile will be an integral unit. Two-color tiles are commercially available where one color represents positive values and the other color represents negative values. One-color tiles may also be used by marking a large X on one side to represent a negative unit; the plain side would be for a positive unit. One-inch paper squares with an X on one side also make effective manipulatives for this objective.

2. Students will use their tiles and coffee stirrer to model the actions in each exercise on Worksheet 2–3a. When tiles are set up to show an initial overall effect, opposite tiles matched as zero-pairs may be needed, along with unmatched tiles that will represent the overall effect of the actions in the initial situation.

3. When a removal or reduction is required by the story situation, the appropriate amount and type of tile will be removed from the initial set of tiles. This will represent the subtraction process. The final effect of the actions will then be found by combining the remaining tiles. Zero-pairs may need to be considered again to simplify the tiles and find which tiles produce the final effect.

4. Below each exercise on the worksheet, students should write a word sentence stating the final overall effect of the combined actions involved in the problem.

5. Discuss Exercise 1 on Worksheet 2–3a with the class before allowing students to work the other exercises on their own.

Consider Exercise 1, along with the introduction to the exercises: "Two teams of students are playing tug-of-war. The teams are pulling in opposite directions on the same rope, trying to move the other team from its initial position. Team A is considered to be pulling in the positive direction, and each person is pulling with one unit (+1) of force. Team B is pulling in the opposite or negative direction; similarly, each person is pulling with one unit (– 1) of force. If one person on team A matches to one person on team B, then their pulling forces balance or neutralize each other, and their collective effect is 0; that is, neither team moves from its initial position as a result of these two people. Now consider the following initial effect and make the given adjustment in the teams: Initial effect on rope pull: +4; remove 5 people from team A. What is the final overall effect on the team positions? That is, which team has the advantage and by how much?"

Have students place the coffee stirrers on their desktops horizontally in front of them. Then have them place 1 positive tile at the left end of the coffee stirrer and 1 negative tile at the right end. The tiles at the left end represent members of team A, and tiles at the right end represent members of team B (these positions are arbitrary choices). Discuss the idea that if each person pulls on the "rope" with an equal unit of force, then the matched pair will not cause either team to move. Hence, this first pair is a zero-pair.

Now have the students place two more zero-pairs of tiles on the desktop with the first pair. These extra pairs are being added on to show that any number of zero-pairs can be used and the problem will not be affected. The tiles will appear as shown (plain tiles are for positive tiles and shaded tiles are for negative tiles):

Since the problem calls for an initial effect of (+4) on the rope pull, students should place 4 more positive tiles on the left end of the coffee stirrer. This indicates that team A is pulling initially with 4 more units of force than team B is. The tiles will appear as follows:

The problem asks for 5 people to be removed (subtracted) from team A, so have students remove 5 positive tiles from the left end of the coffee stirrer. This leaves 2 positive tiles on the left end and 3 negative tiles on the right end. The final effect should now be determined by first identifying which positive and negative tiles form zero-pairs and then seeing what tiles remain. Students may simply account for the zero-pairs; they do not have to remove the pairs from their locations by the coffee stirrer unless they prefer to do so. Two zero-pairs are present, leaving 1 extra negative tile on the right end of the coffee stirrer. This means that the final effect will be 1 unit of force in the direction of team B, resulting in team A's "losing ground" to team B. Students should write a word sentence below Exercise 1 on Worksheet 2–3a as follows: "Removing (+5) from (+4) has a final effect of (–1) in favor of team B." The final tile arrangement is shown here:

Discuss the idea that students need to add on only enough zero-pairs to allow them to remove any required tiles. In the steps presented for Exercise 1, 3 zero-pairs (3 positive and 3 negative tiles) were used for discussion purposes. One zero-pair would have been sufficient for this particular problem. Then the initial effect of (+4) would have been shown by 5 positive tiles and 1 negative tile. This would provide enough positive tiles for 5 positive tiles to be removed. One negative tile would remain on the right end of the coffee stirrer with no positive tiles remaining on the left end. The final effect would still be 1 unit of force in favor of team B.

Do not try to make any connections between the subtraction process and the addition of the additive inverse during this activity.

Answer Key for Worksheet 2–3a

The answer key gives possible word sentences to use for the exercises.

1. Removing (+5) from (+4) has a final effect of (–1) in favor of team B.

2. Removing (–3) from 0 has a final effect of (+3) in favor of team A. [Note: An initial effect of 0 requires an equal number of tiles at both ends of the coffee stirrer.]

3. Removing (+4) from (– 2) has a final effect of (–6) in favor of team B.

4. Removing (–5) from (–1) has a final effect of (+4) in favor of team A.

5. Removing (–2) from (+3) has a final effect of (+5) in favor of team A.

154

WORKSHEET 2–3a

Building with Tiles to Subtract

Name _____

Date _____

Build with tiles and a coffee stirrer to model the actions occurring in each problem. Write a word sentence below each exercise to represent the final overall effect of the actions in the exercise.

For Exercises 1 through 5: Two teams of students are playing tug-of-war. The teams are pulling in opposite directions on the same rope, trying to move the other team from its initial position. Team A is considered to be pulling in the positive direction, and each person is pulling with one unit (+1) of force. Team B is pulling in the opposite or negative direction; similarly, each person is pulling with one unit (–1) of force. If one person on team A matches to one person on team B, then their pulling forces balance or neutralize each other, and their collective effect is 0; that is, neither team moves from its initial position as a result of these two people. Now consider different team sizes and adjustments in the teams, and try to determine the final overall effect on the team positions. That is, in each case, which team has the advantage and by how much?

1. Initial effect on rope pull: +4; remove 5 people from team A.

2. Initial effect on rope pull: 0; remove 3 people from team B.

3. Initial effect on rope pull: –2; remove 4 people from team A.

4. Initial effect on rope pull: –1; remove 5 people from team B.

5. Initial effect on rope pull: +3; remove 2 people from team B.

Activity 2: Pictorial Stage

Materials
 Worksheet 2–3b
 Regular pencil

Procedure
1. Give each student a copy of Worksheet 2–3b.

2. Students will draw small squares to model the actions in each exercise on Worksheet 2–3b. Plain squares will represent positive integral units, and squares with large X's will represent negative integral units. When an initial effect needs to be shown, several pairs of opposite squares (positive and negative) may be drawn for zero-pairs, but unmatched squares will be drawn to represent the overall effect of the actions in the initial situation.

3. To show any removals, the required squares will be marked out with single slash marks. Enough zero-pairs must be drawn to guarantee that enough squares are visible for the amount to be marked out.

4. After the required squares are removed, students will consider the remaining squares. After any zero-pairs are identified, the remaining unmatched squares will represent the final overall effect of the actions. This will be the overall change that occurs in the initial condition.

5. Below each exercise on the worksheet, students should write an equation with integers showing the final effect of the actions involved in the problem.

6. Discuss Exercise 1 on Worksheet 2–3b with the class before allowing students to work the other exercises on their own.

 Consider Exercise 1: "Initial effect: (–3); remove (+5)."
 Have students draw three X-squares (3 negative units) below Exercise 1 on Worksheet 2–3b to represent the initial effect. Five plain squares (5 positive units) need to be removed, but no plain squares are visible at first. Thus, students must draw several zero-pairs until enough plain squares are visible for 5 of them to be marked out. The diagram should appear as shown:

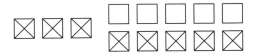

 Once 5 plain squares are visible, students should mark out the 5 squares to show the removal. Then the initial 3 X-squares and an additional 5 X-squares will remain, representing 8 negative units total.

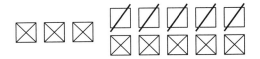

Since no extra plain squares are visible, no final zero-pairs need to be formed. If some plain squares had been present because students had drawn more than 5 zero-pairs initially, then students would just connect opposite squares in pairs to show that they were being excluded from the squares producing the final effect. An example of such a diagram might be the following:

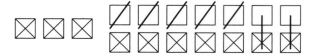

The remaining 8 X-squares in the diagram represent 8 negative units, which will be the final effect of the actions stated in the problem. Therefore, students should write the following equation below Exercise 1 on Worksheet 2–3b: "(–3) – (+5) = (–8)."

If this result is interpreted with respect to the rope pull used in Activity 1, it indicates that team B initially had the advantage of 3 units of force in its direction. Then team A lost 5 of its members, causing team B to have a final advantage of 8 units of force in its direction. Discuss this interpretation with the students.

Continue to present subtraction as the *removal* process in this activity. In Activity 3, students will be introduced to an alternative process: addition of the additive inverse.

Answer Key for Worksheet 2–3b
In the answer key, only equations are given. No diagrams are shown here.

1. (–3) – (+5) = (–8)

2. (+2) – (–2) = (+4)

3. 0 – (+4) = (–4) [Note: An initial effect of 0 requires an equal number of both plain squares and X-squares at the beginning.]

4. (–3) – (–3) = 0

5. (–1) – (–4) = (+3)

6. (+5) – (–2) = (+7)

WORKSHEET 2–3b

Drawing with Squares to Subtract Signed Numbers

Name _____

Date _____

Draw with squares to model the actions occurring in each problem. Write an equation with integers below each exercise to represent the overall effect of the actions in the exercise.

1. Initial effect: (–3); remove (+5).

2. Initial effect: (+2); remove (–2).

3. Initial effect: 0; remove (+4).

4. Initial effect: (–3); remove (–3).

5. Initial effect: (–1); remove (–4).

6. Initial effect: (+5); remove (–2).

Activity 3: Independent Practice

Materials
Worksheet 2–3c
Regular pencil

Procedure
Give each student a copy of Worksheet 2–3c. Before having students work the exercises on the worksheet, write several equations in pairs on the board where each pair is related in a certain way and their answers are not given. Ask students to solve or complete each equation, and then compare the components within each related pair. The equations involving addition should be solved using the combining approach from Objective 2. Those involving subtraction should be solved with the removal approach discussed in Activities 1 and 2 of the current objective. Here are three possible related pairs, which have already been completed:

$$(+3)-(-5)=(+8) \qquad (-6)-(-2)=(-4) \qquad (+1)-(+7)=(-6)$$
$$(+3)+(+5)=(+8) \qquad (-6)+(+2)=(-4) \qquad (+1)+(-7)=(-6)$$

Have several students share their ideas about how the equations within a pair are alike and how they are different. Guide them to discover that the first numbers are alike (or equal) and the answers are alike. Then observe that the two operations are *inverses* of each other and that the second numbers are *additive inverses* of each other. It is because of these specific comparisons or contrasts that the two equations are considered related.

Discuss the idea that since the two related equations have the same answer, one of the equations may be used as an alternative way to solve the other equation. This substitution method is used quite often in mathematics. For example, instead of solving $(-38) + (+20) = ?$ by combining, students might prefer to solve $(-38) - (-20) = (-18)$ by removal, where (-18) is also the answer to the first equation. Similarly, $(+16) - (-14) = ?$, a removal problem, might be solved by combining in $(+16) + (+14) = (+30)$ instead.

Now have students work the exercises on Worksheet 2–3c. Encourage them to use related equations when appropriate or helpful.

Answer Key for Worksheet 2–3c
1. +24

2. –8

3. –21

4. 0

5. B

6. C

7. C

8. D

Possible Testing Errors That May Occur for This Objective

- Students attempt to use the related addition equation as an alternative to the subtraction equation occurring in the problem, but they fail to use the required inverse forms properly. In other words, to solve $(-5) - (+4)$, they might try to use $(-5) + (+4)$ or $(+5) + (+4)$ as the alternative approach.

- Students make fact errors when subtracting integers. For example, $(-17) - (-9)$ is considered to equal (-6) instead of (-8).

- The signs of the integers being subtracted are ignored and the difference merely found between the absolute values of the integers. For example, $(-14) - (+8)$ is viewed as $14 - 8 = 6$.

160

WORKSHEET 2–3c   Name _____

Subtracting Integers to Solve Problems   Date _____

Solve the exercises provided.

1. $(+18) - (-6) = ?$

2. $(-23) - (-15) = ?$

3. $(-9) - (+12) = ?$

4. $(+10) - (+10) = ?$

5. Find the *related* equation for $(+3) - (-7) = ?$

   A. $(-3) - (+7) = ?$ B. $(+3) + (+7) = ?$ C. $(+3) - (+7) = ?$ D. $(-3) + (-7) = ?$

6. Find the *related* equation for $(-8) + (+6) = ?$

   A. $(-8) - (+6) = ?$ B. $(+8) + (-6) = ?$ C. $(-8) - (-6) = ?$ D. $(-8) + (-6) = ?$

7. In a rope-pulling contest, team A pulls in the negative direction, and team B pulls in the positive direction. If the initial pulling effect on the rope equals (-3) but then 5 members of team B release the rope, which expression represents the final pulling effect on the rope?

   A. $(-3) + (+5)$ B. $(+5) - (-3)$ C. $(-3) - (+5)$ D. $(+5) + (+3)$

8. Initially there are 6 metal washers of equal weight on each of the two pans of a balance scale, making the two pans level with each other. Two more washers are placed on the left pan, which lowers the left pan. Later, 1 washer is removed from the right pan. How is the scale finally changed from its initial leveled position?

   A. Right pan lower by 7 washers   C. Right pan lower by 1 washer
   B. Left pan lower by 8 washers   D. Left pan lower by 3 washers

Objective 4
Multiply and divide integers to solve word problems.

Many actions in our everyday lives involve opposite actions, such as opening-closing, raising-lowering, increasing-decreasing, and reversing directions. These actions can be represented with signed numbers, or positive and negative numbers. Some actions may occur both individually and collectively. Such is the case with situations involving multiplication or division. Students need experience with activities that help them describe physical situations that involve multiplication or division of signed numbers.

Activity 1: Manipulative Stage

Materials
Packets of positive and negative tiles (30 tiles per packet)
Building Mat 2–4a (1 per pair of students)
Worksheet 2–4a
Regular pencil

Procedure
1. Give each pair of students a copy of Building Mat 2–4a, two copies of Worksheet 2–4a, and a packet of 30 positive and negative tiles. Each tile will be an integral unit. Two-color tiles are commercially available where one color represents positive values and the other color represents negative values. One-color tiles may also be used by marking a large X on one side to represent a negative unit; the plain side represents a positive unit. One-inch paper squares with an X on one side also make effective manipulatives for this objective.

2. Students will use their tiles and Building Mat 2–4a to model the actions in each exercise on Worksheet 2–4a. The building mat should be positioned so that the bar on the mat is vertical as seen by the student using the mat.

3. It is assumed that students are familiar with *arrays*, or row-column arrangements of objects. Arrays are commonly used to teach the multiplication and division facts for whole numbers. Review the idea that the notation "2 × 3" is read as "2 of 3" and may be modeled with two rows of three (positive) tiles each. This would yield a product of 6 tiles. To be consistent with other mathematical practices, always consider a *row* as going from left to right, not up and down (which is a *column*). Similarly, for the notation "8 ÷ 4," read as "8 divided into 4 equal groups," 8 random (positive) tiles would be arranged into 4 equal rows, yielding 2 tiles per row as the quotient.

4. The initial collective or group action in a story situation will be modeled with tiles on the left side of the vertical bar on Building Mat 2–4a. When a reversing action is required on the entire group by the story situation, a new group of tiles will be built on the right side of the vertical bar with tiles that are opposites of the original tiles.

5. Below each exercise on the worksheet, students should write a word sentence stating the result of the actions involved in the problem.

6. Discuss Exercises 1 and 4 on Worksheet 2–4a with the class before allowing students to work the other exercises on their own.

Consider Exercise 1 on Worksheet 2–4a: "Describe an entire band's movement as shown by the expression: (–3)(–7)."

Have students place negative tiles in three rows on the left side of the vertical bar of Building Mat 2–4a, using 7 negative tiles per row. The (–7) indicates that there are 7 band members in each row and that each member is marching backward. The tiles will appear initially as follows:

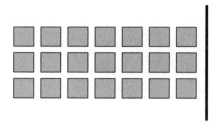

Discuss the idea that the multiplier is shown as a negative number. Since generally a multiplier is considered positive because it counts only the rows (that is, it is an *absolute* number), we will interpret the negative on the multiplier to mean that a change occurs *after* the band begins to march. That is, a reversal occurs that affects the entire band. Hence, have students build another array on the right side of the mat like the array on the left side of the mat, but reverse the tiles. The new array on the right will have 3 rows of 7 positive tiles per row. This final arrangement indicates that the entire band will have 21 members, all marching forward after the group reversal occurs. Students should write a word sentence below Exercise 1 on Worksheet 2–4a similar to the following: "3 rows of 7 members marching backward reverse to become 21 members marching forward, or (+21)." The final building mat appearance is shown here:

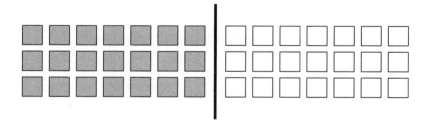

Now consider Exercise 4 on Worksheet 2–4a: "Describe the movement of each row in a band as shown by the expression: (+18) ÷ (–6)."

The focus is now on one row of the band instead of the entire band, so separation or division is involved. Have students place 18 positive tiles randomly on the left side of Building Mat 2–4a. The divisor is the counter of rows to be built, but it is negative. Since the counter of rows is usually an *absolute* number, we will interpret the negative divisor to mean that a reversal occurs during the marching that affects the entire band.

To show the initial situation for the band, have students arrange the 18 positive tiles into 6 equal rows on the left side of the mat. This indicates that 3 band members in each row start off marching forward. To show the reversal, students should build 6 rows of 3 tiles each on the right side of the building mat, but change the positive tiles to negative tiles. Here is the completed mat arrangement:

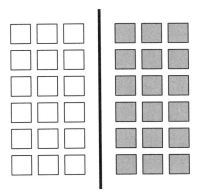

Since the new array on the right side of the building mat contains 3 negative tiles in each row, this shows that each row of the band will have 3 members marching backward (−3) after the group reversal occurs. Students should write a word sentence below Exercise 4 on Worksheet 2–4a similar to the following: "18 band members marching forward in 6 equal rows reverse so that each row has 3 members marching backward, or (−3)."

Answer Key for Worksheet 2–4a
The answer key gives possible word sentences.

1. 3 rows of 7 members marching backward reverse to become 21 members marching forward, or (+21).

2. 4 rows of 5 members marching backward make 20 members total marching backward, or (−20).

3. 2 rows of 8 members marching forward reverse to become 16 members marching backward, or (−16).

4. 18 band members marching forward in 6 equal rows reverse so that each row has 3 members marching backward, or (−3).

5. 20 band members marching backward in 5 equal rows have 4 members marching backward (−4) in each row.

6. 12 band members marching backward in 2 equal rows reverse so that each row has 6 members marching forward, or (+6).

Building Mat 2–4a

WORKSHEET 2–4a

Building with Tiles to Multiply or Divide Signed Numbers

Name _____

Date _____

Build with tiles on Building Mat 2–4a to model the actions represented by each exercise. Write a word sentence below each exercise to describe the result of the actions in the exercise.

Example for Exercises 1–3

$(-4)(+6) = ?$

Initial action: Build 4 equal rows of 6 positive tiles: 4 rows of 6 band members each march forward.

Reverse action: Build 4 rows of 6 negative tiles [for (–) on (–4)].

Final action: 24 band members reverse to march backward (–24).

Example for Exercises 4–6

$(-16) \div (+2) = ?$

Initial action: Build 16 negative tiles as 2 equal rows: 16 band members march backward in 2 equal rows.

Reverse action: Not needed since divisor (+2) is positive.

Final action: 8 band members march backward in each row (–8).

Describe an entire band's movement as shown by each expression:

1. $(-3)(-7)$

2. $(+4)(-5)$

3. $(-2)(+8)$

Describe the movement of each row in a band as shown by each expression:

4. $(+18) \div (-6)$

5. $(-20) \div (+5)$

6. $(-12) \div (-2)$

Activity 2: Pictorial Stage

Materials
   Worksheet 2–4b
   Regular pencil

Procedure
1. Give each student a copy of Worksheet 2–4b.

2. Students will draw small squares to model the actions in each exercise on Worksheet 2–4b. Plain squares will represent positive integral units, and squares with large X's will represent negative integral units. Students will draw arrays similar to those built with tiles in Activity 1. Always consider a row in an array as going from left to right, not up and down (which is a column).

3. The initial collective or group action in a story situation will be modeled with squares drawn on the left side of the vertical bar on Worksheet 2–4b. When a reversing action is required on the entire group by the story situation, a new group of squares will be drawn on the right side of the vertical bar using squares that are opposites of the original squares.

4. Exercises 1 and 2 focus on the final collective group action (the product) and Exercises 3 and 4 on the final row action (the quotient).

5. Below each exercise on the worksheet, students should write an equation with integers showing the result of the actions involved in the problem. A word phrase should also be recorded that explains the result in terms of the situation.

6. Discuss Exercise 1 on Worksheet 2–4b with the class before allowing students to work the other exercises on their own.

   Consider Exercise 1 on Worksheet 2–4b: "Initial action: 4 rows of 3 people moving forward. Reverse. Final total action?"
   Have students draw 4 rows of 3 plain (positive) squares per row on the left side of the vertical bar below Exercise 1 on Worksheet 2–4b. This represents the initial action of the drill team. Since the drill team later reverses its direction while marching, draw another 4 rows of 3 squares per row on the right side of the vertical bar, but draw X-squares (negative) instead. The X-squares are opposites of the plain squares, which the reversal process requires. If the initial squares on the left side had been X-squares, then the reversal squares on the right side would have been plain squares. Here is the final diagram:

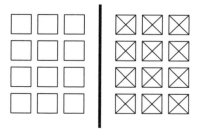

The squares drawn on the right side of the vertical bar represent the final collective or total group action. Hence, 12 drill team members will be marching backward (–12) after the reversal occurs. If no reversal had been required, only the squares on the left side of the vertical bar would have been used for the final total group action.

Students should now write beside the completed diagram an equation and a word phrase that describe the result: "$(-4)(+3) = (-12)$; 12 people total marching backward."

Do not write $(+4)(+3)$ initially for the array on the left side of the vertical bar. This is confusing to students. The total process, including both the left and the right sides of the vertical bar, is represented by $(-4)(+3)$. Students need to associate just one equation with the total process.

Answer Key for Worksheet 2–4b
In this answer key, only equations and possible phrases are given. No diagrams are shown.

1. $(-4)(+3) = (-12)$; 12 people *total* marching backward.

2. $(+2)(-5) = (-10)$; 10 people *total* marching backward.

3. $(-14) \div (-2) = (+7)$; 7 people *in each row* marching forward.

4. $(+15) \div (-3) = (-5)$; 5 people *in each row* marching backward.

168

WORSHEET 2–4b

WORKSHEET 2–4b

Drawing with Squares to Multiply
or Divide Signed Numbers

Name _____

Date _____

Draw with squares to model the actions occurring in each problem involving a school
drill team. The initial action of the drill team will be given. Find the final *total* action or
the final *row* action of the drill team. Along with the diagram, write an equation with
integers and a word phrase beside each exercise to represent the results of the actions
in the exercise.

1. Initial action: 4 rows of 3 people moving forward. Reverse. Final total action?

2. Initial action: 2 rows of 5 people moving backward. No reversal. Final total
    action?

3. Initial action: 14 people moving backward in 2 equal rows. Reverse. Final row
    action?

4. Initial action: 15 people moving forward in 3 equal rows. Reverse. Final row
    action?

Activity 3: Independent Practice

Materials

Worksheet 2–4c

Regular pencil

Procedure

Give each student a copy of Worksheet 2–4c. Encourage the students to visualize each equation as a physical action, like a band or a drill team used in Activities 1 and 2. Before having students complete the worksheet, however, write several equations on the board, and ask students if they can predict the sign on the answer by looking at the signs on the original two numbers (factor-factor or dividend-divisor). The pattern is usually easy for students to recognize. Have them write in their own words a description of the pattern (their language will vary). Ask several students to share their descriptions with the rest of the class. Here are some possible equations to use, followed by a possible description of the pattern:

$$(+3)(+5) = (+15) \qquad (+14) \div (+2) = (+7)$$
$$(+2)(-4) = (-8) \qquad (-12) \div (+3) = (-4)$$
$$(-4)(+2) = (-8) \qquad (+10) \div (-5) = (-2)$$
$$(-6)(-3) = (+18) \qquad (-15) \div (-3) = (+5)$$

Pattern: If the signs on the first two numbers in the equation are both positive or both negative, then the sign on the answer will be positive. If the signs on the first two numbers are different, then the sign on the answer will be negative.

Answer Key for Worksheet 2–4c

1. –70

2. +160

3. –4

4. –10

5. D

6. C

7. A

8. D

Possible Testing Errors That May Occur for This Objective

- Students attempt to use sign patterns to find the sign for the answer, but they fail to use the patterns properly. For example, students use $(-3)(-7) = (-21)$ because they think two negative factors have a negative product.

- Students make fact errors when multiplying or dividing integers. For example, $(-24) \div (-4)$ is considered to equal $(+8)$ instead of $(+6)$.

- The signs of the integers being multiplied or divided are ignored and the answer merely found by using the absolute values of the integers. For example, $(-2)(+7)$ is viewed as $2 \times 7 = 14$.

WORSHEET 2–4c

Name _____

Multiplying or Dividing
with Signed Numbers

Date _____

Solve the exercises provided.

1. (+5)(–14) = ?

2. (–8)(–20) = ?

3. (+24) ÷ (–6) = ?

4. (–100) ÷ (+10) = ?

5. As discussed in Activity 2, the *reversal* of the action represented by (+3)(–8) = ?
    is shown by:

    A. (–3)(+8) = ?   B. (+3)(+8) = ?   C. (+3)(+8) = ?   D. (–3)(–8) = ?

6. As discussed in Activity 2, the *reversal* of the action represented by (–18) ÷ (+6) = ?
    is shown by:

    A. (–18) ÷ (+6) = ?   B. (+18) ÷ (+6) = ?   C. (–18) ÷ (–6) = ?   D. (+18) ÷ (–6) = ?

7. Joggers are running in 5 groups of 3 people each toward Lookout Point. They
    reach a barrier and have to turn around and run in the opposite direction from
    the Point. Which single expression best represents all of these actions by the
    joggers?

    A. (–5)(+3)   B. (–3)(–5)   C. (–3)(+5)   D. (+5)(+3)

8. Fresh loaves of bread are moving in rows of 4 loaves each along the bakery
    conveyor belt to the cutting room. When 10 rows are on the belt, the belt
    malfunctions and reverses its direction. What is happening to the bread now?

    A. 10 rows of 4 loaves move forward   C. 4 rows of 10 loaves move backward
    B. 4 rows of 10 loaves move forward   D. 10 rows of 4 loaves move backward

Objective 5

Model situations with linear equations of the form: $aX + b = c$, where a, b, and c are integers or decimals and X is an integer.

Linear relationships are very common in everyday life. They involve constant rates of change. Students need experience recognizing tables of value for such relationships and writing expressions for linear physical situations. The activities for this objective provide these experiences.

Activity 1: Manipulative Stage

Materials

Set of tiles with building mat (described in step 1 of the procedure) per pair of
    students
Worksheet 2–5a
Regular pencils

Procedure

1. Give each pair of students two copies of Worksheet 2–5a, a set of tiles, and a sheet of white paper 8.5 inches by 14 inches to use as a building mat. Each set of tiles should contain 4 of the same variable tile and 30 positive integer or unit tiles. Such tiles are available commercially or may be teacher-made.

2. Have students model each expression on Worksheet 2–5a with their tiles, then replace the variable tiles with the given amount of unit tiles. They will then count all the unit tiles on the building mat to find the total value of the expression.

3. Below each exercise, students should write an equation that shows the numerical substitution made in the given expression, as well as the total value found for the expression.

4. Discuss Exercise 1 on Worksheet 2–5a with the class before allowing students to work the remaining exercises on their own.

    Consider Exercise 1: "$3p + 8 = ?$ when $p = 4$."
    Have students place 3 variable tiles on the building mat for 3p, then place 8 positive unit tiles on the mat beside the variable tiles. They need to substitute 4 positive unit tiles for each variable tile on the mat. To show this, they should remove each variable tile, and in its initial position on the mat place 4 of the positive unit tiles. Possible mat arrangements of the initial variable tiles and unit tiles, followed by the replacements, are shown here:

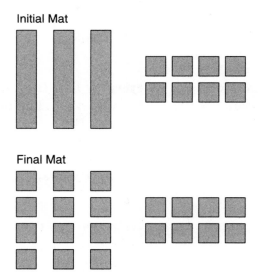

After the substitution has been made, students should count the total unit tiles now on the building mat. There will be 20 positive unit tiles in all, so the total value of the expression is 20 when p = 4. Students should write the following number sentence below Exercise 1 to show the substitution made and the total value found: "3(4) + 8 = 20."

In Exercises 5 and 6, students are asked to make three substitutions for each expression. This will prepare them to work with sequences. They should write a number sentence for each substitution, thereby writing three different equations below each exercise.

Answer Key for Worksheet 2–5a

1. 3(4) + 8 = 20

2. 5 + 2(3) = 11

3. (1) + 12 = 13

4. 5(5) + 2 = 27

5. 3 + 4(1) = 7; 3 + 4(2) = 11; 3 + 4(3) = 15

6. 3(1) + 7 = 10; 3(2) + 7 = 13; 3(3) + 7 = 16

WORKSHEET 2–5a

Building and Evaluating Algebraic
Expressions with Tiles

Name _____

Date _____

Build with tiles on a building mat to show the expression in each exercise. Substitute unit tiles for the variable tiles to find the total value of the expression. Write a number sentence below the exercise to show each substitution used and the total value found.

1. $3p + 8 = ?$ when $p = 4$

2. $5 + 2C = ?$ when $C = 3$

3. $M + 12 = ?$ when $M = 1$

4. $5x + 2 = ?$ when $x = 5$

5. $3 + 4n = ?$ when $n = 1, 2,$ and 3

6. $3n + 7 = ?$ when $n = 1, 2,$ and 3

Activity 2: Pictorial Stage

Materials

    Worksheet 2–5b

    Red pencil and regular pencil

Procedure

1. Give each student a copy of Worksheet 2–5b and a red pencil. Students will draw long, narrow rectangles to represent variables in the given algebraic expressions and draw small squares to represent the positive units.

2. Have students model each expression on Worksheet 2–5b by first drawing the necessary shapes for the stated variables and positive units below the expression. Then they should "replace" each variable bar by drawing small squares in red pencil on top of the variable bar to represent the amount of positive units being substituted for the variable. Students will then count all the positive unit squares, both plain and red, shown in the diagram to find the total value of the expression.

3. Below each exercise, students should write an equation that shows the numerical substitution made in the given expression, as well as the total value found for the expression.

4. Discuss Exercise 1 on Worksheet 2–5b with the class before allowing students to work the remaining exercises on their own.

    Consider Exercise 1: "p + 5 + 4p = ? when p = 3."

Below the exercise on Worksheet 2–5b, students should draw a long, narrow rectangle for each variable p in the expression and draw 5 small squares for the positive constant, 5. The initial diagram should appear as shown:

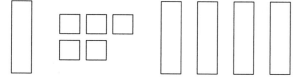

    After the initial diagram is drawn, students should draw small squares in red pencil on top of each variable bar to show the substitution of p = 3. They should then count all the small squares, both red and plain, in the final diagram to find the total value of the expression after the substitution. The following equation should be recorded on the worksheet with the final diagram to show the numerical substitution: "(3) + 5 + 4(3) = 20." An alternate equation for this particular exercise might be: "1(3) + 5 + 4(3) = 20." The final diagram is shown here:

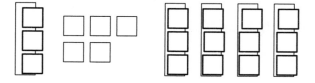

Answer Key for Worksheet 2–5b
No diagrams are shown in this answer key.

1. $(3) + 5 + 4(3) = 20$

2. $8 + 2(4) = 16$

3. $3(2) + 6 + (2) = 14$

4. $5(3) + 1 = 16$

5. $7 + 2(1) = 9$; $7 + 2(2) = 11$; $7 + 2(3) = 13$; table entries 9, 11, 13

WORKSHEET 2–5b   Name _____

Drawing and Evaluating   Date _____
Algebraic Expressions

Below each exercise, draw large and small rectangles to show the expression in the exercise. Draw unit squares in red pencil over the variable bars, and find the total value of the expression. Then write a number sentence below the exercise to show each substitution used and the total value found.

1. $p + 5 + 4p = ?$ when $p = 3$

2. $8 + 2m = ?$ when $m = 4$

3. $3N + 6 + N = ?$ when $N = 2$

4. $5A + 1 = ?$ when $A = 3$

5. Draw diagrams for $7 + 2n = ?$ when $n = 1, 2,$ and 3. Then record the values found in the appropriate boxes of the following table:

n	1	2	3
7 + 2n			

Activity 3: Independent Practice

Materials

> Worksheet 2–5c
> Regular pencil

Procedure

Give each student a copy of Worksheet 2–5c. Discuss the idea that an expression may involve decimals, rather than just integers, but the process of multiplying and then adding remains the same. For example, if the expression $5 + $0.75T is given for the total taxi fee and it needs to be evaluated for T = 2 hours, students should write $5 + $0.75(2) = $5 + $1.50 = $6.50 for the total taxi fee for a two-hour trip. Remind students that when an expression or an equation is given in a word problem, quite often they can test for the correct response to the problem by using the substitution method. Have students share their results when all have completed Worksheet 2–5c.

Answer Key for Worksheet 2–5c

1. D

2. A

3. C

4. B

5. D

Possible Testing Errors That May Occur for This Objective

- Students make only one substitution in an expression where the variable occurs more than once. For example, to evaluate 5m – 2 + 3m for m = 4, students use only 5(4) – 2, omitting the last group, 3(4).

- When substituting for a variable that has a coefficient, students add the substituted value and the coefficient instead of multiplying them. As an example, for 7x when x = 5, students will compute 7 + 5, not 7(5).

- Students will forget to add the constant given in the expression after they make the substitution for the variable. For example, when they evaluate 2y + 3 for y = 6, they compute 2(6), but they fail to add the 3 to get the final value for the expression.

WORKSHEET 2–5c   Name _____

Evaluating Formulas and   Date _____
Algebraic Expressions

Copyright © 2005 by John Wiley & Sons, Inc.

Solve the exercises provided.

1. Sharla's weekly fee for walking a dog daily is based on the equation $T = 5 + 2B$, where T is the total fee in dollars and B is the number of blocks she has to walk the dog. If she has to walk Mr. Johnson's terrier 6 blocks, how much will she be paid?

   A. $11   B. $12   C. $15   D. $17

2. Kerry bought a new motor scooter for $475. The value of the scooter will decrease $80 each year after the purchase. Kerry plans to keep the scooter for at least 3 years. Which expression could be used to find the value in dollars for the scooter after n years?

   A. $475 - 80n$ B. $475 + 3n$ C. $80n - 475$ D. $475 - 3n$

3. The equation $c = 0.55t$ represents the total cost c of t tickets on a city bus. Which set of numbers represents the values that fit in this table for the equation?

t	1	2	3
c = 0.55t			

   A. 0.55, 0.80, 1.05   C. 0.55, 1.10, 1.65

   B. 1.55, 2.10, 2.65   D. 1.55, 2.55, 3.55

4. Which expression can be used to find the Nth term in the following arithmetic sequence, where N is a number's position in the sequence? Use substitution to test each expression.

Position	1	2	3	4	N
Term	5	8	11	14	?

   A. $N + 3$ B. $3N + 2$ C. $5N$ D. $4N + 1$

5. Evaluate $5x - 3 + 6x$ when $x = 7$.

   A. 14   B. 32   C. 41   D. 74

Objective 6

Identify linear and nonlinear functions and contrast their properties using tables, graphs, or equations.

Linear functions involve constant rates of change, whereas nonlinear functions do not. Students need experience recognizing the graphs and the tables of values for both types of functions. The activities for this objective provide these needed experiences.

Activity 1: Manipulative Stage

Materials

    1-inch square tiles (commercial or teacher-made; 100 tiles per pair of students)
    Worksheet 2–6a
    Red pencil and regular pencil

Procedure

1. Give each pair of students two copies of Worksheet 2–6a, a red pencil, and a packet of 100 1-inch square tiles. The tile color is not important.

2. For each exercise on Worksheet 2–6a, students will build different rows of tiles, varying the row length according to the directions given in the exercise.

3. For each exercise, students will plot points on the grid to represent their data found, using ordered pairs of the type: (number of the row, total tiles in the row). For each grid, the vertical axis will need to be labeled as "Total Tiles" and marked off with an appropriate scale.

4. Students will use a red pencil to connect, in order, the 5 points plotted on each grid. The 5 plotted points should not be connected to the origin of the grid, however, since there is no ordered pair included for that point.

5. After all exercises are completed, discuss the appearance of each red path drawn. Each path should be straight because of the *constant* change in amount of tiles occurring from row to row. This is a characteristic of a *linear function*.

6. Discuss Exercise 1 on Worksheet 2–6a with the entire class before allowing students to work the other exercises on their own.

    Consider Exercise 1 on Worksheet 2–6a: "Row 1: 4 tiles; for each new row, increase previous tiles by 3."

    Have students build a row of 4 tiles for row 1. Then below that row, they should build another row with 4 + 3, or 7, tiles; this is row 2. For row 3, have them build a row of 7 + 3, or 10, tiles. Row 4 will have 10 + 3, or 13 tiles, and row 5 will have 13 + 3, or 16 tiles. Here is the final arrangement of the tiles:

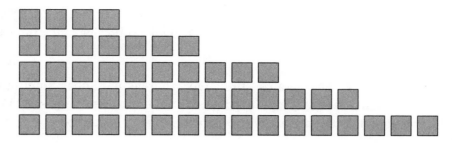

Below Exercise 1, have students list in a column to the left of the grid the ordered pairs that represent the rows and their amounts of tiles: (1,4), (2,7), (3,10), (4,13), and (5,16). Then points should be plotted on the grid to represent the ordered pairs. The vertical axis should be numbered with multiples of 2 to accommodate the range of values from 4 to 16 and should be labeled "Total Tiles." The points should then be connected in red pencil to show a straight path. Do not connect the points to the origin of the grid. Here is the completed grid:

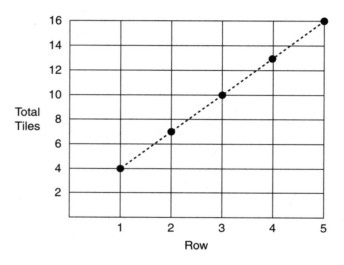

Answer Key for Worksheet 2–6a
The completed graphs are not shown.

1. (1,4), (2,7), (3,10), (4,13), (5,16)

2. (1,5), (2,7), (3,9), (4,11), (5,13)

3. (1,0), (2,4), (3,8), (4,12), (5,16)

WORKSHEET 2–6a   Name _____

Building Functions with Square Tiles   Date _____

Build with square tiles to make 5 different rows as directed in each exercise. Plot points on each grid for ordered pairs found and connect the points with red pencil.

1. Row 1: 4 tiles; for each new row, increase previous tiles by 3

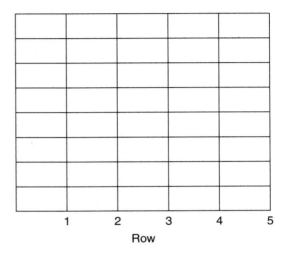

2. Row 1: 5 tiles; for each new row, increase previous tiles by 2

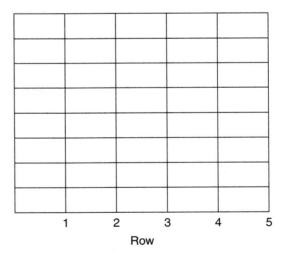

182

WORKSHEET 2–6a Continued

Name _____

Date _____

3. Row 1: 0 tiles; for each new row, increase previous tiles by 4

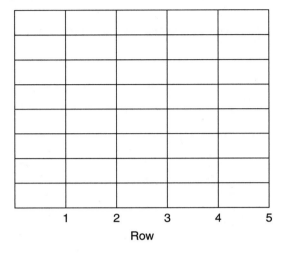

Activity 2: Pictorial Stage

Materials

Worksheet 2–6b
Red pencil and regular pencil
5-mm or 5-cm grid paper
Ruler (inch or centimeter)

Procedure

1. Give each student a copy of Worksheet 2–6b, a ruler, two sheets of grid paper, and a red pencil.

2. For each exercise, have students find the ordered pairs needed, and record them in a table. They should then plot points for the ordered pairs on their grid paper. Guide them to properly label and mark the two axes of each grid.

3. Have them use a ruler to draw a path in red pencil to connect adjacent pairs of plotted points for each exercise. Do not connect to the origin unless that point is included in the list of ordered pairs for the exercise.

4. Discuss the idea that some of the resulting graphs of points will form straight paths, and others will not. The graphs that are straight represent linear functions, which are special sets of ordered pairs. The other graphs are nonlinear functions.

5. Have students identify how the first numbers change and how the second numbers change within the table of ordered pairs for each exercise. As the first numbers (abscissa) increase by the same amount each time, the second number (ordinate) will also change by a constant amount if the ordered pairs belong to a linear function.

6. Discuss Exercise 1 on Worksheet 2–6b with the class before allowing students to work on their own.

Here is Exercise 1 to consider: "Audrey needs to buy ears of corn to sell at the school concession stand. The Farmer's Market has the following price table that shows the cost for different amounts of corn. Will Audrey save on the cost per ear of corn by buying larger quantities?"

Number of ears	10	20	30	40
Total cost	$3	$6	$9	$12

Have students prepare a grid with "Number of Ears" as the horizontal axis and "Total Cost" as the vertical axis. The horizontal axis should be numbered from 0 to 40, and the vertical axis should be numbered from $0 to $12. Points should be plotted on the grid to represent the ordered pairs from the table: (10,$3), (20,$6), (30,$9), and (40,$12). The points should then be connected in red pencil, using a ruler to join each pair of adjacent points. The final red path should be straight.

Ask students to look at the numbers in each row of the table and notice how those numbers change from one column to the next. In the top row, the numbers increase by 10 each time. In the bottom row, the amounts increase by $3 each time. Now ask students to look at the graph of the four points and notice how the horizontal distance of each point changes to that of the next point to the right; a constant change of 10 occurs horizontally. Similarly, the vertical distance from one point to the next will change by 3 units each time; there is a constant change of 3 vertically. These constant changes produce the straight graph.

These constant changes in both directions on the graph, as well as on the table, indicate that every 10 ears of corn will cost $3, no matter how many ears Audrey buys. Students should now write below Exercise 1 a response similar to the following: "Each price in the table is based on every 10 ears of corn costing $3, so Audrey will not save by buying larger quantities of corn." Here is the completed graph:

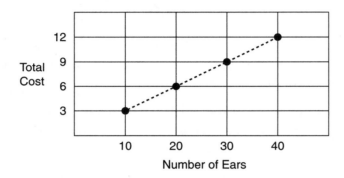

Answer Key for Worksheet 2–6b

No completed graphs are shown here; only ordered pairs are listed with possible sentence responses.

1. (10,$3), (20,$6), (30,$9), (40,$12)

   Each price in the table is based on every 10 ears of corn costing $3, so Audrey will not save by buying larger quantities of corn.

2. (1,5), (2,8), (3,12), (4,14), (5,20)

   The ordered pairs do not represent a linear function because their graph is not a straight path.

3. (1996,$5), (1997,$10), (1998,$15), (1999,$20), (2000,$25)

   Each year the price increases by $5, so in 4 more years, the price will increase by 4 × $5, or $20, making the new price $25 + $20, or $45 in 4 more years.

4. (1,$0.75), (2,$1.25), (3,$1.75), (4,$2.25)

   The ordered pairs represent a linear function because their graph is a straight path.

WORKSHEET 2–6b

**Graphing Linear Functions
and Nonlinear Functions**

Name _____

Date _____

For each exercise, prepare a table of values when needed. Plot points on grid paper for all ordered pairs in the table, and connect the points with red pencil. Label the axes of each graph appropriately. Answer the questions, and write a sentence justifying each answer.

1. Audrey needs to buy ears of corn to sell at the school concession stand. The Farmer's Market has the following price table that shows the cost for different amounts of corn. Will Audrey save on the cost per ear of corn by buying larger quantities?

Number of ears	10	20	30	40
Total cost	$3	$6	$9	$12

2. On a grid, plot the ordered pairs given in the table, and connect the points to form a path. Do the ordered pairs represent a linear function? Why or why not?

X	1	2	3	4	5
Y	5	8	12	14	20

3. Plot the following ordered pairs on a grid: (1996,$5), (1997,$10), (1998,$15), (1999,$20), (2000,$25). If the price per year continues to increase at a constant rate, predict what the price might be in 2004. Explain your reasoning.

4. The cost, C, for the number of trips, t, taken on a bus is found by the formula: $C = \$0.50t + \$0.25$. Prepare a table of values for C, using t = 1, 2, 3, and 4, and plot the ordered pairs (t,C) on a grid. Do the ordered pairs represent a linear function? Why or why not?

Activity 3: Independent Practice

Materials
    Worksheet 2–6c
    Regular pencil

Procedure
Give each student a copy of Worksheet 2–6c to complete. Remind students that a set of ordered pairs, whose graph is a straight path, will be called a *linear function*. A special feature of a linear function is the constant change in the dependent value (ordinate) as the independent value (abscissa) changes by some constant; for example, by 1 each time. This constant change may be negative, thereby causing a decrease in the dependent values rather than an increase. Often the known change allows us to predict the dependent values for larger independent values not provided in an initial table of values. Some nonlinear functions are also included on the worksheet. After students have finished the worksheet, have several students share their results with the entire class.

Answer Key for Worksheet 2–6c
   1. B

   2. C

   3. B

   4. A

   5. D

   6. Missing pairs: (20,60), (25,75), (30,90)

Possible Testing Errors That May Occur for This Objective
   * Students will plot the ordered pairs incorrectly, using the first number as the vertical distance and the second number as the horizontal distance on the grid.

   * When looking for a pattern in a table of values, students will find the difference between the first two numbers in a row (or column) and assume that all other adjacent pairs in that row (or column) have the same difference. This would be incorrect reasoning in cases of nonlinear functions.

   * When the constant of change is known and students need to complete a table based on that change, they will use incorrect facts when computing the missing entries for the table.

WORSHEET 2–6c

Solving Word Problems About
Linear Functions

Name _____

Date _____

Solve each exercise provided.

1. Which store's price table is based on a constant unit price for CDs?

Store A

Number of CDs	2	4	6	8
Total cost	$10	$15	$18	$20

Store B

Number of CDs	2	4	6	8
Total cost	$10	$20	$30	$40

Store C

Number of CDs	2	4	6	8
Total cost	$5	$8	$12	$17

Store D

Number of CDs	2	4	6	8
Total cost	$5	$10	$15	$18

2. The graph of the line representing $y = 3x + 1$ is drawn on the coordinate grid to the right below. Which table (A, B, C, or D) contains only ordered pairs for points on this line? [grid segment = 1 unit]

A

x	−2	−1	+1	+2
y	−5	−2	0	+3

B

x	−1	0	+2	+3
y	−2	+1	+3	−1

C

x	−2	−1	0	+1
y	−5	−2	+1	+4

D

x	−2	−1	0	+2
y	0	−2	+1	+4

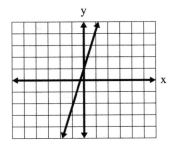

WORSHEET 2–6c Continued

Name _____

Date _____

3. A new baseball card was worth $4 in the year 2000. The table shows its value each year for several years after its issue. Based on the table's information, what is a reasonable prediction of the card's value in 2006?

Year	2000	2001	2002	2003
Value of card	$4.00	$4.40	$4.85	$5.35

A. Between $8 and $9

C. Between $6 and $7

B. Between $7 and $8

D. Between $5 and $6

4. Which set of ordered pairs represents a linear function?

A. (2,9), (4,13), (6,17), (8,21)

C. (2,5), (4,10), (6,12), (8,15)

B. (3,8), (4,8), (5,10), (6,14)

D. (3,6), (4,5), (5,2), (6,1)

5. Which set of ordered pairs for (week number, average weekly temperature) does not reflect a constant change in temperature?

A. (1,80), (2,84), (3,88), (4,92)

C. (1,98), (2,95), (3,92), (4,89)

B. (1,55), (2,56), (3,57), (4,58)

D. (1,75), (2,84), (3,79), (4,81)

6. Complete the table so that its ordered pairs represent a linear function.

Number of cookies	5	10	15	20	25	
Total cost in cents	15	30	45			

Name _____

Date _____

PROPORTIONAL AND ALGEBRAIC REASONING: PRACTICE TEST ANSWER SHEET

Directions: Use the Answer Sheet to darken the letter of the choice that best answers each question.

1. ○ A ○ B ○ C ○ D   7. ○ A ○ B ○ C ○ D

2. ○ A ○ B ○ C ○ D   8. ○ A ○ B ○ C ○ D

3. ○ A ○ B ○ C ○ D   9. ○ A ○ B ○ C ○ D

4. ○ A ○ B ○ C ○ D   10. ○ A ○ B ○ C ○ D

5. ○ A ○ B ○ C ○ D   11. ○ A ○ B ○ C ○ D

6. ○ A ○ B ○ C ○ D   12. ○ A ○ B ○ C ○ D

SECTION 2: PROPORTIONAL AND ALGEBRAIC REASONING: PRACTICE TEST

1. A car is traveling at an average speed of 55 miles per hour. At this rate of speed, which is the best estimate for how long it will take the car to travel 209 miles?

   A. 3 hrs.   B. 4 hrs.   C. 5 hrs.   D. 6 hrs.

2. Charla saved $18 when she bought a jacket on sale. If the discount was 30% of the regular price, what was the regular price of the jacket?

   A. $45   B. $54   C. $60   D. $75

3. $(+15) + (-36) = ?$

   A. +51   B. +21   C. -51   D. -21

4. On Saturday, 10 gallons of water were drained from the large aquarium at the museum. Then 7 gallons of fresh water were released into the aquarium. What overall change was produced in the initial amount of water in the aquarium?

   A. Decreased 3 gal.   B. Decreased 17 gal.   C. Increased 17 gal.   D. Increased 3 gal.

5. Find the *related* equation for $(+4) - (-9) = ?$

   A. $(-4) - (+9) = ?$ B. $(+4) + (+9) = ?$ C. $(+4) - (+9) = ?$ D. $(-4) + (-9) = ?$

6. In a rope-pulling contest, team A pulls in the negative direction and team B pulls in the positive direction. If the initial pulling effect on the rope equals (-2), but then 6 members of team A release the rope, which expression represents the final pulling effect on the rope?

   A. $(-2) + (-6)$ B. $(-6) - (-2)$ C. $(-2) - (-6)$ D. $(-6) + (+2)$

7. $(+28) \div (-7) = ?$

   A. -4   B. +21   C. +4   D. Not shown here

8. New car wheels are moving in rows of 4 wheels each along the factory conveyor belt to the paint room. When 9 rows are on the belt, the belt malfunctions and reverses its direction. What is happening to the wheels now?

   A. 9 of 4 wheels move forward   C. 4 of 9 wheels move backward

   B. 4 of 9 wheels move forward   D. 9 of 4 wheels move backward

SECTION 2: PROPORTIONAL AND ALGEBRAIC REASONING: PRACTICE TEST (Continued)

9. Juan's weekly fee for walking a dog daily is based on the equation T = 4 + 3D, where T is the total fee in dollars and D is the number of blocks he has to walk the dog. If he has to walk Mr. Mack's terrier 5 blocks, how much will he be paid each week?

   A. $7   B. $12   C. $15   D. $19

10. Which expression can be used to find the Nth term in the following arithmetic sequence, where N is a number's position in the sequence? Use substitution to test each expression.

Position	1	2	3	4	N
Term	3	5	7	9	?

   A. 2N + 1   B. 3N + 2   C. 5N   D. 4N + 3

11. If ordered pairs in the incomplete table below represent a linear function, which ordered pair will not belong to the table when the table is extended?

Number of stickers	4	8	12	16	20	
Total cost in cents	12	24	36			

   A. (32,96)   B. (28,56)   C. (24,72)   D. (20,60)

12. A new baseball card was worth $5 in the year 2000. The table shows its value each year for several years after its issue. Based on the table's information, what is a reasonable prediction of the card's value in 2006?

Year	2000	2001	2002	2003
Value of card	$5.00	$5.20	$5.45	$5.75

   A. Between $8 and $9   C. Between $6 and $7

   B. Between $7 and $8   D. Between $5 and $6

Section 2: Proportional and Algebraic Reasoning: Answer Key for Practice Test

The objective being tested is shown in brackets beside the answer.

1. B [1]	7. A [4]
2. C [1]	8. D [4]
3. D [2]	9. D [5]
4. A [2]	10. A [5]
5. B [3]	11. B [6]
6. C [3]	12. C [6]

GEOMETRY, SPATIAL REASONING, AND MEASUREMENT

Objective 1

Sketch side views (orthogonal views) of solids and identify different perspectives of solids that satisfy the side views.

Matching two-dimensional orthogonal views (line of sight at 90 degrees to surface being viewed) to other orthogonal views or perspective views of the same shape or to their corresponding three-dimensional shapes or solids is difficult for students of any age to do. It is a skill necessary for reading and interpreting blueprints and other types of construction drawings. To develop this skill, students need experience touching and observing different solids, describing the faces or surfaces of the solids, and drawing various orthogonal and perspective views. The following activities provide such experience.

Activity 1: Manipulative Stage

Materials

Commercial set of plastic or wooden geometric solids (1 shape per pair of students)

Connectable cubes (0.75-inch or 1-inch size preferred; 10 cubes per pair of students)

Regular pencil and paper

Procedure

1. Give each pair of students 1 geometric solid and 10 connectable cubes.

2. Vary the solids given to the pairs of students. Sets of plastic or wooden geometric solids are available commercially through educational catalogues. These sets usually include cones, cylinders, pyramids, spheres, ellipsoids, truncated cones and pyramids, and right rectangular prisms. Each solid is approximately 2 to 4 inches high.

3. Students should write a description about their solid on their own paper, including the solid's correct geometric name. It may be helpful to review such

terms as *vertex, lateral surface, base*, and *edge*. General shape names like *pyramid, prism*, and *cone* may also need to be reviewed.

4. Have partners take turns, with one person holding the solid up at eye level while the other person draws different orthogonal views of the solid. Generally, an orthogonal view includes the surface(s) seen by the eyes when the line of sight is perpendicular to the viewed surface. Therefore, students must view their solid at eye level in order to see the different sides properly. They should rotate their solid so that they can easily see the top, lateral, and bottom faces or surfaces at the correct angle.

5. Students should build a free-form or irregular structure using the 10 connectable cubes. The structure should not be a prism; it should have various appendages in its design and possibly two or more levels of cubes involved in some way.

6. Have students repeat the previous writing-drawing sequence using their connectable cube structure. It will be helpful when drawing the cube structure if students place the structure on a sheet of paper with its edges labeled as "front," "back," "left end," and "right end." Then the paper may be easily rotated to change the viewpoint, and the drawings may be labeled with the corresponding titles.

7. Students should draw a perspective view of their cube structure. This requires them to look at the structure from one of its corners rather than from a direct side or orthogonal view.

8. Have students share their descriptions and drawings with the entire class. At other times throughout the school year, have students repeat this activity with various solids until they have had experience with most of the solids in the original set. Have them occasionally repeat the activity with the connectable cubes as well.

9. Discuss samples of the geometric solids and a 10-cube structure with the class before allowing students to work on their own.

As examples of solids, when a cone (one whose height is perpendicular to the circular base) is viewed from the top or from the bottom, a circular shape is seen. Because the cone's "top" is a vertex or point, the line of sight from the top will actually be perpendicular to the cone's base. When the cone's lateral surface is viewed, a somewhat triangular shape will appear. Because of the orthogonal viewing angle, the lower edge of the "triangle" will look slightly curved. All surfaces of a right rectangular prism will look like rectangles, which include squares. The lateral surfaces of truncated pyramids will look like trapezoids or generic quadrilaterals. Below is an example of orthogonal views for a square pyramid; that is, the base of the pyramid is a square.

Bottom

Lateral/Side

Top

Here is a sample perspective view of a square pyramid:

Here are examples of a perspective view and three orthogonal views for a 10-cube structure:

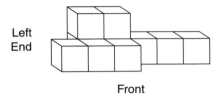

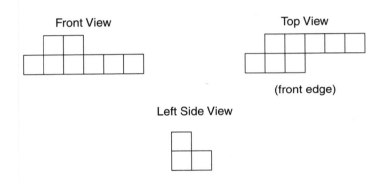

Activity 2: Pictorial Stage

Materials

Worksheet 3–1a
Worksheet 3–1b
Connectable cubes (0.75-inch or 1-inch size preferred; 10 cubes per pair of
   students)
Commercial set of plastic or wooden geometric solids from Activity 1
Regular pencil

Procedure

1. Give each team of 4 students 4 copies of Worksheet 3–1a and Worksheet 3–1b. If preferred, these two worksheets may be completed at different class times.

2. For Worksheet 3–1a, give each team of 4 students the 4 solids that correspond to the exercises on the worksheet (cylinder, triangular pyramid, hexagonal prism, truncated cone), along with one or two extra solids not described on the worksheet. Each exercise of 2 or 3 orthogonal views should correspond to a solid in the set used previously at the manipulative stage. Do not tell the students which solids are the correct ones for Worksheet 3–1a. An extra set of solids may be needed in order to have enough for all teams.

3. For Worksheet 3–1a, each team must work together to examine their set of solids and decide which one matches the views provided in each exercise on the worksheet. When students make a match, they should write the geometric name of the solid in the blank shown on the worksheet. Review the names of various geometric solids before students begin the worksheet.

4. For Worksheet 3–1b, give each pair of students 10 connectable cubes. For each exercise on the worksheet, partners must build a cube structure that corresponds to the views shown in the exercise, using 10 or fewer cubes. Each exercise consists of three orthogonal views. A given side view may be for the left or the right side; students must determine which side will lead to a solution. When students complete a structure, inspect the structure for its agreement with the provided views. Have students make changes where necessary. It is possible for several different structures to have the same set of orthogonal views. Students who have already demonstrated strength in this type of visualization may serve as "class inspectors" to speed up the checking.

5. When students have found a cube structure that satisfies the three views of an exercise, they should label the squares of the top view with the number of cubes in the stack represented by that square. Labeling the diagram in this manner will allow students to compare their cube structures to those of other students even after the actual structures are dismantled.

6. Have several teams share their results with the entire class when the worksheets are completed. For each exercise on Worksheet 3–1b, one pair of students might show their particular cube structure for that exercise. If another pair of students has a different structure for the same exercise, ask that pair to share their structure as well.

Answer Key for Worksheet 3–1a

1. cylinder

2. triangular pyramid

3. hexagonal prism

4. truncated cone

Answer Key for Worksheet 3–1b

Possible structures are shown using top views with the number 2 or 3 inside squares to indicate the number of cubes in each stack; blank squares indicate only one cube in the stack.

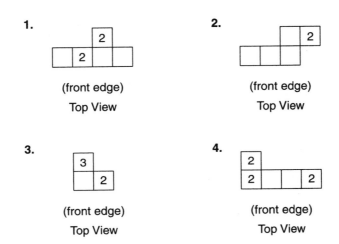

1.

(front edge)

Top View

2.

(front edge)

Top View

3.

(front edge)

Top View

4.

(front edge)

Top View

WORKSHEET 3–1a

**Matching Side Views
to Geometric Solids**

Name _____

Date _____

For each exercise, identify the geometric solid that matches the two or three views provided. Write the name of the solid in the blank beside or below the exercise.

1.

Side View

Top/Bottom
View

Shape Name: _____

2.

Top View

Bottom View

Shape Name: _____

3.

Side View

Top/Bottom
View

Shape Name: _____

4.

Bottom View

Top View

Side View

Shape Name: _____

WORKSHEET 3–1b

Matching Side Views to Cube Structures

Name _____

Date _____

For each exercise, build a cube structure that matches the three orthogonal views provided. Show each completed structure to your teacher. Label each top view as instructed. Is there more than one way a structure might be built?

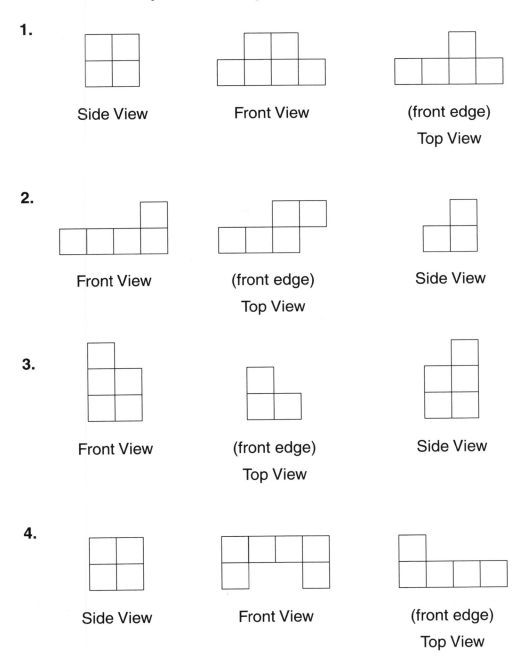

1.

Side View   Front View   (front edge)
                              Top View

2.

Front View   (front edge)   Side View
               Top View

3.

Front View   (front edge)   Side View
               Top View

4.

Side View   Front View   (front edge)
                             Top View

Activity 3: Independent Practice

Materials
    Worksheet 3–1c
    Regular pencil

Procedure
Give each student a copy of Worksheet 3–1c. After students have completed the worksheet, have several students share their answers with the entire class.

Answer Key for Worksheet 3–1c
  1. B

  2. A

  3. D

  4. B

  5. C

  6. C

Possible Testing Errors That May Occur for This Objective
- When asked to select a front view that matches to a given three-dimensional (3D) shape, students match to the top or end or side face of the shape instead.

- When given orthogonal views to match to the name of the corresponding geometric solid, students select the wrong name for the shape because they do not recognize the different orthogonal views of the shape or do not know the formal names of the shapes they have studied.

- Students select the wrong side view for a given 3D shape because they mentally flip the view they have selected to make it match the side of the given shape.

WORKSHEET 3–1c

Matching Side Views
with Their 3D Shapes

Name _____

Date _____

Complete each exercise.

1. Which top view belongs to the cube structure represented below?

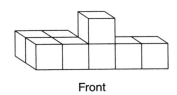

Front

A.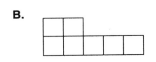

C.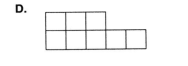

B.

D.

2. Which side view might belong to a solid 3D block having the given top view and front view?

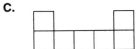

Front
View

Top
View

(front edge)

A.

C.

B.

D.

202

WORSHEET 3–1c Continued

Name _____

Date _____

3. Which geometric solid would have both of the following orthogonal views?

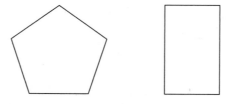

A. Triangular pyramid   C. Tetrahedron

B. Right cylinder   D. Pentagonal prism

4. A square pyramid has a lateral side view that looks like a:

A. Square   B. Triangle   C. Hexagon   D. None of these

5. A cylinder sitting on one of its bases has a lateral side view that looks like a:

A. Circle   B. Pentagon   C. Rectangle   D. Triangle

6. A cone sitting on its base and viewed directly from above will look like a(n):

A. Triangle   B. Square   C. Circle   D. Octagon

Objective 2

Identify or graph reflections (flips), rotations (turns), and translations (slides) on a coordinate plane.

Transformations exist in our daily lives. *Translations* occur when we ride on an escalator or slide down a slide, or a vacuum cleaner is pushed back and forth. *Reflections* happen when pancakes or playing cards are turned over. *Rotations* occur when a doorknob is turned or a person walks in a revolving door. In the coordinate plane, students need experience with locating points that are reflections (mirror images) of other points across the different axes, the origin, or a specific line, such as y = x. They should be able to reflect individual points, as well as simple planar shapes. Similarly, they need to be able to locate new points that result from translations or rotations of planar shapes. The following activities provide experience with such transformations. It is assumed that students have already mastered the plotting of points for given ordered pairs.

Activity 1: Manipulative Stage

Materials

> Small tagboard cutouts of irregular shapes (approximately 1.5 to 2 inches in width and length; one cutout per pair of students)
> 5-mm grid paper
> Small index cards
> Red pencil and regular pencil

Procedure

1. Give each pair of students a red pencil, an index card, two copies of the 5-mm grid paper, and a tagboard cutout of an irregular shape. All students may have the same shape or a different shape, whichever is preferred.

2. Have students draw a pair of coordinate axes for x and y in the upper half of each sheet of grid paper and another pair of axes in the lower half of the grid paper. Each axis should be numbered from –8 to +8. Students should label the four grids 1 through 4.

   For the following exercises in Activity 1, grid and ordered pair work will need to be assessed individually or by pairs of students since the cutout shapes used and the initial positioning of the shapes may vary among the students. Steps 3 to 9 refer to reflections, steps 10 and 11 to translations, and steps 12 and 13 to rotations.

3. *Reflections:* On grid 1, have students place their cutout shape so that it overlaps quadrants II and III, and trace around the shape in regular pencil. Ask them to label each vertex of the traced shape with a letter and the appropriate ordered pair.

4. Have students reflect each labeled point across the y-axis and mark its image appropriately in quadrant I or quadrant IV. They should label each image point with its own ordered pair and the letter in prime format of its corresponding point in quadrant II or III (for example, A' is the image of A).

5. The cutout shape should then be placed in quadrants I and IV so that its vertices align with the image points marked there. Students should discover that their cutout shape must be flipped over in order for its vertices to fit the image points. Have students trace around the cutout shape in this new position with red pencil. Here is an example of two such traced shapes on a partial grid with only one vertex labeled on each shape. Students should label all vertices on their shapes. The broken-line figure represents the cutout traced in red pencil:

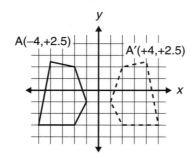

6. When all are finished, discuss the differences and likenesses between the two traced shapes in quadrants I and IV and quadrants II and III. Students should notice that the two shapes are congruent, but their left-right orientation in the plane is reversed. Their corresponding ordered pairs differ in that their x-values, or abscissas, are opposites or additive inverses.

7. Now have students draw a line on grid 2 to represent the graph of y = x. They should trace their cutout shape in regular pencil on one side of the drawn line and label the vertices with letters and ordered pairs as they did on grid 1. Each vertex point should be reflected across the y = x line and its image marked and labeled accordingly. The index card may be used to line up each original point with its proposed image point so that the path connecting the two points is perpendicular to the y = x line on the grid (a reflection property). It is difficult for students to visualize reflective paths across slanted lines. On grid 1, however, they are able to easily follow the horizontal lines of the grid when reflecting points across the y-axis. Here is an example of the index card in use:

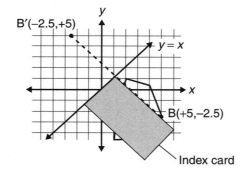

8. The cutout shape should be placed on the image points so that its vertices align with the appropriate points. Again, the cutout shape will need to be flipped in

order for all image points to match. The shape should then be traced in the new position with red pencil. Here is a sample of a partially completed diagram:

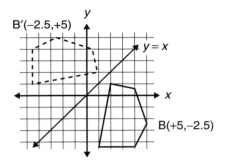

9. When all students are finished, discuss the differences and likenesses between the two traced shapes. The two shapes are congruent, but their orientation in the plane with respect to the y = x line is reversed. Their corresponding ordered pairs differ in that the x-value, or abscissa, of the original point becomes the y-value, or ordinate, of the image point, and the y-value of the original point becomes the x-value of the image point.

10. *Translations:* On grid 3, have students make a new tracing of their cutout shape in regular pencil, positioning the shape in quadrants II and III. Each vertex of the tracing should be marked and labeled as done previously. Have students find image points of the vertices by moving each vertex point 5 steps to the right and 2 steps down. Thus, if one vertex is at (–3,+5), its image point will be at (+2,+3).

11. After students have found all the image points for the vertices, they should place the cutout shape on the points and align its vertices with their image points. The cutout shape should be traced in this new position with red pencil. Students should observe that the two drawn shapes are congruent and oriented in the plane in the same manner, just in different locations of the plane. Each original ordered pair has been changed by adding +5 to the x-value and adding –2 to the y-value. Here is a sample of a partially completed diagram:

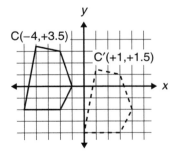

12. *Rotations:* On grid 4, have students place their cutout shape mostly in quadrant I, positioning it so that one vertex point touches the origin of the grid. Have them trace the cutout shape in regular pencil and then, holding the selected vertex at the origin, slowly rotate the shape counterclockwise until it overlaps some of

quadrant II and quadrant III. Students should trace the cutout shape in its new position with red pencil. Do not have them label the vertices in this case. Here is a sample of finished tracings:

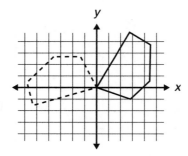

13. Guide students to observe that the new image is not in the same orientation as the original shape, but the two shapes are still congruent. Also notice that the new image has *not* been formed by flipping over the original shape, as was done on grids 1 and 2. In this particular exercise, the image has been formed by rotating the original shape around the origin. Therefore, the origin is called the *center of rotation*. Other points besides the origin might serve as the center of rotation, if preferred.

Activity 2: Pictorial Stage

Materials

Worksheet 3–2a
Red pencil and regular pencil

Procedure

1. Give each student a copy of Worksheet 3–2a and a red pencil. Have students work in pairs.

2. Each exercise on the worksheet will provide experience with the transformations studied in Activity 1.

3. Review the idea that a reflection across the y-axis changes the x-value of each ordered pair being reflected to its inverse. Similarly, a reflection across the x-axis changes the y-value of the ordered pair being reflected to its inverse. In a reflection across the line for y = x, the original x-value and y-value are interchanged. In translations, no flips occur, and all original points are changed in the same way. Rotations do not involve flips, but they do change the orientation of the original shape and have a center of rotation.

4. After students have completed the worksheet, ask several students to explain their results to the entire class.

Answer Key for Worksheet 3–2a

1. Selected ordered pairs should be of the forms (a,b) and (a,–b).

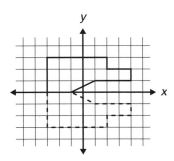

2. Selected ordered pairs should be of the forms (a,b) and (b,a).

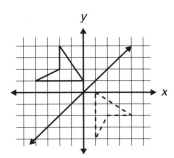

3. The center of the circle slides from (+1,+1) to (−3,−2), so each point of the original circle will slide left 4 steps and down 3 steps.

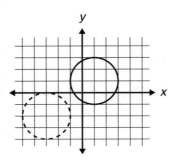

4.

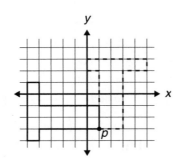

WORSHEET 3–2a   Name _____

**Drawing Transformations
of Planar Shapes**   Date _____

Complete each exercise. Draw each image with red pencil.

1. Draw the image when the given shape is reflected across the x-axis. Label one original vertex and its image point with their proper ordered pairs.

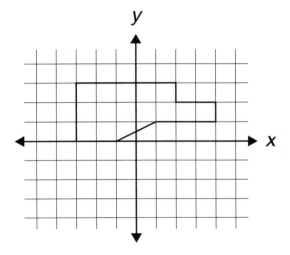

2. Draw the image of the shape's reflection across the line, y = x. Label one original vertex and its image point with their proper ordered pairs.

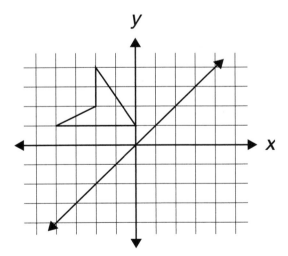

210

Name _____

Date _____

3. If the circle is translated so that its image is centered at (–3, –2), locate and draw the circle's image. How does each point on the circle change horizontally and vertically to become its image point?

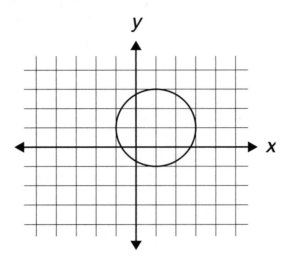

4. Draw a 90-degree rotation clockwise of the given shape, using point P as the center of rotation.

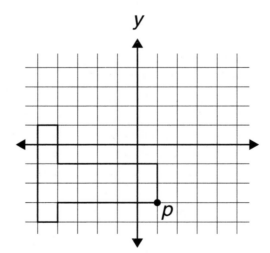

Activity 3: Independent Practice

Materials
Worksheet 3–2b
Regular pencil

Procedure
Give each student a copy of Worksheet 3–2b. After all have completed the worksheet, have several students share their results with the rest of the class.

Answer Key for Worksheet 3–2b
1. B

2. C

3. A

4. C

5. D

Possible Testing Errors That May Occur for This Objective
- When reflecting a point on a grid, students may reflect it across the wrong axis; for example, across the x-axis instead of the y-axis.

- In translations, students may fail to slide all points of the original shape in the same manner. For example, they might slide point A three steps to the right and two steps down, but then slide point B two steps to the right and three steps down.

- In rotations, students may rotate the original shape in the wrong direction. For example, they might rotate the shape 45 degrees counterclockwise instead of 45 degrees clockwise.

212

WORKSHEET 3–2b   Name _____

Reflections, Translations, and   Date _____
Rotations of Planar Shapes

Complete each exercise.

1. A circle with a radius of 4 units has its center at (–3,+2) on a coordinate grid. If
    the circle is translated 5 units to the right and 2 units up, what will be the
    ordered pair for the new center?

    A. (+5,+2)   B. (+2,+4)   C. (+1,+6)   D. (+4,+2)

2. If the triangle is reflected across the y-axis, the coordinates of the new vertices
    will be (–1,+2), (–5,+3), and _____.

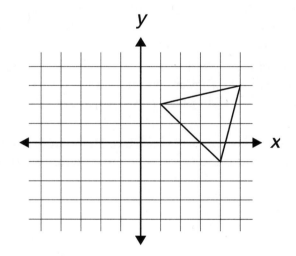

    A. (+1,–2)   B. (+5,–3)   C. (–4,–1)   D. (–1,–2)

3. If the point A(–2,+3), is reflected across the line y = x, the ordered pair for its
    image, A', will be _____.

    A. (+3,–2)   B. (+2,+3)   C. (–2,–3)   D. (–3,+2)

Name _____

Date _____

4. Which figure is a rotation of the top figure?

A.    B.    C. 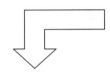   D.

5. If the rectangle is rotated counterclockwise about its vertex, P, then possible coordinates for the image of another vertex will be _____.

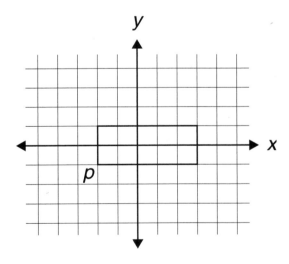

A. (+1,–1)   B. (+4,0)   C. (–3,+2)   D. (–2,+4)

Objective 3

Use dilations to generate similar two-dimensional shapes, and compare their side lengths, angles, and perimeters; find missing measurements using proportional relationships.

Students have great difficulty understanding that as side measures of polygons increase by a constant factor, the perimeter increases proportionately by the same factor. This proportional change is a characteristic of dilations, or the process of forming similar shapes. For example, if all sides are doubled (a factor of 2), the perimeter will also double (a factor of 2). For an extension of this characteristic, when the side measures increase, the area of the polygon increases by the *square* of the factor used to change the side lengths. That is, if the side lengths are tripled (a factor of 3), the area is multiplied by 3×3, or 9. The activities described below will help students understand the special relationship between the sides of a polygon and the perimeter of the polygon when a similar polygon is generated by a dilation.

Activity 1: Manipulative Stage

Materials

Packets of 1-inch flat straw pieces (100 pieces per packet per pair of students)
Rectangular pieces of felt material (approximately 12 inches by 18 inches; 1 per pair of students)
Worksheet 3–3a
Regular pencil

Procedure

1. Give each pair of students a packet of 100 1-inch pieces cut from flat plastic straws or coffee stirrers, a piece of felt for a building mat, and a copy of Worksheet 3–3a as a recording sheet. This activity involves similar shapes. It is assumed that students already know the basic definition of *similar polygons*: two polygons that have the same shape and same corresponding angle measures but whose corresponding sides taken pairwise form equivalent ratios. Dilations and similarity will be connected in this activity.

2. Consider a single straw piece as the unit of measure (approximately 1 inch) for building polygons. Have students work on a piece of felt material, so that the straw pieces do not slide around too freely during the building process.

3. For each initial polygon (A) built according to the directions on the worksheet, students should record on Worksheet 3–3a the number of straw units used to make each side. They should then count all the unit pieces used to make the shape in order to find the perimeter of the polygon. The perimeter should also be recorded on Worksheet 3–3a.

4. After students have built an initial polygon and recorded its measures, have them build another larger polygon (B) having the same shape as the first one (that is, the first shape will be *dilated* to form a larger similar shape) by doubling (2×), tripling (3×), or forming other multiples of all the original sides as indicated on

Worksheet 3–3a. The side lengths and perimeter of the new shape should then be found by counting the straw pieces, and these new measures should be recorded in the appropriate spaces on Worksheet 3–3a.

5. Repeat the above process for each new initial polygon built. After four pairs (A and B) of polygons have been built and their measures recorded, ask students to look for patterns among the side lengths and perimeters of each pair of polygons built. They should discover that as all side lengths are changed, so also is the perimeter changed in the same way. Have students record their ideas at the bottom of Worksheet 3–3a.

6. Discuss Exercise 1 on Worksheet 3–3a with the class before allowing the students to work the other exercises involving pentagons, quadrilaterals, and triangles.

For Exercise 1 on Worksheet 3–3a, students are asked to build a small hexagon (preferably an irregular hexagon) with their straw pieces, then record the different side lengths and the perimeter on the worksheet in the row for 1A. For row 1B, students are directed to build a larger hexagon by doubling each side length of the first hexagon. That is, if they used 3 straw pieces for one side, then they must use 2×3, or 6, straw pieces for the corresponding side in the larger hexagon.

Once the larger hexagon is built, each of its side lengths and its perimeter should be recorded in row 1B of Worksheet 3–3a. Here is a sample of a pair of hexagons where the side lengths of the first hexagon have been doubled to make the second, larger hexagon. The side lengths and perimeters of the two hexagons should be recorded on their respective rows, 1A and 1B, on Worksheet 3–3a:

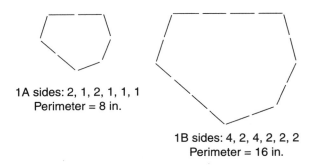

1A sides: 2, 1, 2, 1, 1, 1
Perimeter = 8 in.

1B sides: 4, 2, 4, 2, 2, 2
Perimeter = 16 in.

Answer Key for Worksheet 3–3a

Entries in the table will vary depending on how students build their required polygons. The final results, however, should be the same; whatever factor is used to enlarge the sides of a polygon will also be used to enlarge the perimeter.

WORSHEET 3–3a

Building Similar Polygons and
Comparing Their Perimeters

Name _____

Date _____

As you build the required polygons with your straw pieces, record their measurements on the table provided. Not all side columns will be needed for every polygon.

Polygon	Side 1	Side 2	Side 3	Side 4	Side 5	Side 6	Perimeter
1A Hexagon							
1B (2×)							
2A Pentagon							
2B (3×)							
3A Quadri-lateral							
3B (4×)							
4A Triangle							
4B (5×)							

As the side lengths of polygon A change to make the new similar polygon B, how does the perimeter of polygon A compare to the perimeter of polygon B?

Activity 2: Pictorial Stage

Materials
Worksheet 3–3b
Regular pencil

Procedure

1. Give each pair of students two copies of Worksheet 3–3b.

2. For each polygon on Worksheet 3–3b, have students draw a similar polygon according to the dilating instructions provided. Two shapes will be enlarged, and two shapes will be reduced. The amount of change required will be stated as a scale factor. The horizontal or vertical distance between adjacent dots on a worksheet grid will be 1 unit of length. The diagonal distance between two dots is greater than 1 unit in length.

3. For each polygon on Worksheet 3–3b, both those provided and those drawn, students should label each side with its length and record the perimeter inside the shape.

4. After the required polygons have been drawn and all polygons have been labeled and their perimeters found, ask students to describe in their own words how changing all side lengths in a polygon by the same scale factor, thereby obtaining another *similar* polygon, will affect the original perimeter. Have them write a statement on the back of the worksheet telling what they have discovered. Have several students share their statements with the entire class.

5. Discuss Exercise 1 with the class before allowing students to work the other exercises on their own.

Consider Exercise 1 on Worksheet 3–3b. Students must apply a scale factor of $\frac{1}{2}$ to dilate the polygon and form a new similar polygon. That is, they must find half of each original side length in order to draw the new shape. Since the scale factor is less than 1, the new shape will be a reduction of the original shape. The side lengths of the original polygon are 6, 4, 2, 2, 4, and 2 units, respectively. These measures should be labeled on their corresponding sides of the figure on the worksheet. The perimeter should be recorded inside the figure as "p = 20 units." Be sure that students count the spaces between adjacent dots as units and not the dots themselves.

When the new side lengths are found, their measures will be 3, 2, 1, 1, 2, and 1 units, respectively. The new perimeter will be 10 units, which should be recorded inside the newly drawn polygon. Here is an example of the original shape and the new shape with their perimeters recorded. The original shape is shown with a solid line and the new shape with a broken line. The side measures are not shown in the illustration.

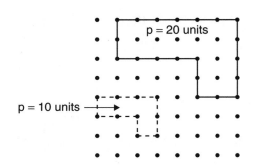

Answer Key for Worksheet 3–3b

1. Original: 6, 4, 2, 2, 4, and 2 units; p = 20 units

    New: 3, 2, 1, 1, 2, and 1 units; p = 10 units

2. Original: 3, 1, 1, 1, 1, 1, 1, and 1 units; p = 10 units

    New: 6, 2, 2, 2, 2, 2, 2, and 2 units; p = 20 units

3. Original: 1, 2, 1, and 2 units; p = 6 units

    New: 3, 6, 3, and 6 units; p = 18 units

4. Original: 4, 2, 2, 2, 2, and 4 units; p = 16 units

    New: 1, $\frac{1}{2}$, $\frac{1}{2}$, $\frac{1}{2}$, $\frac{1}{2}$, and 1 units; p = 4 units

WORKSHEET 3–3b

Drawing Similar Polygons and Comparing Their Perimeters

Name _____

Date _____

Draw the required polygons. Record the side measures and perimeter of each polygon on the drawing.

1. Scale factor of $\frac{1}{2}$

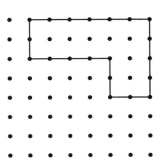

2. Scale factor of 2

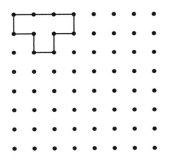

3. Scale factor of 3

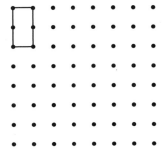

4. Scale factor of $\frac{1}{4}$

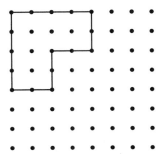

Activity 3: Independent Practice

Materials
  Worksheet 3–3c
  Regular pencil

Procedure
Give each student a copy of Worksheet 3–3c. Encourage students to draw and label shapes to help them solve the problems on the worksheet that do not provide illustrations. When all have completed the worksheet, have various students share their reasoning and their answers for each of the exercises.

Answer Key for Worksheet 3–3c
  1. C

  2. B

  3. A

  4. C

Possible Testing Errors That May Occur for This Objective
  • Students view the change between corresponding side lengths of similar shapes as addition rather than multiplication.

  • When finding the new measures for an enlargement, students multiply to find one new side length but divide to find another side length for the same new shape. They do not change all side lengths the same way.

  • Students fail to realize that in a dilation (enlargement or reduction), the side lengths and the perimeter change by the same scale factor.

WORSHEET 3–3c

Dilation: Reducing and
Enlarging Polygons

Name _____

Date _____

Complete the exercises provided. Drawing diagrams to solve the problems may be helpful.

1. A right triangle has a perimeter of 16 centimeters. The length of each side is increased to 3 times its original length to form a larger triangle. What is the perimeter of the larger triangle?

    A. 19 cm   B. 25 cm   C. 48 cm   D. 56 cm

2. △ABC is similar to △FGH. Find the length of side AC.

    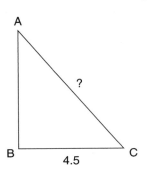 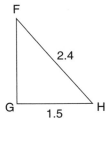

    A. 6.0 units   B. 7.2 units   C. 8.4 units   D. 9.0 units

3. The larger quadrilateral was dilated to form the smaller quadrilateral. Two corresponding side lengths are shown. What was the scale factor used to change the larger into the smaller shape?

    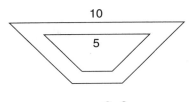

    A. $\frac{1}{2}$ B. $\frac{1}{4}$ C. 2   D. 3

4. Rectangle A is similar to rectangle B. The longer side length of rectangle A is 5 inches. The longer side length of rectangle B is 20 inches and its area is 240 square inches. Find the area of rectangle A.

    A. 3 sq. in.   B. 12 sq. in.   C. 15 sq. in.   D. 25 sq. in.

Objective 4

Model and apply the Pythagorean theorem to solve real-life problems.

To fully understand the Pythagorean theorem, students need to explore both right and nonright triangles and the relationships among their three sides. The following activities provide such opportunities and will lead students to discover the famous theorem for themselves.

Activity 1: Manipulative Stage

Materials

Worksheet 3–4a

Large 1-inch grids (approximately 14 inches by 16 inches; 1 grid per pair of students)

Packets of 100 1-inch paper squares (1 packet per student)

Long bamboo skewers (1 per pair of students)

Tape (optional)

Regular pencil

Procedure

1. Give each pair of students a large grid sheet, two packets of 100 paper squares (1 inch by 1 inch), a bamboo skewer, and two copies of Worksheet 3–4a. The grid may be drawn on heavy bulletin board or butcher paper to form a grid approximately 14 inches by 16 inches (unit length of 1 inch), or it may be drawn on two sheets of paper 8.5 inches by 14 inches, which can be taped together at their longer edges to make the larger grid that is needed. Laminating the final grids will make them more durable. Worksheet 3–4a should have at least ten lines for recording the data.

2. In Activity 1, students will work only with right triangles. In Activity 2, the pictorial stage, they will investigate other triangles in order to determine which conditions of the theorem are really necessary. Allow students to find patterns for themselves. The same recording table, Worksheet 3–4a, will be used for both activities.

3. The large grid should be positioned so that the longer edge appears as a horizontal axis and the shorter edge appears as a vertical axis on the left. Students will arrange paper squares as square regions at the left and the bottom edges of the grid. The sizes of these two square regions are shown on Worksheet 3–4a for the first three exercises. The grid edge from each of these two square regions together will form the legs of a right triangle. Students will then try to build a square region, whose edge will be the hypotenuse of the same triangle.

4. For each exercise, after the assigned pair of square regions is in place along the two adjacent grid edges, have students place the bamboo skewer on the large grid so that it touches the corner of the top paper square along the left edge of the grid and the corner of the right-most paper square along the bottom edge

of the grid. The skewer will form a right triangle with the left-edge portion and bottom-edge portion of the grid bounded by the skewer. The students may find it helpful to tape the ends of the skewer in place on the grid to keep it from sliding during the exercise.

5. Now ask students if all the paper squares forming the two regions touching the large grid will be enough to form another square region along the skewer, or longer side of the triangle. Students should move all the paper squares from the two regions onto the grid and try to form a new square region. A square region will be possible each time because of the assigned lengths used for the shorter sides of the triangle.

6. The edge of the new square region will coincide with the hypotenuse (skewer segment) of the right triangle. Students should record their results on a line of the table on Worksheet 3–4a. The question in the right-most column of the table simply asks whether the combined paper squares from the first two square regions were enough to make the third square region. It will be possible for all exercises in Activity 1.

7. Follow the above procedure for each pair of side lengths shown in Exercises 1 through 3 on Worksheet 3–4a. Record the results in the table each time. Students will continue to use this same table during the pictorial stage in Activity 2.

8. Guide students through Exercise 1 from Worksheet 3–4a before allowing them to work the other two exercises on their own.

For Exercise 1, students will use the side lengths of 3 inches and 4 inches to build their first pair of square regions on the grid. Have students place 3 paper squares along the shorter edge of the large inch grid, starting from the lower left corner of the grid. Then have them place 4 paper squares along the longer edge of the grid, starting from the same corner as the 3 paper squares. Ask them to use more paper squares to build a square region (3 inches by 3 inches) that has the first 3 paper squares along one side; repeat the process with the 4 paper squares. Now have students place the bamboo skewer on the large grid so that it touches the corner of the top paper square along the left edge of the grid and the corner of the right-most paper square along the bottom edge of the grid. The skewer now forms a right triangle with the left-edge portion (3 inches) and bottom-edge portion (4 inches) of the grid bounded by the skewer. Tape the skewer in place if needed. Here is an example of the finished square regions and the skewer on the grid:

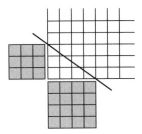

Now ask students if all the paper squares forming the 3×3 region and the 4×4 region touching the large grid will be enough to form another square region along the skewer, or longer side of the triangle. Students should move the 9 paper squares and the 16 paper squares onto the grid and form a new square region that is 5 inches by 5 inches in size. The new square region is shown below:

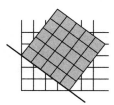

The 5-inch edge of the new square region will coincide with the hypotenuse (skewer segment) of the right triangle. Students should now record their results on the first line of their table in the following order: right, 3 inches, 4 inches, 5 inches, 9 square inches, 16 square inches, 25 square inches, yes. The question in the right-most column of the table simply asks whether the combined paper squares from the first two square regions were enough to make the third square region. It was possible for this exercise, and will also be possible for Exercises 2 and 3.

Alternative materials for this activity might be commercial colored square tiles, along with a large sheet of paper containing an L-frame (14-inch vertical bar with 16-inch horizontal bar) with no grid lines shown. The bamboo skewer would still be used in the described manner. The previous illustrations would remain the same, just without the grid lines.

Answer Key for Worksheet 3–4a

The answers are given for the first three exercises only.

1. right, 3 in., 4 in., 5 in., 9 sq. in., 16 sq. in., 25 sq. in., yes

2. right, 6 in., 8 in., 10 in., 36 sq. in., 64 sq. in., 100 sq. in., yes

3. right, 5 in., 12 in., 13 in., 25 sq. in., 144 sq. in., 169 sq. in., yes

WORSHEET 3–4a

Name _____

Modeling the Pythagorean Theorem
with Triangles

Date _____

Build square regions with 1-inch paper squares on a grid or with cutout grid shapes.
Follow the teacher's instructions to make different triangles. Record your results in the
table. Side lengths for Exercises 1 through 3 are shown.

Type of Triangle	Edge Lengths			Areas			Area 1 + Area 2 = Area 3? Yes/No
	Short Side 1	Short Side 2	Long Side 3	Short Side 1	Short Side 2	Long Side 3	
1. right	3	4					
2. right	6	8					
3. right	5	12					
4.							
5.							
6.							
7.							
8.							
9.							
10.							

Activity 2: Pictorial Stage

Materials

Worksheet 3–4a (from Activity 1)
5-mm grid paper
Small index cards (1 per pair of students)
Scissors (1 per pair of students)
Transparent tape (1 roll per pair of students)
Plain paper
Regular pencil

Procedure

1. Give each pair of students three sheets of 5-mm grid paper, four sheets of plain paper, a small index card, scissors, and a roll of transparent tape. They will continue to use the recording table on Worksheet 3–4a from the manipulative stage.

2. In Activity 2, students will cut various square regions from the grid paper. They will form new triangles by arranging three selected square regions, so that only their vertices or corners touch in a prescribed way (see the illustration on the next page). The edge between each pair of touching vertices will form a side of the new triangle. The paper regions will then be taped down on a plain sheet of paper, carefully preserving the triangle that has been formed.

3. The index card should be used to test the triangle's three angles for a possible right angle. The triangle should be identified as obtuse, acute, or right, and the triangle's side lengths and the areas of the corresponding paper grid squares recorded on a line of the table on Worksheet 3–4a. Students should also answer the question about the areas in the right-most column.

4. For Exercises 4 through 10 on Worksheet 3–4a, use the following sets of side lengths for the paper squares. The type of triangle the side lengths will produce is also given:

   Exercise 4: 5, 5, 8—obtuse triangle
   Exercise 5: 6, 6, 6—acute triangle
   Exercise 6: 9, 12, 15—right triangle
   Exercise 7: 5, 8, 10—obtuse triangle
   Exercise 8: 4, 4, 4—acute triangle
   Exercise 9: 10, 10,12—acute triangle
   Exercise 10: 12, 16, 20—right triangle

5. After the table on Worksheet 3–4a is completed for all 10 triangles (3 from the manipulative stage and 7 from the pictorial stage), ask the students to notice which types of triangles have "yes" in the right-most column of the table. Only the right triangles should have "yes." Have students write a statement below their table stating that "only for *right* triangles does the sum of the squares of the shorter two side lengths equal the square of the longest side length," or some similar wording.

6. Before allowing students to work on their own, discuss Exercise 4 with the class.

Consider Exercise 4. The side lengths are 5, 5, and 8 units. Students should make cutouts of two 5 × 5 squares and one 8 × 8 square from their 5-mm grid paper. A triangle should be formed with the 3 paper squares, then the paper squares taped down on a sheet of plain paper. The corner of the index card will not fit exactly into any angle (therefore, no right angle exists), and one angle of the triangle opens wider than the corner of the index card, indicating an obtuse angle. So the triangle formed will be an obtuse triangle with side lengths 5, 5, and 8 units, with corresponding areas 25, 25, and 64 square units, all to be recorded in line 4 of the table on Worksheet 3–4a. Since (25 + 25) does not equal 64, the word "no" will be written in the right-most column. Have students write the side lengths and the triangle name below the taped-down paper squares.

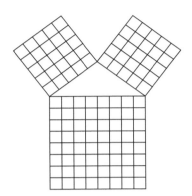

Answer Key for Worksheet 3–4a

1. right, 3 in., 4 in., 5 in., 9 sq. in., 16 sq. in., 25 sq. in., yes

2. right, 6 in., 8 in., 10 in., 36 sq. in., 64 sq. in., 100 sq. in., yes

3. right, 5 in., 12 in., 13 in., 25 sq. in., 144 sq. in., 169 sq. in., yes

4. obtuse, 5 units, 5 units, 8 units, 25 sq. units, 25 sq. units, 64 sq. units, no

5. acute, 6 units, 6 units, 6 units, 36 sq. units, 36 sq. units, 36 sq. units, no

6. right, 9 units, 12 units, 15 units, 81 sq. units, 144 sq. units, 225 sq. units, yes

7. obtuse, 5 units, 8 units, 10 units, 25 sq. units, 64 sq. units, 100 sq. units, no

8. acute, 4 units, 4 units, 4 units, 16 sq. units, 16 sq. units, 16 sq. units, no

9. acute, 10 units, 10 units, 12 units, 100 sq. units, 100 sq. units, 144 sq. units, no

10. right, 12 units, 16 units, 20 units, 144 sq. units, 256 sq. units, 400 sq. units, yes

Activity 3: Independent Practice

Materials
    Worksheet 3–4b
    Regular pencil

Procedure
Give each student a copy of Worksheet 3–4b to complete. Encourage students to draw and label diagrams to help them solve the word problems. After all are finished, have several students share their answers with the entire class.

Answer Key for Worksheet 3–4b
    1. B

    2. A

    3. D

    4. C

    5. B

Possible Testing Errors That May Occur for This Objective
- Students will find the mean of the two given side lengths of the triangle instead of finding the length of the hypotenuse. The hypotenuse must be longer than either of the two legs of the triangle.

- Students will find the sum of the two given side lengths of the triangle instead of finding the length of the hypotenuse. If the hypotenuse were to equal the sum of the lengths of the two shorter sides, a triangle would not be possible.

- When the lengths of the hypotenuse and a leg of the triangle are given and the length of the other leg of the triangle is sought, students add the squares of the two given lengths instead of subtracting to find the square of the missing leg of the triangle.

WORSHEET 3–4b

Name _____

Solving Word Problems with the
Pythagorean Theorem

Date _____

Complete each exercise provided. Draw and label diagrams to solve the problems, if needed. A calculator may be helpful.

1. Josh drove 20 miles due north from Akron to Timberline, then drove 21 miles due east to Fort Davis. If he drove the shortest distance from Akron northeast to Fort Davis without going through Timberline, how far would he drive?

   A. 41 mi.   B. 29 mi.   C. 18 mi.   D. 10 mi.

2. A right triangle has a leg length of 6 centimeters and a hypotenuse length of 10 centimeters. Find the length of the other leg of the triangle.

   A. 8 cm   B. 10 cm   C. 12 cm   D. 16 cm

3. Which figure best represents a triangle with side lengths a, b, and c in which the relationship $a^2 + b^2 = c^2$ is always true?

   A.

   C.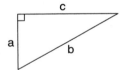

   B.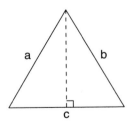

   D.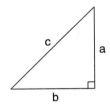

WORKSHEET 3–4b Continued

Name _____

Date _____

4. If k = 18.4 and n = 23.5, find the value of m to the nearest tenth if $k^2 + m^2 = n^2$.

A. 41.9   B. 29.8   C. 14.6   D. 5.1

5. A television tower is located 80 miles due north of a straight road. The tower has a transmission range of 100 miles. Find d, the length of the section of road that is within the transmission range of the tower.

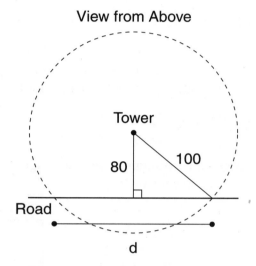

View from Above

A. 100 mi.   B. 120 mi.   C. 180 mi.   D. 200 mi.

Objective 5

Generate the formulas for the circumference and the area of a circle; apply the formulas to solve word problems.

Applications of the circle occur in many situations of our daily lives. Students need to view the formulas of a circle as more than just some letters to memorize. The role of pi in both circumference and area is unique to the circle and should be developed carefully. The activities for this objective provide the necessary experience with pi.

Activity 1: Manipulative Stage

Materials

Assorted plastic circular lids (3- to 5-inch diameters; 1 lid per pair of students)
Cotton string (nonstretchable; 1 20-inch piece per pair of students)
Scissors (1 per pair of students)
Centimeter grid paper (on colored paper; 1 sheet per pair of students)
Transparent tape (1 roll per pair of students)
Worksheet 3–5a
Regular pencil and paper

Procedure

1. Give each pair of students a plastic circular lid, 1 piece of 20-inch cotton string, scissors, 1 sheet of colored centimeter grid paper, tape, and Worksheet 3–5a. This activity is more effective if students have different-sized lids instead of all having the same size.

2. Have students wrap the string around the outer rim of their plastic lid to measure the lid's circumference. Students should mark the string to show where the end point falls or the wrapping stops.

3. Ask students to predict how many times the diameter length of their lid might be made from the newly marked-off portion of string. Write their predictions on the board.

4. Have students place the marked-off portion (circumference) of the string across the diameter of the plastic lid, starting with one end of the string touching the edge of the lid. They should slide the string across the lid, matching or counting off each diameter length until the marked-off portion of string has been used as much as possible. Three diameter lengths should be counted or matched with the string, with a small portion of string left over, regardless of the lid size used.

5. Compare the final diameter count of "3 and a little more" to the predictions made earlier by students. Have students write on the back of Worksheet 3–5a the following results: "The circumference of a circle equals the length of 3 and a little more of the circle's diameter." Here is an example of the wrapping of a lid and the measuring or counting off of the lid's diameter with the string:

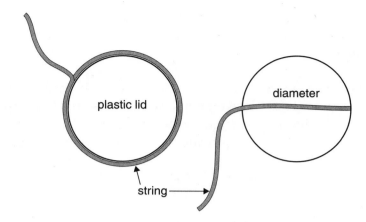

6. Have students continue to work with Worksheet 3–5a. For each circle on the work-sheet, from the colored centimeter paper have students cut out 4 large squares, whose edges equal the length of the circle's radius. Circle A requires 2-cm by 2-cm squares and circle B requires 3-cm by 3-cm squares. Each circle's special squares will be called the circle's *related squares*.

7. Ask students to predict how many of each circle's related squares will be needed to cover the interior of that circle. Write their predictions on the board.

8. For each circle, each large colored paper square should be cut apart in various ways in order to fit inside the circle, but the squares should not be cut apart into individual square centimeter units. Students should strive to use a minimal number of cuts on each large square. One paper square should be cut apart and all its pieces placed inside the circle before another paper square is cut apart. As students place cut paper pieces inside a circle, they should tape down the small pieces to hold them in place. The paper pieces should not overlap each other. Students should also try to cover a circle so that no gaps are left between paper pieces.

9. After students have finished each circle, have them compare the number of paper squares they actually used to the number they predicted. The actual covering should use 3 large whole squares plus a small part of a fourth square, regardless of which circle is being covered.

10. Discuss the relationship of the related square's area to the area of its circle. At the bottom of Worksheet 3–5a, have students write a statement about the two areas like the following: "A circle's area equals 3 and a little more of the area of the circle's related square, where the edge length of the related square equals the radius length of the circle." Here is an example of a covered circle (centimeter grid marks are not shown):

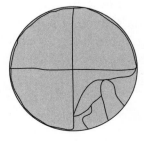

WORKSHEET 3–5a

Modeling the Area of a Circle

Name _____

Date _____

For each circle, from colored centimeter grid paper cut out 4 large squares, whose edge lengths equal the radius length of the circle. Cover the interior of the circle with as many of these related squares as needed, completely using one full square before starting the next square.

Circle A (radius = 2 cm):

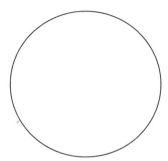

Circle B (radius = 3 cm):

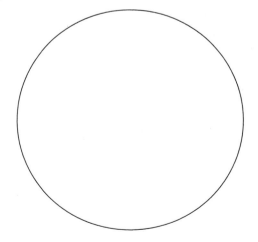

Activity 2: Pictorial Stage

Materials
Worksheet 3–5b
Adding machine tape
Centimeter rulers
Calculators (optional)
Red pencil and regular pencil

Procedure

1. Give each pair of students two copies of Worksheet 3–5b, a centimeter ruler, a calculator (optional), a red pencil, and a strip of adding machine tape about 18 inches long.

2. Students are to use the paper strip to form a stand-up "collar" around each circle to find its circumference. They should mark off the paper to show where the wrapping stops. This marked-off distance should be measured with the centimeter ruler in order to find the circumference in centimeters to the nearest tenth.

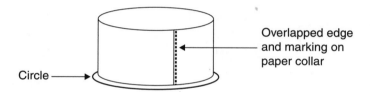

Circle →

Overlapped edge and marking on paper collar ←

3. The diameter of each circle should be measured by counting the centimeter grid units across the circle *through the center point* of the circle. Ask students to compute how many diameters (d) will equal the circumference (c) of each circle. Have them compute c ÷ d to the nearest hundredth. The equation should be recorded on Worksheet 3–5b beside the appropriate circle.

4. Since the measurement for the circumference of the same circle will vary slightly among the students, their quotient for c ÷ d will also vary. Collect all their quotients for the same circle and have the class compute the mean for these values. The mean of these quotients should be close to 3.14 for each circle. Have students write on the back of Worksheet 3–5b the following statement: "A circumference equals about 3.14 of the diameter's length." Then have them write with abstract symbols: $c \approx 3.14 \times d$ or $3.14(d)$. This is the formula used when computing circumference.

5. Now have students estimate the area of each circle on Worksheet 3–5b by counting the whole or partial unit squares in the interior of the circle. The total unit squares found will vary. Encourage students to mentally combine various parts of unit squares to form a "whole" unit square when estimating. Have each pair of students record their own totals beside the appropriate circles on their copies of Worksheet 3–5b.

6. For each circle, students should find the area of the related square, whose edge length equals the radius of the circle. They should find how many times the area of the related square may be removed or subtracted completely from the estimated

area of the circle. Each time they subtract, have them draw with red pencil a related square overlapping the circle. After this area has been subtracted a possible three times, have students compare the remaining portion of the circle's area to the square's area to find what fractional part of another related square will be needed to finish matching the square's area to the circle's total area. The fractional part should be computed to the nearest hundredth.

7. For each circle, all students should have used three areas of the related square plus a decimal portion of another area of the related square to equal their circle's estimated area. On the board, write the different amounts of squares used for each circle, and have students compute the mean of these amounts. The mean should be close to 3.14 for each circle on Worksheet 3–5b. On the back of the worksheet, have students write the statement: "The area of a circle equals about 3.14 of the area of the circle's related square."

8. Now guide students to transform their statement about area to a more abstract formula. Have them write the following sequence of statements below the initial area statement:

Area of circle of radius r ≈ 3.14 of area of square of edge r
Area of circle of radius r ≈ 3.14 × (r × r) or 3.14(r²)

Discuss the idea that the last statement represents the formula that is often used when computing the area of a circle. Advanced mathematics is needed to find the actual formula, which uses pi, but since pi is an irrational number, we must use an approximation of its value, here 3.14, when computing a circle's area.

As an example of finding area, consider circle A on Worksheet 3–5b. A possible estimate of its area in square centimeters might be 28 square centimeters. Since the circle has a radius of 3 centimeters, its related square will be 3 centimeters by 3 centimeters, which has an area of 9 square centimeters.

The related square's area may be subtracted from the circle's estimated area three times: 28 − 9 = 19, 19 − 9 = 10, and 10 − 9 = 1. Then three areas of the related square will "cover" or equal most of the circle's area, leaving 1 square centimeter of the circle still to be matched. Some students may want to divide 28 by 9, instead of subtracting 9 repeatedly. This is acceptable as long as they understand what the remainder means in this situation.

Students should draw with red pencil the three related squares overlapping the circle as shown below. This helps students to visualize that the entire area of a fourth related square will not be needed because the external "corners" of the 3 drawn squares must be moved inside the circle, thereby leaving only a small portion of the circle uncovered.

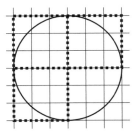

Only 1 square centimeter out of a fourth related square's area is needed to complete the circle's area. This is 1 square centimeter out of 9 square centimeters of area, which equals $\frac{1}{9}$, or about 0.11, of the fourth related square's area. Therefore, 3 + 0.11, or 3.11 of the areas of the related square equal the estimated area of the circle. The students with an estimate of 28 square centimeters for circle A's area should record the following beside their circle A on Worksheet 3–5b: "3.11 of $(3 \times 3) \approx 28$ sq cm of area."

For this same circle, other students may have estimates of 27 or 29 square centimeters for the circle's area, so they will have different decimal numbers for their results. For 27, they will have 3.00, and for 29, they will have 3.22. The class mean of all such decimal numbers found by all pairs of students, including any repeats, should be close to 3.14.

Answer Key for Worksheet 3–5b
Possible statements are given for each circle; equations may vary.

   Circle A: 18.9 cm ÷ 6 cm = 3.15 diameters in circumference;
      3.11 of $(3 \times 3) \approx 28$ sq cm of area
   Circle B: 24.9 cm ÷ 8 cm = 3.11 diameters in circumference;
      3.19 of $(4 \times 4) \approx 51$ sq cm of area

WORKSHEET 3–5b

**Finding the Circumference
and Area of a Circle**

Name _____

Date _____

For each circle, use a ruler and a paper collar to find the circumference. Find the area by overlaying the circle with related squares drawn on the grid and counting their unit squares.

Circle A (radius = 3 cm)

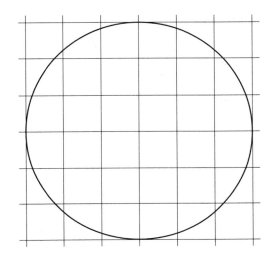

Circle B (radius = 4 cm)

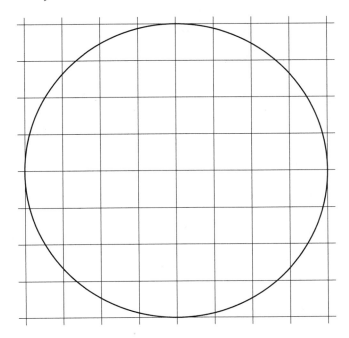

Activity 3: Independent Practice

Materials
   Worksheet 3–5c
   Regular pencil

Procedure
Give each student a copy of Worksheet 3–5c to complete independently. Encourage students to draw and label diagrams when solving word problems. Also remind them to write the needed formula in words or symbols, including 3.14 instead of pi, before substituting the numbers and performing the computation. When all have completed the worksheet, have several students share their results with the entire class.

Answer Key for Worksheet 3–5c
   1. B

   2. D

   3. C

   4. B

   5. C

Possible Testing Errors That May Occur for This Objective
   - Students confuse the two concepts of area and circumference and apply one when the other is needed.

   - A single radius value is used to compute the circumference instead of doubling the radius value or using the diameter value. That is, students use 3.14r, instead of 3.14(2r) or 3.14d, when finding the circumference.

   - The area of a circle is computed by squaring the radius value, but this product is not then multiplied by 3.14 or some other approximation for pi. That is, students use (r)(r) for the area, instead of 3.14(r)(r).

WORSHEET 3–5c

Applying the Circumference
and Area of a Circle

Name _____

Date _____

Solve the exercises provided.

1. A bicycle wheel travels about 75 inches for each full rotation. Find the diameter
    of the wheel to the nearest inch.

    A. 26 in.   B. 24 in.   C. 15 in.   D. 10 in.

2. A circular flower garden has a radius of 5 feet. What total area, to the nearest
    square foot, is needed to determine the amount of fertilizer to purchase?

    A. 16 sq. ft.   B. 25 sq. ft.   C. 63 sq. ft.   D. 79 sq. ft.

3. The figure below shows a circle inside a rectangle:

    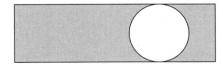

    Which procedure should be used to find the area of the shaded region?

    A. Find the area of the circle and then subtract the area of the rectangle from it.

    B. Find the circumference of the circle and then subtract the perimeter of the
       rectangle from it.

    C. Find the area of the rectangle and then subtract the area of the circle from it.

    D. Find the perimeter of the rectangle and then subtract the circumference of the
       circle from it.

4. A 6.0-cm square is inscribed in a circle with a radius of approximately
    4.2 centimeters. What is the area of the shaded region to the nearest tenth?

    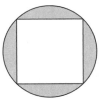

    A. 17.6 sq cm   B. 19.4 sq cm   C. 36.0 sq cm   D. 55.4 sq cm

5. A goat grazes in a circular path around a stake to which it is tied. If the goat can
    eat grass at a maximum distance of 10 feet from the stake, what is the maximum
    path to the nearest foot that it can make around the stake?

    A. 20 ft.   B. 31 ft.   C. 63 ft.   D. 100 ft.

Objective 6
Generate and apply the area formula for a parallelogram (including rectangles); extend to the area of a triangle.

Students seem to have much experience with the area of a rectangle, but not with the area of a parallelogram and its corresponding triangles. They are efficient in working with the adjacent side lengths of a rectangle, but often are unable to identify the perpendicular dimensions of nonrectangular parallelograms. They need more experience in locating these special dimensions. The following activities focus on ways to find the appropriate measures for computing area.

Activity 1: Manipulative Stage

Materials
> Worksheet 3–6a (patterns for parallelograms)
> Scissors (1 per pair of students)
> Transparent tape (1 per pair of students)
> Red and blue markers (1 set per pair of students)
> Regular paper and pencil

Procedure
1. Give each pair of students a copy of Worksheet 3–6a, scissors, transparent tape, and a red and a blue marker.

2. Ask students to cut out the two parallelograms drawn on Worksheet 3–6a and trace around each cutout shape on a plain sheet of paper.

3. For each cutout parallelogram, ask students to find a *simple* way to rearrange the shape into a rectangle without losing any of the original area. This should be done by cutting the grid shape apart, making the least number of cuts possible. To prevent possible confusion, point out that all cuts should be made along grid segments that are perpendicular to one of the longer sides of the parallelogram. One major strategy is to try to rearrange the more obvious triangular sections of the parallelogram. A cut closer toward the center of the shape is also possible.

4. Once students have converted a grid shape into a rectangle, have them temporarily tape the parts together and mark off a line segment or bar in red along the rectangle's longer side or edge. Have them also mark off another segment in blue along the shorter or adjacent edge.

5. They should then find the rectangle's area, using the grid units to measure the red and blue segments. Below the traced outline of the parallelogram, students should write the number sentence used to find the area of the rectangle and, hence, the area of the parallelogram.

6. Now have the students untape and move the parts back into their original positions to reform the original parallelogram by placing the parts on the shape's outline traced previously. The parts can now be taped down on this tracing of the parallelogram.

7. Ask students what they notice about the locations of the colored line segments or bars on the reformed shape. One colored segment should be in a perpendicular direction to the second colored segment. One colored segment should correspond to one edge of the parallelogram. The other colored segment will be perpendicular to that edge of the parallelogram and extend to the edge of the parallelogram that is opposite to the first edge.

8. Guide students to understand that each parallelogram and its corresponding rectangle have the same area. One shape has just been rearranged to form the other shape. Preservation of area is not intuitively obvious to some students.

The first parallelogram will be discussed below in detail.

As an example, shape I from Worksheet 3–6a should be cut out and traced onto a plain sheet of paper. Then the parallelogram should be cut apart to form a rectangle. Here are two possible ways that this first parallelogram might be cut *one time* and rearranged into a rectangle. Other cuts are possible as well. The arrow indicates how the section to the left of the cut might be moved to the extreme right in order to form a rectangle:

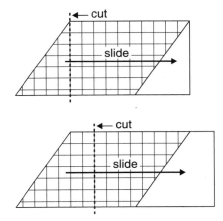

After the rectangle has been formed by either cutting method, a colored bar (red or blue) should be drawn along each of two adjacent edges of the rectangle, using a different color for each edge. Counting the grid units (approximately centimeters), the two dimensions of the rectangle are found to be about 6.3 units (length of the cutting edge) and 9.7 units (the adjacent edge). The area of the rectangle, and hence the parallelogram, may now be computed to the nearest tenth with the equation or number sentence: $6.3 \times 9.7 = 61.11$, or 61.1 square units (or square centimeters). This equation should be recorded below the traced outline of shape I. The rectangle with its two differently colored edges is shown here:

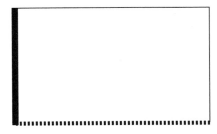

The two sections of the rectangle should now be rearranged as the original parallelogram and taped onto the traced copy of the parallelogram. Depending on which cutting method was used, the two differently colored bars from the rectangle will appear on the original parallelogram in one of the following ways:

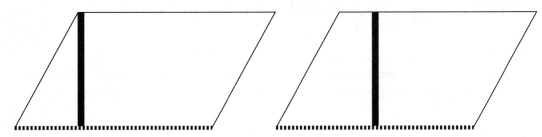

Guide students to observe that the two colored bars are perpendicular to each other in either case. One colored bar is drawn along one of the edges of the parallelogram. The other colored bar is drawn between that edge and its opposite edge. The two colored bars represent the lengths on the original parallelogram that need to be measured directly in order to find the area of the parallelogram.

Answer Key for Worksheet 3–6a
Possible equations are shown below; measures may vary.

Shape I: $6.3 \times 9.7 = 61.11$, or 61.1 square units (or square centimeters)
Shape II: $3.5 \times 8.2 = 28.70$, or 28.7 square units (or square centimeters)

WORKSHEET 3–6a

Rearranging Parallelograms into Rectangles

Cut out each parallelogram. Follow the teacher's instructions to change each shape into a rectangle.

Shape I:

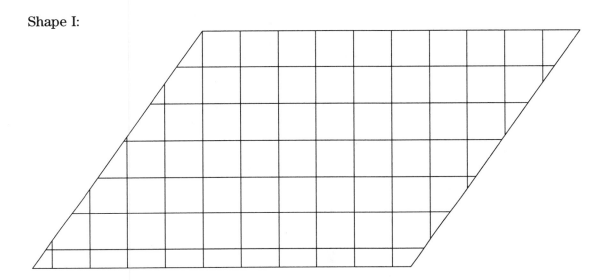

Shape II:

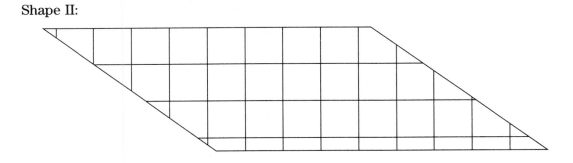

Activity 2: Pictorial Stage

Materials

Worksheet 3–6b
Centimeter rulers (1 per pair of students)
Small index cards
Red and blue markers (1 set per pair of students)
Calculators (optional)
Regular pencil

Procedure

1. Give each pair of students two copies of Worksheet 3–6b, an index card, a centimeter ruler, a red and a blue marker, and a calculator (optional). Guide students through the steps provided for each shape on the worksheet.

2. For shape I on Worksheet 3–6b, students should select a longer side of the parallelogram and draw a red bar along that entire side. They should then place an edge of the index card against the red bar and use the card's adjacent edge to draw a blue bar that connects perpendicularly from the red bar to the opposite side of the shape:

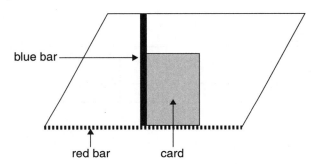

3. The red and blue bars should be measured in centimeters to the nearest tenth and then labeled. These measures (the dimensions for area) should be multiplied to find the area of the parallelogram. Have students round their product to the nearest tenth and then write an equation below shape I on Worksheet 3–6b to show their results (numbers may vary): "Area of parallelogram = 10.1×7.2 = $72.72 \approx 72.7$ square centimeters."

4. Now have students draw a diagonal on shape I. Two triangles will be formed. Ask students how the areas of the triangles compare to each other and to the area of the related parallelogram. They should notice that the triangles are congruent, so their areas are equivalent. Consequently, each triangle's area is equal to half the area of the related parallelogram. Using their own value found for the parallelogram's area, have students write another equation below shape I like the following: "Area of triangle = $\left(\frac{1}{2}\right)(72.7)$ = $36.35 \approx 36.4$ square centimeters."

5. Consider shape II on Worksheet 3–6b. Two segments should be drawn parallel to two sides of the triangle, respectively, to show a parallelogram that contains two of the given triangle. A parallel segment may be drawn by aligning the ruler with a side of the triangle and carefully sliding the ruler, without rotating it, until it touches the vertex opposite to the aligning side. A red and a blue bar should be drawn similarly to those on shape I. Here is a diagram that shows the changes to shape II. The blue bar drawn perpendicular to the red bar along the parallelogram's side or the triangle's side might also be drawn so that it lies completely in the interior of the triangle and intersects a vertex of the triangle. Discuss this idea with the students:

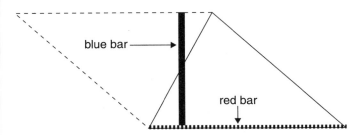

6. As done with shape I, the red and blue bars on shape II should be measured in centimeters to the nearest tenth and then labeled. These measures should be multiplied to find the area of the parallelogram. Have students round their product to the nearest tenth and then write an equation below shape II on Worksheet 3–6b to show their results (numbers may vary): "Area of parallelogram = 5.9×8.2 = $48.38 \approx 48.4$ square centimeters." Another equation should be written to show the area of the related triangle: "Area of triangle = $\left(\frac{1}{2}\right)(48.4) = 24.2$ square centimeters."

7. Remind students that rectangles are members of the parallelogram family and that finding the area of a rectangle is equivalent to finding the area of a parallelogram: the length of one side of the rectangle is multiplied by the perpendicular distance from that side to its opposite parallel side; the perpendicular distance corresponds to the length of the side of the rectangle adjacent to the first side measured. Perpendicular measures are always needed to find area. As with all other parallelograms, the diagonal of a rectangle will form two congruent triangles.

Answer Key for Worksheet 3–6b
See the text for details; numbers may vary.

246

WORSHEET 3–6b

WORKSHEET 3–6b

Measuring Parallelograms and
Triangles to Find Area

Name _____

Date _____

Follow the teacher's instructions to measure each shape and find its area.

Shape I:

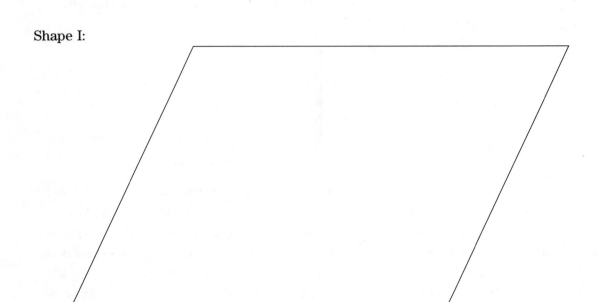

Shape II:

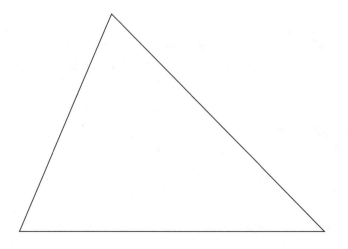

Activity 3: Independent Practice

Materials
Worksheet 3–6c
Regular pencil
Calculators (optional)

Procedure
Give each student a copy of Worksheet 3–6c and a calculator (optional). Remind students that every triangle is part of some related parallelogram. Also, every rectangle is a parallelogram. Encourage students to draw and label diagrams when they are solving word problems. After all have completed the worksheet, have several students share their results with the entire class.

Answer Key for Worksheet 3–6c
1. C

2. B

3. A

4. C

5. D

Possible Testing Errors That May Occur for This Objective
- When finding the area of a parallelogram, students multiply the lengths of two adjacent sides that are not perpendicular to each other.

- To find a triangle's area, students find the area of the related rectangle or parallelogram, but fail to take half of that product for the triangle's area.

- Students find the perimeter of a parallelogram instead of finding the area required by the problem.

248

WORKSHEET 3–6c   Name _____

Applying the Areas of   Date _____
Parallelograms and Triangles

Solve the exercises provided.

1. The two shorter sides of a right triangle are 8 inches and 5 inches long. What is
    the area of the triangle?

    A. 89 sq. in.   B. 40 sq. in.   C. 20 sq. in.   D. 13 sq. in.

2. A lawn design has flower beds around two sides of the lawn. The largest section
    has only grass, as shown in the diagram. How many square meters are in the area
    of the grass section?

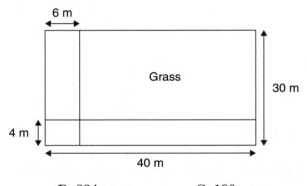

    A. 1,200 sq m   B. 884 sq m   C. 180 sq m   D. 160 sq m

3. The total area of the floor of a parallelogram-shaped room is 405 square yards. If
    the length of one edge of the floor is 27 yards, what is the perpendicular distance
    from that edge across to the opposite edge of the floor?

    A. 15 yds.   B. 27 yds.   C. 54 yds.   D. None of these

4. Find the area, to the nearest tenth, of the shaded triangle shown in the diagram.
    The outer shape containing the triangle is a parallelogram.

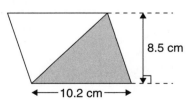

    A. 86.7 sq cm   B. 80.0 sq cm   C. 43.4 sq cm   D. 18.7 sq cm

5. A square platform has an area of 900 square feet. What is the perimeter of the
    platform?

    A. 900 ft.   B. 300 ft.   C. 225 ft.   D. 120 ft.

Objective 7
Generate and apply the area formula for a trapezoid.

The trapezoid is not a familiar shape to most students. They often mistake it for a parallelogram and thus apply the parallelogram's area formula when looking for the area of the trapezoid. The following activities show students how to transform a trapezoid into a parallelogram and modify the more familiar area formula of the parallelogram into a new formula for the trapezoid. For these activities, the trapezoid will be considered to have exactly one pair of parallel sides. It is assumed that students have already mastered the concept of area of a parallelogram.

Activity 1: Manipulative Stage

Materials
> Worksheet 3–7a
> Scissors (1 per pair of students)
> Transparent tape (1 per pair of students)
> Red and blue markers (1 set per pair of students)
> Small index cards
> Regular paper and pencil

Procedure
1. Give each pair of students a copy of Worksheet 3–7a, scissors, transparent tape, an index card, and a red and a blue marker.

2. Ask students to cut out the two trapezoids drawn on Worksheet 3–7a and trace around each cutout shape on a plain sheet of paper.

3. For each cutout trapezoid, guide students to find a *simple* way to rearrange the shape into a parallelogram without losing any of the original area. This should be done by folding one parallel edge over onto its opposite parallel edge, then cutting along the fold. One of the two parts should be rotated around so that one of its nonparallel edges matches one of the nonparallel edges of the other part, thereby forming a parallelogram. This process is shown here in the diagram:

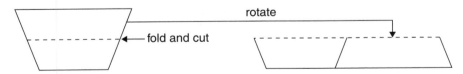

4. Once students have converted a grid shape into a parallelogram, have them temporarily tape the parts together and draw a red bar along the parallelogram's longer side or edge. Have them use the index card, if necessary, to draw a blue bar perpendicular to the red bar, connecting from the red bar to the opposite edge of the parallelogram. The blue bar might be drawn along a grid segment that is perpendicular to the red bar.

5. Students should find the parallelogram's area, using the grid units to measure the red and blue segments. Below the traced outline of the original trapezoid, students should write the number sentence or equation used to find the area of the parallelogram.

6. Have the students untape and move the parts back into their original positions to reform the original trapezoid by placing the parts on the shape's outline traced previously. The parts can now be taped down on this tracing of the trapezoid.

7. Ask students what they notice about the locations of the colored bars on the reformed trapezoid. The red bar from the parallelogram will be split between the two parallel edges of the trapezoid. The blue bar should be in a perpendicular direction to the red bars, but the blue bar will extend only half the perpendicular distance between the two parallel edges of the trapezoid:

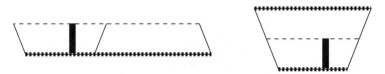

8. Guide students to write another equation for area, using measures directly from the trapezoid, which produced the parallelogram's measures needed for finding area. This new equation should be written below the first equation for area. (See the discussion concerning shape I on Worksheet 3–7a for the type of equation to write.)

9. Help students to understand that each trapezoid and its corresponding parallelogram have the same area. One shape has just been rearranged to form the other shape. Preservation of area is not intuitively obvious to some students.

10. The first trapezoid on Worksheet 3–7a will be discussed below in detail.

As an example, shape I from Worksheet 3–7a should be cut out and traced onto a plain sheet of paper. Then the trapezoid should be cut apart and rearranged to form a parallelogram. This may be done by rotating one part clockwise 180 degrees and then sliding it beside the other part:

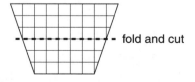

After the parallelogram has been formed, a red bar should be drawn along one of the longer edges of the parallelogram, and a blue bar should be drawn along one of the grid segments perpendicular to the red bar. The blue bar should extend from the red bar to the opposite side of the parallelogram. Counting the grid units (approximately centimeters), the two dimensions of the parallelogram are found to be 5 + 9, or 14 units (length of the longer edge or red bar) and 3 units (the perpendicular distance or blue bar's length). The area of the parallelogram, and hence the trapezoid, may now be computed with the equation or number sentence: "Area of parallelogram = 3 × 14 = 42 square units." This equation should be recorded below the traced outline of shape I. The parallelogram with its red and blue bars is shown here:

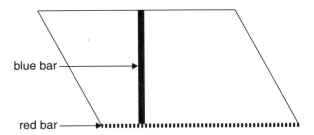

The two sections of the parallelogram should now be rearranged as the original trapezoid and taped onto the traced copy of the trapezoid. The colored bars from the parallelogram will appear on the original trapezoid as shown here, but the position of the blue bar may vary from left to right:

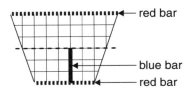

Guide students to observe that the original red bar has been separated and now appears as drawn along each of the two parallel edges of the trapezoid. Each red bar is also perpendicular to the blue bar. The blue bar is drawn perpendicular between the two parallel edges, but is only drawn half the distance between the two parallel edges.

Ask students what length they might measure on the trapezoid to find the length of the blue bar without measuring the blue bar itself. The perpendicular distance (6 units) between the two parallel edges should be measured on the trapezoid. Half of that distance will equal the length of the blue bar (3 units). To find the length of the red bar, students will need to measure both parallel edges (5 units and 9 units) of the trapezoid and add those lengths together (14 units). Once they have determined the lengths of the red and blue bars, their product will yield the area of the trapezoid. Below the first equation written to show the area of the parallelogram, write the following equation to show how the area of the trapezoid would be found directly from the trapezoid itself: "Area of trapezoid = $\left(\frac{1}{2}\right)(6)(5+9) = 3(14) = 42$ square units."

Answer Key for Worksheet 3–7a
Possible equations are shown below:

Shape I: Area of parallelogram = 3 × 14 = 42 square units. Area of trapezoid = $\left(\frac{1}{2}\right)(6)(5+9) = 3(14) = 42$ square units.

Shape II: Area of parallelogram = 2.5 × 12 = 30 square units. Area of trapezoid = $\left(\frac{1}{2}\right)(5)(4+8) = 2.5(12) = 30$ square units.

WORKSHEET 3–7a

**Rearranging Trapezoids into
Parallelograms**

Cut out each trapezoid. Follow the teacher's instructions to change each shape into a parallelogram.

Shape I:

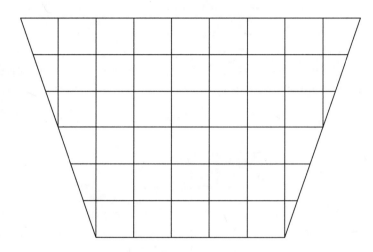

Shape II:

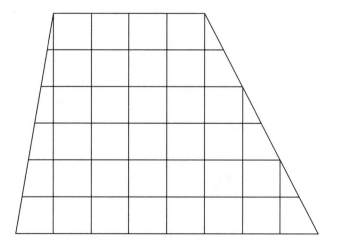

Activity 2: Pictorial Stage

Materials

Worksheet 3–7b
Small index cards
Centimeter rulers (1 per pair of students)
Red and blue markers (1 set per pair of students)
Calculators (optional)
Regular pencil

Procedure

1. Give each pair of students two copies of Worksheet 3–7b, an index card, a centimeter ruler, a red and a blue marker, and a calculator (optional).

2. For each trapezoid on Worksheet 3–7b, have students draw a red bar along each parallel side of the trapezoid. They should use an index card to help them draw a blue bar that connects the two parallel sides and is perpendicular to those two sides.

3. Have them measure each colored bar to the nearest tenth of a centimeter and use the measures appropriately to find the area of the trapezoid. They should write the area equation used below its shape on the worksheet.

4. Shape I on Worksheet 3–7b will be discussed to clarify the procedure to follow.

Shape I on Worksheet 3–7b might be discussed in the following way. Students should draw a red bar along each of the parallel sides of the trapezoid. Then one edge of an index card should be aligned with one of the red bars in order to draw a blue bar along the adjacent edge of the card. The blue bar should extend across the trapezoid from one red bar to the other red bar. The blue bar will be perpendicular to each of the red bars. Here is a diagram showing the positions of the colored bars:

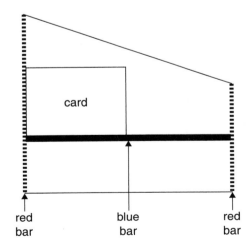

red   blue   red
bar   bar   bar

Using the centimeter ruler, students should measure and label each colored bar to the nearest tenth of a centimeter. The red bars should be about 4.2 centimeters and 6.2 centimeters in length. The blue bar should measure about 7.5 centimeters.

To find the area of shape I, students should first combine the two red bar lengths for the sum, 10.4 centimeters. Then they should find half of the blue bar's length, which will be 3.75 centimeters. Do not round to the nearest tenth until the final computation step. The product of 3.75×10.4 will be the area of the trapezoid. To record their results, students should now write the following equation below shape I on Worksheet 3–7b: "Area of trapezoid $= \left(\frac{1}{2}\right)(7.5)(4.2+6.2) = (3.75)(10.4) = 39.0$ sq cm." The area value should be rounded to the nearest tenth when necessary.

Answer Key for Worksheet 3–7b
Here are possible equations to use; measures used in equations may vary.

Shape I: Area of trapezoid $= \left(\frac{1}{2}\right)(7.5)(4.2+6.2) = (3.75)(10.4) = 39.0$ sq cm

Shape II: Area of trapezoid $= \left(\frac{1}{2}\right)(5.3)(4.3+11.4) = (2.65)(15.7) = 41.605 \approx$ 41.6 sq cm

255

WORKSHEET 3–7b

Measuring Trapezoids to Find Their Areas

Name _____

Date _____

For each trapezoid, draw a red bar along each parallel side of the trapezoid. Use an index card to help you draw a blue bar that connects the two parallel sides and is perpendicular to those two sides. Measure the colored bars to the nearest tenth of a centimeter and use the measures appropriately to find the area of the trapezoid. Write the area equation used below its shape.

Shape I:

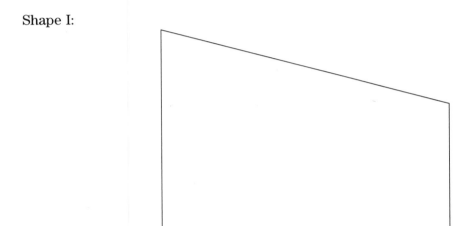

Shape II:

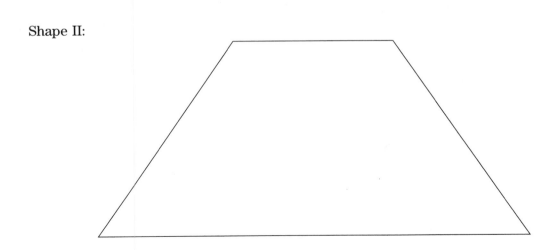

Activity 3: Independent Practice

Materials
Worksheet 3–7c
Calculators (optional)
Regular pencil

Procedure
Give each student a copy of Worksheet 3–7c and a calculator (optional). As review, have several students state in their own words how to find the area of a trapezoid. Tell the class that the parallel sides of a trapezoid are sometimes called the *bases* of the trapezoid and the perpendicular distance is called the *altitude* or *height* of the trapezoid. Encourage students to draw and label diagrams when they solve word problems. After all have completed the worksheet, have several students share their results with the entire class.

Answer Key for Worksheet 3–7c
1. C

2. C

3. B

4. A

5. B

Possible Testing Errors That May Occur for This Objective
- Students use the length of only one of the parallel bases when finding the area of a trapezoid. They forget to use both bases.

- When computing the area, students multiply the whole altitude by the total length of the two bases but do not divide by 2.

- Students multiply the lengths of the two parallel bases together instead of adding them.

WORKSHEET 3–7c

Applying the Areas of Trapezoids

Name _____

Date _____

Solve the exercises provided.

1. The two parallel sides of a trapezoid are 3 inches and 5 inches long. Its altitude is 4.6 inches. What is the area of the trapezoid?

    A. 69 sq. in.   B. 34.5 sq. in.   C. 18.4 sq. in.   D. 15 sq. in.

2. A rectangular lawn design has a large terrace at one corner of the lawn. The larger section has only grass, as shown in the diagram. How many square meters are in the area of the grass section?

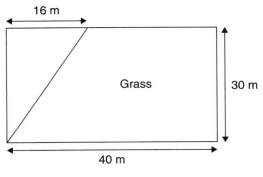

    A. 14,400 sq m   B. 1,200 sq m   C. 960 sq m   D. 720 sq m

3. The surface area of a trapezoid-shaped table top is 33 square feet. If the sum of the lengths of the two parallel edges is 11 feet, what is the perpendicular distance or altitude between those parallel edges?

    A. 22 ft.   B. 6 ft.   C. 3 ft.   D. None shown here

4. Find the area, to the nearest tenth, of the shaded trapezoid shown in the diagram. The outer shape containing the trapezoid is a parallelogram.

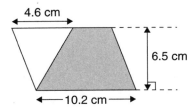

    A. 51.4 sq cm   B. 66.3 sq cm   C. 46.9 sq cm   D. 29.9 sq cm

5. A trapezoid has an area of 300 square feet and an altitude of 20 feet. What is the total length of its parallel bases?

    A. 40 ft.   B. 30 ft.   C. 20 ft.   D. 10 ft.

Objective 8
Apply nets and concrete models to find total or partial surface areas of prisms and cylinders.

Identifying the three-dimensional shapes that can be made from various patterns or nets is difficult for students. They need to work with a variety of nets by folding them and taping their edges together. Such construction experiences are necessary for students to be able to visualize and find the surface areas of the different geometric solids. The following activities provide experience with nets for rectangular prisms and cylinders. It is assumed that students have mastered the area of a rectangle and the area of a circle.

Activity 1: Manipulative Stage

Materials
Worksheet 3–8a
Scissors (1 per pair of students)
Transparent tape (1 roll per pair of students)
Centimeter rulers (1 per pair of students)
Calculators (optional)
Regular paper and pencil

Procedure
1. Give each pair of students two copies of Worksheet 3–8a, a pair of scissors, a roll of transparent tape, a centimeter ruler, and a calculator (optional).

2. Have students cut out each pattern on Worksheet 3–8a. They should try to fold and lightly tape the pattern together to form a cylinder or a prism. Folds should be made along line segments only, and circles should remain attached to adjacent parts. No parts or edges should overlap when the solid is formed. Not all patterns or nets will make a geometric solid.

3. For each pattern that successfully yields a solid, have students flatten the pattern back out and measure the necessary edges or radii to the nearest half-centimeter. They should then compute the area of each face or surface of the solid. The dimensions and area of each separate face or surface should be recorded directly on that face or surface as an equation.

4. After the area equations of all faces or surfaces of a solid have been recorded on the cutout pattern, the net or pattern should be taped onto a plain sheet of paper.

5. The sum of all the individual areas should be computed to find the total surface area represented by the pattern or net. Below the labeled net or pattern, students should write an equation that represents the sum of the different areas involved.

6. The surface area of pattern 1 from Worksheet 3–8a will be discussed here.

Consider pattern 1 from Worksheet 3–8a, which will successfully form a cylinder. Have students measure the diameter of each circle to find the radius more easily. Measuring to the nearest half-centimeter, the diameter for each circle will be about 2 centimeters, so the radius will be about 1 centimeter. The rectangle will measure about 6.5 by 2.5 centimeters.

Students should label each part with the equation used to compute the area for that part. The equation should reflect the measures found for that part. Here is a diagram that shows the labeling on the cylinder's net:

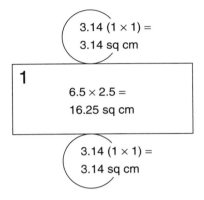

The labeled net should be taped on a plain sheet of paper. An equation for the sum of all the areas found should be recorded below the labeled net. For pattern 1, students should write the following equation: "Surface area of cylinder = 3.14 (1 × 1) + 3.14 (1 × 1) + (6.5 × 2.5) = 3.14 + 3.14 + 16.25 = 22.53 sq cm." Do not round off the final sum.

Discuss the idea that the longer length of the rectangle (here, 6.5 centimeters) corresponds to the circumference of the cylinder's circular base. If students had not measured that longer length directly on the net, they could also have found the length by using the circle's diameter and computing the circumference. In this case, the computation would yield 3.14 × 2, or 6.28, which rounds to 6 centimeters, not the 6.5 centimeters found when students measured the length directly on the rectangle of the net. This is because of the early rounding to the nearest half-centimeter during the measuring process.

Answer Key for Worksheet 3–8a

1. Surface area of cylinder = 3.14 (1 × 1) + 3.14 (1 × 1) + (6.5 × 2.5) = 3.14 + 3.14 + 16.25 = 22.53 sq cm

2. Surface area of prism = 4 (3 × 2) + 2 (2 × 2) = 24 + 8 = 32 sq cm

3. No solid possible

4. No solid possible

5. Surface area of prism = 6 (1.5 × 1.5) = 13.5 sq cm

WORKSHEET 3–8a

Building Cylinders and Prisms
from Nets

Cut out each net provided. Try to make a cylinder or a prism from each net by folding and taping the edges together. For each successful solid made, measure its dimensions to the nearest half-centimeter and compute its surface area.

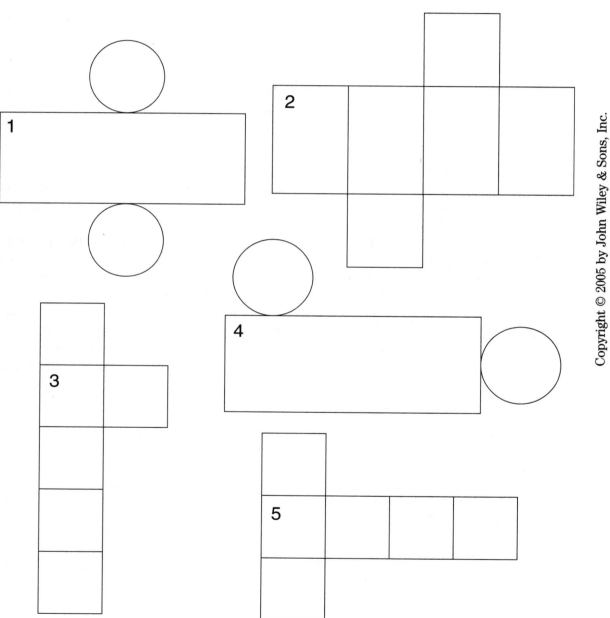

Activity 2: Pictorial Stage

Materials

    Worksheet 3–8b
    Centimeter rulers (1 per pair of students)
    Calculators (optional)
    Regular paper and pencil
    Compass (1 per pair of students)

Procedure

1. Give each pair of students two copies of Worksheet 3–8b, a centimeter ruler, a compass, and a calculator (optional).

2. For each figure on Worksheet 3–8b, have students draw a net on their own plain paper that will produce the geometric solid shown. The net should be drawn according to the actual measures given on the solid. Students should also transfer the given dimensions to the appropriate segments on the net. Either a diameter or a radius should be drawn on each circle of the net for the cylinder.

3. Students should use the given dimensions to compute the area for each distinct part of the net and write the equation for the area inside the part. Remind students that only one dimension for the lateral surface of the cylinder is shown on the diagram on the worksheet. Since this lateral surface becomes a rectangle in the net, the other dimension needed to find its area must come from the circumference of the circular base of the cylinder.

4. After all areas have been found, have students find the surface area, which is the sum of all the areas, and write an equation for that sum below the net.

5. Here is a discussion for the rectangular prism on Worksheet 3–8b.

    The rectangular prism on Worksheet 3–8b has the dimensions of 3 inches, 2 inches, and 1 inch. Since all faces of this prism are rectangles, any face may be considered as a base. For purposes of discussion, the 2-inch by 1-inch face will be used as the base. The drawing of the net reflects this choice by showing these two faces as appendages to the other four parts, which are connected together in a row. Other arrangements of the six parts are possible.

    Students should label enough measures on the net so that each part has its own two dimensions labeled. Here is a possible way to label the net and to record the area equation for each part:

After each area of the six parts or faces of the prism has been found, have students find the surface area of the prism by writing an equation that sums the six areas together. This equation should be written below the diagram of the net. Since each distinct area occurs twice for this particular net, a possible equation might be the following: "Surface area of prism = $2(3 \times 1) + 2(3 \times 2) + 2(2 \times 1) = 6 + 12 + 4 = 22$ sq. in."

Answer Key for Worksheet 3–8b

Prism: Surface area of prism = $2(3 \times 1) + 2(3 \times 2) + 2(2 \times 1) = 6 + 12 + 4 = 22$ sq. in.

Cylinder: Surface area of cylinder = $3.14(1 \times 1) + 3.14(1 \times 1) + 5(3.14 \times 2) = 3.14 + 3.14 + 31.4 = 37.68$ sq. in.

WORKSHEET 3–8b

Drawing Nets for Prisms and Cylinders

Name _____

Date _____

Draw a net for each solid. Label the dimensions of the solid in appropriate places on the net. Find the area of each part of the net, and write its equation on the part. Find the surface area of the solid. Note that the solids are not drawn to scale, but the nets should be drawn according to the measures shown.

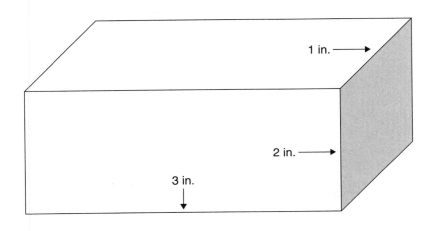

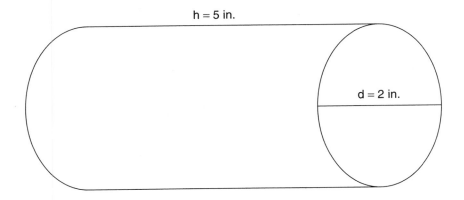

Activity 3: Independent Practice

Materials
Worksheet 3–8c
Regular pencil

Procedure
Give each student a copy of Worksheet 3–8c. Encourage students to draw nets and label their dimensions to help them solve word problems involving the surface area of a geometric solid. Remind them that the rectangle in the net for a cylinder will have a dimension that corresponds to the circumference of the cylinder's circular base. When all have completed the worksheet, have several students share their results with the entire class.

Answer Key for Worksheet 3–8c
1. B

2. A

3. C

4. D

5. A

Possible Testing Errors That May Occur for This Objective
- Students use the given dimensions of the prism or cylinder to find the volume instead of the required surface area.

- When adding the areas of the different parts of the net of a geometric solid to find the surface area, students omit the area of one or more of the parts.

- Students apply formulas incorrectly to find the area or the circumference of the circular base of a cylinder.

WORSHEET 3–8c

Using Nets of Prisms and Cylinders
to Find Surface Area

Name _____

Date _____

Solve the exercises provided.

1. For a store window display, Susan needs to cover a box shaped like a rectangular prism. Its base is 8 inches by 8 inches, and its height is 12 inches. If there are no overlaps, how much wallpaper will she need to cover all faces of the box except the bottom face?

   A. 512 sq. in.   B. 448 sq. in.   C. 384 sq. in.   D. Not shown here

2. A cylindrical pipe open at both ends has an interior radius of 3 inches and is 8 feet long. What is the pipe's interior surface area in square feet?

   A. 12.56 sq. ft.   B. 14.13 sq. ft.   C. 25.12 sq. ft.   D. 75.36 sq. ft.

3. A rectangular prism has the dimensions 10 centimeters, 12 centimeters, and 7 centimeters. What is the prism's surface area?

   A. 274 sq cm   B. 408 sq cm   C. 548 sq cm   D. 840 sq cm

4. A wooden cube is 3 centimeters on each edge. What is the surface area of the cube?

   A. 9 sq cm   B. 27 sq cm   C. 36 sq cm   D. 54 sq cm

5. A roller for pressing down new asphalt is 30 inches wide and has a radius of 10 inches. To the nearest square inch, what is the area of pavement with which the surface of the roller will come into contact in one complete rotation?

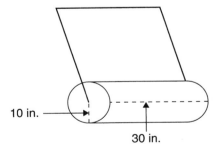

   10 in.

   30 in.

   A. 1,884 sq. in.   B. 1,256 sq. in.   C. 942 sq. in.   D. 300 sq. in.

Objective 9
Find the volume of a right rectangular prism, or find a missing dimension of the prism; find the new volume when dimensions of a prism are changed proportionally.

When studying dilations as transformations, students work with reductions or enlargements of planar shapes and discover that the changes in dimensions produce equivalent changes in perimeter. Experiences with changes in volume are also needed. In the following activities, students will discover the relationship between the change in dimensions and the change in the volume of a rectangular prism. It is not assumed that students have already mastered the formula for the volume of a prism.

Activity 1: Manipulative Stage

Materials
Worksheet 3–9a
Connectable centimeter cubes (270 per 4 students)
Calculators (1 per team of students; optional)
Regular pencil

Procedure
1. Give each team of four students four copies of Worksheet 3–9a, a set of at least 270 connectable centimeter cubes, and a calculator (optional).

2. Have each team of students build three different rectangular prisms with the connectable cubes. They will build the three prisms one at a time. When each prism is built, that prism will be left intact while a specified enlargement of that prism is also built with cubes. The dimensions for each original prism, as well as its required enlargement, are listed on Worksheet 3–9a.

3. After an original prism and its enlargement are built, students should record the volume (total cubes used) of the original prism and also the dimensions and volume of the enlarged prism in the appropriate spaces of the table on Worksheet 3–9a. Once that pair of prisms is recorded, students should dismantle the cubes and proceed to build the next original prism and its enlargement.

4. After all three pairs of prisms have been built, ask students to compare the change in dimensions to the change in volume for each pair of prisms. Have students write a statement about their discovery at the bottom of Worksheet 3–9a. A possible statement might be as follows: "The product of the size changes in the three dimensions equals the size change in volume." For example, if each dimension is multiplied by 3, the original volume will multiply by $3 \times 3 \times 3$, or 27.

5. To check their observations further, ask each team to select their own dimensions for a fourth prism (keep the numbers small) and record the dimensions as prism 4 on the table on Worksheet 3–9a. Students should then record what the new dimensions would be if their fourth prism were enlarged by a factor of 5 and also predict and record what the new volume would be. The volume of the enlargement

will be high for this fourth prism. If enough cubes are available, one team might build the enlargement of their fourth prism to show to the class and thereby confirm their predicted volume.

6. Discuss the procedure for building prism 1 before allowing teams to work on their own.

Consider prism 1 on Worksheet 3–9a. Its dimensions for the base are 2 centimeters and 5 centimeters, and its height dimension is 3 centimeters, assuming that centimeter cubes are being used. If centimeter cubes are not used, then each edge length of a cube should be called a "unit" and the volumes will be in "cubic units."

Each team of four students should first build the 2-cm by 5-cm base with their cubes. The base represents their first or bottom level of cubes. There should be 2 rows of 5 cubes each, or 10 cubes, in the base. Students should then build additional levels like the first level until they have 3 levels in all, which is the height of prism 1. The total number of cubes used to build prism 1 equals the volume of prism 1. Thus, the volume of 30 cubes (or 30 cubic centimeters or 30 cubic units) should be recorded in the "volume" column of the row for "prism 1."

The second row of the table indicates that prism 1 should be doubled (2×); that is, each dimension of prism 1 should be multiplied by 2 in order to create an enlargement of prism 1. On the row for "(2×) prism 1" on the table, students should record the new dimensions: 4, 10, and 6, respectively.

Leaving prism 1 intact, teams should use additional cubes to build a new base (first level) that is 4 centimeters by 10 centimeters. This first level of 4 rows of 10 cubes each, or 40 cubes, should then be repeated until there are 6 levels total, the height of the new prism. Students should use some type of counting strategy, such as 40 + 40 + 40 + 40 + 40 + 40 or 6(40), to find the volume of the new or enlarged prism. Such a strategy eventually evolves into a formula for volume. A volume of 240 cubes should be recorded in the "volume" column of the row for "(2×) prism 1" on the table on Worksheet 3–9a.

Ask students to compare the original volume of 30 cubes to the enlarged volume of 240 cubes. They should notice that $8 \times 30 = 240$. Have them write "8×" to the right of the "volume" column, but vertically between the 30 and the 240 entries. Ask students to reflect on how multiplying each dimension by 2 might be connected to a volume being multiplied by 8. They will need to combine their thoughts on prism 1 with their ideas for the other prisms in order to answer the question at the bottom of Worksheet 3–9a.

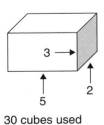

30 cubes used

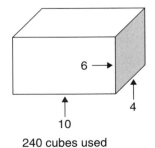

240 cubes used

Answer Key for Worksheet 3–9a

Prism 1: $2 \times 5 \times 3$, volume = 30 cubes

(2×) prism 1: $4 \times 10 \times 6$, volume = 240 cubes

Prism 2: $2 \times 2 \times 2 = 8$ cubes

(3×) prism 2: $6 \times 6 \times 6 = 216$ cubes

Prism 3: $2 \times 2 \times 1 = 4$ cubes

(4×) prism 3: $8 \times 8 \times 4 = 256$ cubes

Answer to question: The volume changes by the cube of the enlarging factor used. For example, if the dimensions are quadrupled, the volume will be multiplied by 4^3.

WORSHEET 3–9a   Name _____

Building Prisms with Cubes   Date _____

Build different solid prisms with small cubes. Record their dimensions and volumes in the table.

Prism	Base Side 1	Base Side 2	Height	Volume (number of cubes)
1	2	5	3	
(2×) prism 1				
2	2	2	2	
(3×) prism 2				
3	2	2	1	
(4×) prism 3				
4				
(5×) prism 4				

As the dimensions of a prism change to form a new prism, how does the original volume change?

_____

_____

_____

_____

_____

Activity 2: Pictorial Stage

Materials
> Worksheet 3–9b
> Straightedge (1 per pair of students)
> Calculators
> Regular pencil

Procedure

1. Give each pair of students two copies of Worksheet 3–9b, a straightedge, and a calculator. The worksheet contains diagrams of two prisms drawn in perspective with their three dimensions labeled on the diagrams.

2. For each original prism, students should draw its specified enlargement on the new frame, which consists of three segments sharing a common vertex. This should be done by marking off on a straightedge each labeled segment on the original prism (actual measuring is not needed here) and transferring the required copies of that segment to its corresponding segment on the new frame.

3. When all three segments have been copied the required number of times on the new frame, have students slide the straightedge from those new segments to other parallel positions to draw the remaining edges of the new enlarged prism. The diagram of the new prism will be a perspective view of the prism.

4. Students should now write the new dimensions on appropriate segments of the new prism's diagram. Beside the pair of prisms, they should also write equations for the following: the original prism's volume, the product of the three dimension changes, the new prism's volume based on its new dimensions, and the new prism's volume based on the original prism's volume. The latter two volumes, of course, should be equivalent.

5. Here is a discussion of the first exercise on Worksheet 3–9b, using prism 1.

Prism 1 on Worksheet 3–9b is shown from a perspective view and has the dimensions of 5, 7, and 3 units labeled on three intersecting edges. A similar set of intersecting edges is shown at the right. This second set will be used to draw a corresponding perspective view of an enlargement of prism 1.

The new prism must be drawn, based on a 2.5 enlargement factor. That is, each dimension of prism 1 must be multiplied by 2.5 to find its corresponding dimension for the new prism. Students should notice, however, that the prism is not drawn to scale. Therefore, to do a freehand sketch of the enlargement, students merely need to copy each segment that represents an edge of prism 1 on a straightedge (a ruler or an edge of a sheet of paper), then mark off that distance twice, followed by half the distance, onto the corresponding segment on the new frame. Here is an illustration of the straightedge being applied to copy prism 1's dimension segment of 5 units onto the new frame. The dimension segment of 7 units has already been copied 2.5 times onto the new frame:

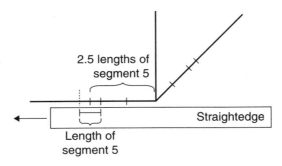

After each of the three dimensions of prism 1 has been copied 2.5 times on the new frame, students should use the straightedge to draw additional segments as edges to complete the perspective view of the enlarged prism. Each new edge should be parallel to one of the three dimensions already marked on the new frame. Here is a completed diagram of the enlarged prism with its three dimensions labeled:

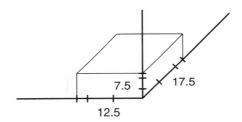

On Worksheet 3–9b, have students record the following equations on or near the completed diagram for prism 1: the original prism's volume, the product of the three dimension changes, the new enlarged prism's volume based on its new dimensions, and the new prism's volume based on the original prism's volume. For prism 1, here are the respective equations:

$5 \times 7 \times 3 = 105$ cubic units, volume of prism 1
$2.5 \times 2.5 \times 2.5 = 15.625$, the change factor for volume
$12.5 \times 17.5 \times 7.5 = 1{,}640.625$ cubic units, enlarged volume
$15.625 \times 105 = 1{,}640.625$ cubic units, enlarged volume

Answer Key for Worksheet 3–9b
Prism 1:

$5 \times 7 \times 3 = 105$ cubic units, volume of prism 1
$2.5 \times 2.5 \times 2.5 = 15.625$, the change factor for volume
$12.5 \times 17.5 \times 7.5 = 1{,}640.625$ cubic units, enlarged volume
$15.625 \times 105 = 1{,}640.625$ cubic units, enlarged volume

Prism 2:

$13 \times 6 \times 12 = 936$ cubic units, volume of prism 2
$3 \times 3 \times 3 = 27$, the change factor for volume
$39 \times 18 \times 36 = 25{,}272$ cubic units, enlarged volume
$27 \times 936 = 25{,}272$ cubic units, enlarged volume

WORKSHEET 3–9b

**Drawing Enlargements of
Rectangular Prisms**

Name _____

Date _____

For each original prism, use a straightedge to mark off multiple copies of the original edge lengths on the new frame. Extend the frame if needed. Draw opposite parallel edges to complete the enlarged prism. Label the dimensions on the new prism. Find the volume of the original prism and its enlarged prism. Original prisms are not drawn to scale. Computations should be based on numbers shown on the diagrams, not on actual measurements.

Prism 1

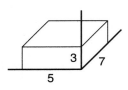

(2.5 ×) Enlargement

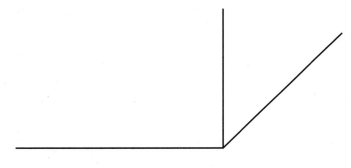

Prism 2

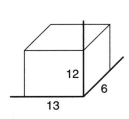

(3 ×) Enlargement

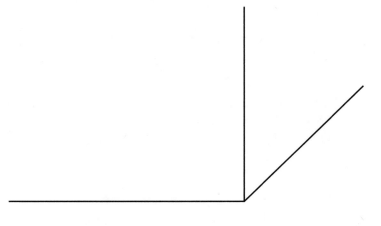

Activity 3: Independent Practice

Materials
Worksheet 3–9c
Calculators (optional)
Regular pencil

Procedure
Give each student a copy of Worksheet 3–9c and a calculator (optional). Remind students how dimension changes affect the volume of a rectangular prism. Encourage them to make freehand sketches of any described prisms and their enlargements. Students should also label all known or inferred measurements on any diagrams being used. When all have completed the worksheet, have several students explain to the rest of the class the steps they used to solve the exercises.

Answer Key for Worksheet 3–9c
1. A

2. D

3. C

4. D

5. A

6. B

Possible Testing Errors That May Occur for This Objective
- To find volume, students add the dimension measures together instead of multiplying them.

- When a prism has been enlarged by multiplying each of its dimensions by the same constant, students find the volume of the enlarged prism by multiplying the original volume by that same constant.

- When the volume and two dimensions of a prism are known, students find the missing dimension by multiplying the volume and the two given dimensions together instead of dividing the volume by the product of the two dimensions.

274

WORSHEET 3–9c

WORKSHEET 3–9c

Applying the Volume of a
Rectangular Prism

Name _____

Date _____

Solve the exercises provided.

1. A box with rectangular faces is 48 inches long, 24 inches wide, and 12 inches high. Which is closest to the volume of the box in cubic feet?

   A. 8 cu. ft.   B. 14 cu. ft.   C. 18 cu. ft.   D. 24 cu. ft.

2. A small cube has a volume of 64 cubic centimeters. If the small cube is enlarged by tripling its dimensions, what will be the volume of the new cube?

   A. 192 cu cm   B. 576 cu cm   C. 1,024 cu cm   D. 1,728 cu cm

3. The volume of a rectangular prism is 280 cubic meters. If the base measures 5 m by 7 m, what is the height or third dimension of this prism?

   A. 40 m   B. 10 m   C. 8 m   D. None of these

4. The dimensions of a rectangular prism are 15 inches, 10 inches, and 6 inches. Find the prism's volume.

   A. 31 cu. in.   B. 150 cu. in.   C. 480 cu. in.   D. 900 cu. in.

5. The water level in an aquarium is 2.5 feet high when the aquarium is full. The area of the base of the aquarium is 6 square feet. If the water drains out until the water level is only 2 feet high, what volume of water has been drained out of the aquarium?

   A. 3 cu. ft.   B. 6 cu. ft.   C. 15 cu. ft.   D. 30 cu. ft.

6. A rectangular prism has a height of 10 centimeters and a volume of 200 cubic centimeters. When the prism is enlarged by increasing all dimensions proportionally, the new volume will be 1,600 cubic centimeters. What will be the height of the new prism?

   A. 10 cm   B. 20 cm   C. 40 cm   D. 80 cm

Name _____

Date _____

GEOMETRY, SPATIAL REASONING, AND MEASUREMENT: PRACTICE TEST ANSWER SHEET

Directions: Use the Answer Sheet to darken the letter of the choice that best answers each question.

1. ○ A ○ B ○ C ○ D   10. ○ A ○ B ○ C ○ D

2. ○ A ○ B ○ C ○ D   11. ○ A ○ B ○ C ○ D

3. ○ A ○ B ○ C ○ D   12. ○ A ○ B ○ C ○ D

4. ○ A ○ B ○ C ○ D   13. ○ A ○ B ○ C ○ D

5. ○ A ○ B ○ C ○ D   14. ○ A ○ B ○ C ○ D

6. ○ A ○ B ○ C ○ D   15. ○ A ○ B ○ C ○ D

7. ○ A ○ B ○ C ○ D   16. ○ A ○ B ○ C ○ D

8. ○ A ○ B ○ C ○ D   17. ○ A ○ B ○ C ○ D

9. ○ A ○ B ○ C ○ D   18. ○ A ○ B ○ C ○ D

276

SECTION 3: GEOMETRY, SPATIAL REASONING, AND MEASUREMENT: PRACTICE TEST

1. Which geometric solid would have both of the following orthogonal views?

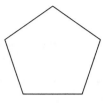

   A. Pentagonal pyramid

   B. Right cylinder

   C. Tetrahedron

   D. Triangular prism

2. A cylinder sitting on one of its bases has a lateral side view that looks like a:

   A. Circle   B. Pentagon   C. Rectangle   D. Triangle

3. A circle with a radius of 3 units has its center at (–1,+4) on a coordinate grid. If the circle is translated 4 units to the left and 5 units down, what will be the ordered pair for the new center?

   A. (–4,+1)   B. (+3,–1)   C. (+2,+7)   D. (–5,–1)

4. If the triangle is reflected across the y-axis, the coordinates of the new vertices will be (–4,–1), (–5,+3), and ____.

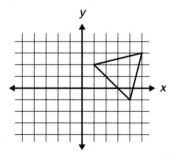

   A. (+1,–2)   B. (–1,+2)   C. (+1,+2)   D. (–1,–2)

SECTION 3: GEOMETRY, SPATIAL REASONING, AND MEASUREMENT: PRACTICE TEST (Continued)

5. A trapezoid has a perimeter of 18 centimeters. The length of each side is increased to 3 times its original length to form a larger trapezoid. What is the perimeter of the larger trapezoid?

   A. 21 cm   B. 36 cm   C. 54 cm   D. 72 cm

6. △ABC is similar to △FGH. Find the length of side AB.

   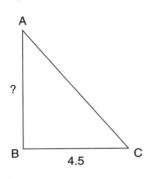   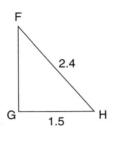

   A. 4.9 units   B. 5.7 units   C. 7.2 units   D. 9.0 units

7. Miriam drove 25 miles due north from Toledo to Junction, then drove 26 miles due west to Fort Smith. If she drove the shortest distance from Toledo northwest to Fort Smith without going through Junction, about how far would she drive?

   A. 36 mi.   B. 45 mi.   C. 51 mi.   D. 60 mi.

8. A right triangle has a leg length of 5 centimeters and a hypotenuse length of 13 centimeters. Find the length of the other leg of the triangle.

   A. 8 cm   B. 10 cm   C. 12 cm   D. 18 cm

9. A 10.0-cm square is inscribed in a circle with a radius of approximately 7.1 centimeters. What is the area of the shaded region to the nearest tenth?

   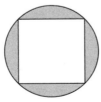

   A. 17.1 sq cm   B. 30.4 sq cm   C. 45.0 sq cm   D. 58.3 sq cm

SECTION 3: GEOMETRY, SPATIAL REASONING, AND MEASUREMENT: PRACTICE TEST (Continued)

10. A goat grazes in a circular path around a stake to which it is tied. If the goat can eat grass at a maximum distance of 13 feet from the stake, what is the maximum path to the nearest foot that it can make around the stake?

    A. 26 ft.   B. 41 ft.   C. 63 ft.   D. 82 ft.

11. The total area of the floor of a parallelogram-shaped room is 690 square feet. If the length of one edge of the floor is 30 feet, what is the perpendicular distance from that edge across to the opposite edge of the floor?

    A. 12 ft.   B. 23 ft.   C. 54 ft.   D. None of these

12. Find the area, to the nearest tenth, of the shaded triangle shown in the diagram. The outer shape containing the triangle is a parallelogram.

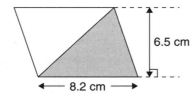

    A. 67.2 sq cm   B. 53.3 sq cm   C. 26.7 sq cm   D. 14.7 sq cm

13. The two parallel sides of a trapezoid are 4 inches and 7 inches long. Its altitude is 3.8 inches. What is the area of the trapezoid?

    A. 53.2 sq. in.   B. 41.8 sq. in.   C. 20.9 sq. in.   D. 13.8 sq. in.

14. A rectangular lawn design has a large terrace at one corner of the lawn. The larger section has only grass, as shown in the diagram. About how many square meters are in the area of the grass section?

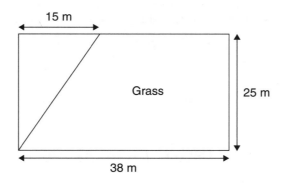

    A. 375 sq m   B. 763 sq m   C. 950 sq m   D. 1,425 sq m

SECTION 3: GEOMETRY, SPATIAL REASONING, AND MEASUREMENT: PRACTICE TEST (Continued)

15. For a store window display, Lydia needs to cover a box shaped like a cylinder. Each base of the cylinder has a diameter of 10 inches, and its height is 12 inches. If there are no overlaps, how much wallpaper will she need to cover all surfaces of the box except the bottom base?

    A. 455.3 sq. in.   B. 376.8 sq. in.   C. 120.0 sq. in.   D. None of these

16. A rectangular prism has the dimensions 8 centimeters, 12 centimeters, and 10 centimeters. What is the prism's surface area?

    A. 960 sq cm   B. 843 sq. cm   C. 670 sq. cm   D. 592 sq. cm

17. A small rectangular prism has a volume of 58 cubic centimeters. If the small prism is enlarged by doubling its dimensions, what will be the volume of the new prism?

    A. 116 cu cm   B. 464 cu cm   C. 512 cu cm   D. None of these

18. The water level in an aquarium is 3 feet high when the aquarium is full. The area of the rectangular base of the aquarium is 6 square feet. If the water drains out until the water level is only 2.5 feet high, what volume of water has been drained out of the aquarium?

    A. 3 cu. ft.   B. 15 cu. ft.   C. 18 cu. ft.   D. 45 cu. ft.

Section 3: Geometry, Spatial Reasoning, and Measurement: Answer Key for Practice Test

The objective being tested is shown in brackets beside the answer.

1. A [1]
2. C [1]
3. D [2]
4. B [2]
5. C [3]
6. B [3]
7. A [4]
8. C [4]
9. D [5]

10. D [5]
11. B [6]
12. C [6]
13. C [7]
14. B [7]
15. A [8]
16. D [8]
17. B [9]
18. A [9]

GRAPHING, STATISTICS, AND PROBABILITY

Objective 1

Locate and name points using ordered pairs of rational numbers or integers on a Cartesian coordinate plane.

To locate a point indicated by a given ordered pair, students must focus on both the horizontal and the vertical distances represented by the ordered pair coordinates. Students need practice in identifying both distances and recording them in the proper order. The following activities provide this practice, as well as introduce students to the logical connectors AND and NOT.

Activity 1: Manipulative Stage

Materials

　　Large 1-inch grid sheets (14 in. by 16 in.; 1 sheet per pair of students)
　　Small markers (centimeter cubes or flat buttons)
　　Flat coffee stirrers in 1-inch pieces (2 colors; 20 pieces per set, 10 per color)
　　One-inch paper squares (4 per set, labeled A, B, C, and D)
　　Regular paper and pencil

Procedure

1. Give each pair of students a large 1-inch grid sheet, a small marker, 20 1-inch pieces cut from flat coffee stirrers (2 colors; 10 pieces per color), and 4 1-inch paper squares (one labeled with A, one with B, one with C, and one with D). Instead of 1-inch pieces cut from flat coffee stirrers, 1-inch by 0.25-inch strips of colored construction paper may be used. Except for the grid, all other materials for each pair of students should be packaged together in a small, closable plastic bag to make distribution easier and quicker. The grid may be drawn on heavy bulletin board paper to form approximately a 14-in. by 16-in. grid (unit length of 1 inch), or a grid may be drawn on two sheets of 8.5-in. by 14-in. paper, which can then be taped together at their longer edges to make the larger grid that is needed. Laminating the final grids will make them more durable.

2. For discussion purposes, assume the coffee stirrer pieces are red or blue. Each grid should be positioned so that the longer edge is the horizontal axis; the lower left corner of the grid will be the origin. Discuss with students that the horizontal axis is traditionally used for the independent value in a relationship, and the vertical axis is used for the dependent value. The independent value is written as the first number in an ordered pair, and the dependent value is the second number.

3. Now write the ordered pair A(3,7) on the board. To represent the first number, 3, have students place three red pieces end-to-end to the right along the horizontal axis, beginning at the origin. Each red piece should lie on a unit segment of the axis.

4. Starting at the right end of the red pieces on the horizontal axis, students should place seven blue pieces vertically upward end-to-end. Each blue piece should lie on a vertical segment of the grid. The upper end of the blue pieces should be at the point (3,7) on the grid. Now have students place the small marker at the upper end of the blue pieces and place the paper square with the letter A on the grid near the marker. Here is an illustration of the completed grid. Only a portion of the grid is shown:

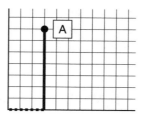

5. Now have students record the ordered pair on their own paper and, beside the ordered pair, record the direction and distance from the origin that each coordinate represents. For this exercise, they should record the following: "A(3,7)—right 3, up 7."

6. Repeat this process with other ordered pairs written on the board, such as B(0,4), C(9,3), and D(6,6). Only zero or positive integers should be used for the coordinates in this activity. Students should build with the colored pieces on the grid until they are consistently and correctly interpreting each ordered pair. Grids should be cleared of materials before the next ordered pair is located. Rotate the paper squares for labels as new ordered pairs are used.

Activity 2: Pictorial Stage

Materials

Worksheet 4–1a
Red and blue markers (1 of each color for each student)
Regular pencil

Procedure

1. Give each pair of students two copies of Worksheet 4–1a and one red and one blue marker per student.

2. On the first page of Worksheet 4–1a, have students identify the ordered pair of each marked point. For each point, they should draw a red arrow from the origin to the left (or right) along the horizontal axis until the red arrowhead is directly below (or above) the marked point. Then they should draw a blue arrow from the head of the red arrow up (or down) until the blue arrowhead touches the point.

3. Ask students how long the red arrow is in grid segments and whether they moved right or left to reach the blue arrow where it touches the horizontal axis. If they moved to the right, the grid steps being counted will be considered positive; if they moved left, the steps will be negative.

4. Now moving from the red arrow to the blue arrow, ask students how long the blue arrow is in grid segments and whether they moved up or down from the horizontal axis in order to reach the marked point on the grid. If they moved upward, the grid steps being counted will be considered positive; if they moved downward, the steps will be negative.

5. Have students record the appropriate ordered pair below the grid, using the red arrow's length and its direction as the first number and the blue arrow's length and its direction as the second number. Write the letter for the point to the left of the ordered pair. Have students tell in which quadrant (or axis) the point lies. Here is a completed grid and recording for Exercise 1 on Worksheet 4–1a. Discuss Exercise 1 as an example before students begin to work on Part I of Worksheet 4–1a:

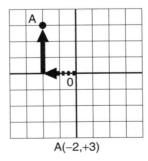

A(−2,+3)

6. Now consider part II of Worksheet 4–1a. For each grid, have students locate and label on the grid the point of the given ordered pair. They should draw red and blue arrows to locate the point.

7. Students should also describe the point's location with respect to the two shapes, using the logical connectors: AND and NOT. The description should be written below the grid.

8. Discuss Exercise 5 before having students work Part II of Worksheet 4–1a.

In Exercise 5 on Worksheet 4–1a, students must graph the ordered pair, N(+2,–2.5). Have students start at the origin and draw a red arrow 2 units long and pointing to the right along the horizontal axis. They should then draw a blue arrow 2.5 units long and pointing vertically downward from the horizontal axis and the head of the red arrow. An arrowhead should be drawn on each bar to show the direction of movement. The head of the blue arrow will locate the point to be labeled with the letter N.

Below the grid, write point N's description with respect to the circle and the triangle. An alternative description may also be given if preferred. Here is the completed grid for Exercise 5 on Worksheet 4–1a:

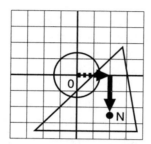

N(+2,–2.5) is inside the triangle <u>and not</u> inside the circle. (Alternative: N is inside the triangle <u>and</u> outside the circle.)

Answer Key for Worksheet 4–1a

1. A(–2,+3)

2. N(+1.5,–2)

3. R(0,+3.5)

4. W(–3,–1)

5. N(+2,–2.5) is inside the triangle *and not* inside (*and* outside) the circle.

6. P(–0.5,+4) is outside the trapezoid *and* outside the circle.

7. B(+2,–2) is inside the triangle *and* inside the pentagon.

8. M(–2,1.5) is inside the rectangle *and not* inside (*and* outside) the hexagon.

WORKSHEET 4-1a

Locating and Describing
Ordered Pairs on Grids

Name _____

Date _____

Part I. On each grid, identify the given point and write its ordered pair below the grid.

1.

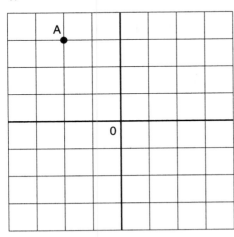

2.

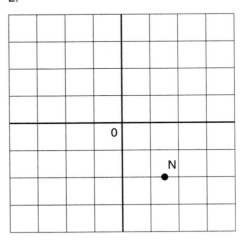

3.

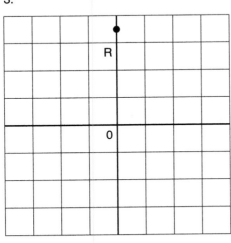

4.

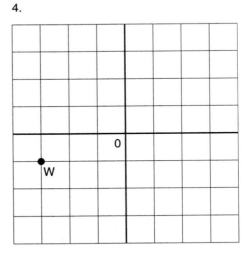

WORSHEET 4–1a Continued

Name _____

Date _____

Part II. On each grid, locate the point for the given ordered pair. Describe its location with respect to the shapes shown on the grid.

5. N(+2,−2.5)

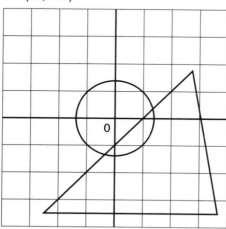

6. P(−0.5,+4)

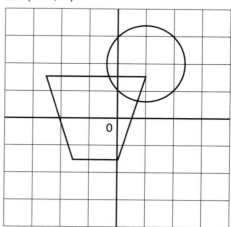

7. B(+2,−2)

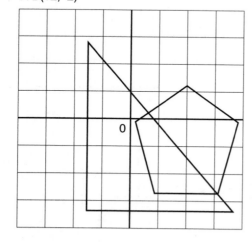

8. M(−2,−1.5)

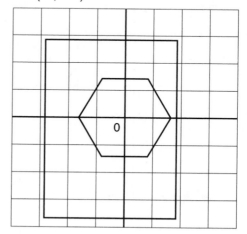

Activity 3: Independent Practice

Materials
Worksheet 4–1b
Regular pencil

Procedure
Give each student a copy of Worksheet 4–1b. Remind them that the first number in an ordered pair indicates the distance to move horizontally and the second number indicates the distance to move vertically. When all have completed the worksheet, have several students share their results with the entire class.

Answer Key for Worksheet 4–1b
1. D

2. B

3. A

4. D

5. C

Possible Testing Errors That May Occur for This Objective
- Students incorrectly match an ordered pair to a point on a grid by applying only one of the coordinates, not both. For example, a point may be located at (+3,−5), but students will match the point to the ordered pair (+3,+1), ignoring the second number in the ordered pair.

- Students reverse the roles of the two coordinates in an ordered pair. They use the first number for the vertical movement and the second number for the horizontal movement.

- Students do not count steps on the grid correctly when locating a point, even though they are interpreting the numbers in the ordered pair correctly.

288

WORKSHEET 4–1b   Name _____

Locating and Applying   Date _____
Ordered Pairs on a Coordinate Plane

Solve the exercises provided. On each grid, 1 segment equals 1 unit.

1. Which point has the coordinates (+2.5,–1.5)?

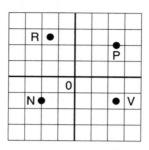

   A. Point R   B. Point N   C. Point P   D. Point V

2. Which statement correctly applies to the triangle on the grid?

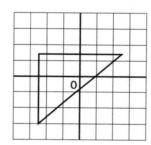

  A. One vertex is in the first quadrant and another vertex is at coordinates (–3,–2.5).

  B. One vertex is in the second quadrant and another vertex is at coordinates (–2.5,–3).

  C. One vertex is in the first quadrant and another vertex is at coordinates (+2.5,+1).

  D. One vertex is in the second quadrant and another vertex is at coordinates (+1,0).

WORKSHEET 4–1b Continued

Name _____

Date _____

3. A circle has its center at (–1,+3) on a coordinate grid. If the circle is translated 5 units to the right and 2 units up, what will be the coordinates of the new center?

A. (+4,+5)   B. (–6,+5)   C. (+1,+8)   D. (–3,+8)

4. The point P(+2.5,–1) is located in which quadrant?

A. Quadrant I   B. Quadrant II   C. Quadrant III   D. Quadrant IV

5. Where is the point, W(–3.5,0), located on the grid?

A. Vertical axis   B. Quadrant II   C. Horizontal axis   D. None of these

Objective 2
Construct and interpret circle graphs.

The interpretation of circle graphs often depends on the relative sizes of the sectors to form visual impressions. Students need experience with comparing sector sizes of a circle graph in general and with relating those sizes to equivalent values in tables or other types of graphs. The following activities provide such experience.

Activity 1: Manipulative Stage

Materials
        Worksheet 4–2a
        Worksheet 4–2b
        Colored markers (1 red, 1 yellow, 1 green, and 1 blue per set; 1 set per pair of
            students)
        Regular pencil

Procedure
1. Give each pair of students three copies of Worksheet 4–2a, three copies of Worksheet 4–2b, and a set of four colored markers (one each of red, yellow, green, and blue).

2. On one copy of Worksheet 4–2a, on the circle have students color 8 sectors red, 2 sectors yellow, 2 sectors green, and 4 sectors blue. Sectors of the same color should be adjacent to each other. Students have now made a circle graph:

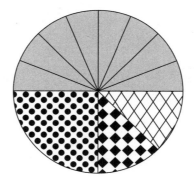

3. Discuss what the students notice about the number of sectors for each color; for example, there are twice as many red sectors as there are blue, four times as many red as green, and the number of yellow sectors equals the number of green sectors. Have students write these comparisons as statements below the completed circle graph.

4. Now have students color bars on a copy of Worksheet 4–2b to correspond to the colored sectors on the circle on Worksheet 4–2a. Use the shorter edge of the grid as the bottom horizontal axis of the new bar graph being made. Leave spacing between each pair of adjacent bars. One space on the grid should match one sector on the circle. So the red bar will be 8 spaces long, the blue bar will be 4 spaces long, and the green bar and the yellow bar will each be 2 spaces long.

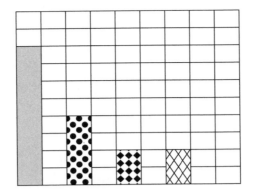

5. Have students compare the different lengths of the bars. The red bar is twice as long as the blue bar, and the red bar is four times as long as the green or the yellow bar. The blue bar is twice as long as either the green bar or the yellow bar, and the green bar and the yellow bar are equal in length. Students should write these comparisons as statements on the back of the grid worksheet. Observe that the descriptions for the bars on the bar graph are the same as those used to compare the sectors on the circle graph.

6. Repeat the above process with the other two circle worksheets and grid worksheets. On one circle, color 6 sectors red, 3 sectors green, 5 sectors blue, and 2 sectors yellow. On the remaining circle, color 10 sectors green; then color 2 sectors each of red, blue, and yellow. Each circle's sectors should be transferred to a grid, and then various comparisons should be made as before.

Answer Key for Worksheets 4–2a and 4–2b
Sample statements are provided here.

1. Red is twice the blue; red is 4 times the green or the yellow; blue is twice the green or the yellow; and green and yellow are equal.

2. Red is twice the green; red is 1 more than blue; red is 3 times the yellow; green is 1 more than yellow; blue is 3 more than yellow; green is 2 fewer than blue.

3. Green is 5 times the red or the blue or the yellow; red, blue, and yellow are equal.

WORKSHEET 4–2a
Constructing a Circle Graph

Name _____

Date _____

Follow the teacher's directions to make a circle graph below.

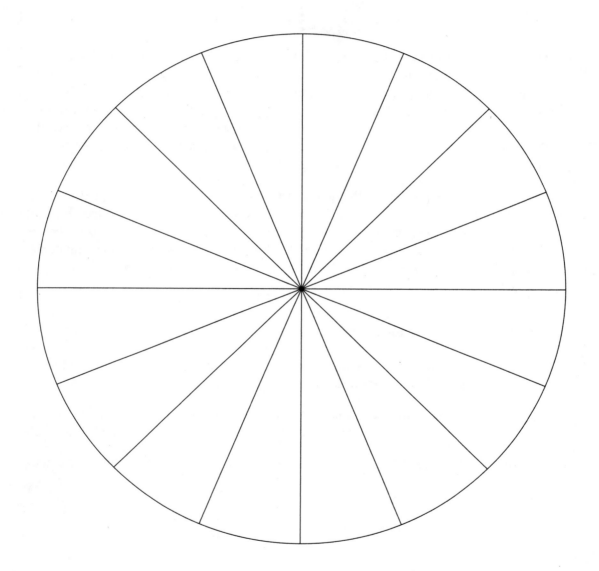

WORKSHEET 4–2b

Grid Pattern

Name _____

Date _____

Follow the teacher's directions to make a bar graph below.

Activity 2: Pictorial Stage

Materials

Worksheet 4–2c
Centimeter grid paper (4 sheets per student)
Regular pencil

Procedure

1. Give each student a copy of Worksheet 4–2c and four sheets of centimeter grid paper. Have students work in pairs.

2. On each circle on Worksheet 4–2c, have students label various amounts of sectors for different colors, using the first letter of a color's name each time (for example, R for red, B for blue). Sectors containing the same letter should be adjacent to each other in the circle. Use the following amounts: circle 1—5 red, 3 blue, and 2 yellow; circle 2—2 red, 2 green, 2 yellow, and 4 blue; circle 3—4 blue, 4 red, 1 green, and 1 yellow; and circle 4—7 green, 1 red, 1 blue, and 1 yellow.

3. After all four circles have been labeled to make circle graphs, have students transfer the information to the grid sheets to make bar graphs, but according to different factors. For circle 1, each sector should correspond to 4 spaces on the grid. For circle 2, each sector should match to 5 spaces on the grid. For circle 3, each sector should match to 3 spaces; and for circle 4, each sector should match to 2 spaces.

4. Since each circle graph has 10 sectors, each sector represents 10 percent of the circle's area. This allows the color sections to be described as a percent of the whole circle and for the bar lengths to be described similarly. For example, on circle 1, the blue section (3 sectors) will represent 30 percent of the "whole" (circle). So the corresponding bar for blue (3 × 4 spaces long) on the bar graph will also represent 30 percent of the "whole." Have students label the vertical axis of each completed bar graph with the appropriate percents.

5. Have students transfer the percents found for each circle graph to the table below the circle graph on Worksheet 4–2c.

6. For each circle graph, have students compare the color sections to each other and then look for similar relationships among the corresponding bars on the partner bar graph. On the back of Worksheet 4–2c, have students write statements about the various relationships they find between each circle graph and its bar graph. Have them share their ideas with the entire class.

Here is an example of the completed graphs and table for Exercise 1 on Worksheet 4–2c, along with possible comparison statements students might write. Encourage students to have a variety of statements. On the bar graph illustration, each space represents 4 spaces on the actual centimeter grid paper.

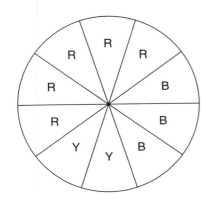
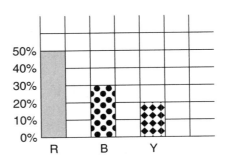

Color	Red	Blue	Yellow	
Percent	50%	30%	20%	

Possible Statements for Exercise 1 on Worksheet 4–2c:

Red is half or 50% of all the color choices made.
Red is 20% more than blue.
Yellow is 10% less than blue.
Red is 30% more than yellow, or two and a half times the yellow.
Blue is 10% more than yellow, or one and a half times the yellow.

Answer Key for Worksheet 4–2c
Only final percents and possible statements are provided; completed graphs are not shown.

1. Red—50%, blue—30%, yellow—20%

    Red is half or 50% of all the color choices made.

    Red is 20% more than blue.

    Yellow is 10% less than blue.

    Red is 30% more than yellow, or two and a half times the yellow.

    Blue is 10% more than yellow, or one and a half times the yellow.

2. Red—20%, green—20%, yellow—20%, blue—40%

    Red, green, and yellow have equal percents.

    Blue is 20% more than the red or the green or the yellow.

    Blue is twice the red or the green or the yellow.

3. Blue—40%, red—40%, green—10%, yellow—10%

   Blue is 30% more than green or yellow.

   Red is 30% more than green or yellow.

   Blue is equal to red, and green is equal to yellow.

   Blue (or red) is 4 times the green, and 4 times the yellow.

4. Green—70%, red—10%, blue—10%, yellow—10%

   Red, blue, and yellow are equal.

   Green is 7 times the red or the blue or the yellow.

   Green is 60% more than the red or the blue or the yellow.

WORKSHEET 4–2c

Finding Percentages with Circle Graphs

Name _____

Date _____

Transfer data from each circle graph to a bar graph and a two-row table of values. Write comparison statements about the data.

1.

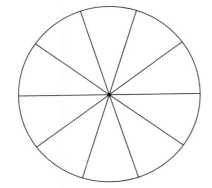

Color				
Percent				

2.

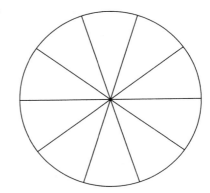

Color				
Percent				

3.

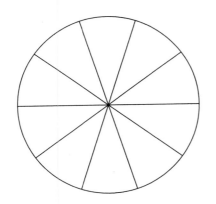

Color				
Percent				

4.

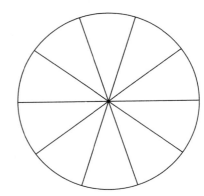

Color				
Percent				

Activity 3: Independent Practice

Materials
Worksheet 4–2d
Regular pencil

Procedure
Give each student a copy of Worksheet 4–2d to work independently. When all are finished, have several students share their results with the entire class.

Answer Key for Worksheet 4–2d
1. C

2. A

3. D

4. C

Possible Testing Errors That May Occur for This Objective
- Students do not realize that numbers (or percents) that are unequal in a set of data must correspond to sectors on the circle graph, which are unequal in size. The greater number (or percent) requires the larger sector on the circle graph.

- Students correctly match the largest value in the given data to the largest sector of a circle graph, but do not notice that the other values do not match to the remaining sectors of the selected graph.

- When one percent (or number) is greater than another, students select a circle graph, which contains one sector larger than another, but the labels on those two sectors do not correspond to the two values being compared.

WORSHEET 4–2d

Solving Problems with Circle Graphs

Name _____

Date _____

Solve the exercises provided.

1. A recycling program reported the following percents by weight of the materials collected and processed for 1 year.

Newspaper	75%
Glass	5%
Plastic	20%

Which circle graph frame might best be used to represent these data?

A.   B.   C.   D.

2. A health clinic recorded each patient's blood type. The results are shown in the circle graph without numbers. Which set of data best corresponds to the graph's sectors?

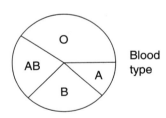

A. A, 12%; B, 30%; AB, 18%; O, 40%

B. A, 10%; B, 35%; AB, 20%; O, 35%

C. A, 40%; B, 20%; AB, 25%; O, 15%

D. A, 13%; B, 40%; AB, 17%; O, 30%

300

WORKSHEET 4-2d Continued

Name _____

Date _____

3. In a survey, 300 students were asked about the type and number of pets they owned. Which circle graph frame best matches the survey data shown in the table?

Type of pet	Cat	Dog	Bird	Fish
Number of pets	80	30	30	160

A.   B.   C.   D.

4. Three sectors on a circle graph compare as follows: P is twice Q, and P = R. How will their respective bars look when shown in P, Q, R order on a bar graph?

A. 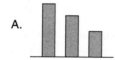   B. 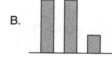   C. 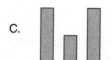   D.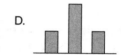

Objective 3

Compare different numerical or graphical models for the same data, including histograms, circle graphs, stem-and-leaf plots, box plots, and scatter plots; compare two sets of data by comparing their graphs of similar type.

Students must be able to equate two very different statistical forms. Often different visual impressions are made by such forms. For example, tallies are arranged in rows when the bars in the bar graph are arranged vertically. In Objective 2, activities are presented that compare circle graphs to tables and to bar graphs. Here are additional activities that will help students connect other statistical forms together.

Activity 1: Manipulative Stage

Materials

> Worksheet 4–3a
> Toothpicks (40 per team of 4 students)
> Worksheet 4–3b
> Colored markers (at least 3 colors; 1 set of 3 colors per team)
> Regular pencil

Procedure

1. Give each team of four students one copy of Worksheet 4–3a, one copy of Worksheet 4–3b, 3 different colored markers, and a packet of 40 toothpicks.

2. Have students take a survey of the entire class, using a question that has only three response choices. Students should write the choices in the left column of Worksheet 4–3a. Each team may collect survey data on its own, going from student to student, or the teacher may survey the class as a whole and record the results on the board for the teams to use for Worksheet 4–3a.

3. For each response choice, students are to build a row of toothpicks (1 toothpick per vote) on the grid of Worksheet 4–3a, but the toothpicks will be placed in groups of 5, or up to 5 toothpicks per grid space. (The groups of 5 will be transferred to a bar graph whose scale uses multiples of 5.) Monitor each team's work carefully.

4. Students should now transfer the information represented by the toothpick groups on Worksheet 4–3a to the grid on Worksheet 4–3b. Guide them to make a vertical bar graph, using multiples of 5 (0, 5, 10, 15, 20, 25) on the vertical scale for the "number of votes" and leaving a blank column between each pair of adjacent bars. Have students create a title for the new graph based on the survey question. The horizontal axis should be labeled for the three response choices. A different color can be used for each bar made. In particular, however, help students focus on how long to make their bar when the value being represented is *not* a multiple of 5.

5. After students have completed their new bar graph, ask them a variety of questions about it. Then have each team write two questions about the completed bar graph on the back of Worksheet 4–3b, such that each question requires computation in order to find the answer. Have each team read their questions out loud for the rest of the class to discuss and answer.

For discussion purposes, suppose the survey question is the following: "What is your favorite movie? *Men in Black*, *Shrek*, or *Lord of the Rings*?" The votes are as follows: *Men in Black*—13, *Shrek*—10, and *Lord of the Rings*—4. Have students write the three movie titles in the spaces of the left-most column of Worksheet 4–3a in the order listed in the survey question.

Students are to build a row of toothpicks (1 toothpick per vote) on Worksheet 4–3a for each movie choice, but the toothpicks will be placed in groups of 5, or up to 5 toothpicks per grid space. Using the top row for 13 *Men in Black* votes, have students count out 13 toothpicks, placing 5 in the second space of the row, 5 more in the next space to the right, and the last 3 in the fourth space. Showing the 10 votes for *Shrek* in the middle row, students should place 5 toothpicks in the second space and 5 more toothpicks in the next space to the right. Finally, on the bottom row, they should put 4 toothpicks in the second space for the 4 votes for *Lord of the Rings*. The final grid with toothpicks on Worksheet 4–3a should have the following appearance:

Choice 1: *Men in Black*																		
Choice 2: *Shrek*															
Choice 3: *Lord of the Rings*									

The data on Worksheet 4–3a will now be transferred to Worksheet 4–3b. The left vertical axis on the new grid should be labeled "Number of Votes" and numbered off in multiples of 5. The bottom horizontal axis should be labeled "Favorite Movie," with the first, third, and fifth columns labeled at the bottom as *MIB*, *Shrek*, and *Lord of the Rings*, respectively.

For the *Men in Black* votes, two spaces on the grid of Worksheet 4–3a held 5 toothpicks each, so on the new grid, students should color in two full spaces of the column for *MIB*. Since the third space held only 3 toothpicks, guide students to color only *about half* of the third space of the column. For the *Shrek* votes, two spaces on the large grid held 5 toothpicks each, so students should color two full spaces of the column for *Shrek*. Finally, the row for *Lord of the Rings* shows only 4 toothpicks, not a complete group of 5, in the second space. Show students how to color *almost* a full space of the column for *Lord of the Rings;* part of the space should be left uncolored near the top of the space.

After students have completed their new bar graph, ask them a variety of questions about it. Each team should write two questions on the back of Worksheet 4–3b and then have the rest of the class answer their questions. Here are some possibilities for the example. Most questions require computation:

- How many more students liked *Men in Black* than liked *Shrek*? (3)
- How many students in all were surveyed? (27)
- How many students did *not* vote for *Shrek*? (17)
- What movie received more than 5 but fewer than 12 votes? (*Shrek*)
- How many students voted for *Shrek* or *Lord of the Rings*? (14)

Here is an example of the completed movie bar graph:

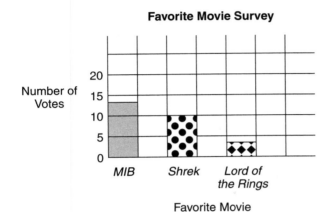

304

WORKSHEET 4–3a Name _____

Using Tallies in Surveys Date _____

Survey the class with 3 choices and place tallies in the table. Use toothpicks as tallies, with 5 toothpicks per space.

Choice 1					
Choice 2					
Choice 3					

WORKSHEET 4–3b
Grid Pattern

Name _____

Date _____

Activity 2: Pictorial Stage

Materials

Worksheet 4–3c

Colored dice (2 per team of 4 students; 2 colors)

5-mm grid paper (or similar size)

Regular pencil

Procedure

1. Give each student a copy of Worksheet 4–3c and a sheet of 5-mm grid paper. Have students work in teams of 4 students each.

2. Give each team 2 dice, each die a different color. The dice will be rolled to generate two-digit numbers. One color should designate the tens digit and the other color should designate the ones digit. For example, if a red die rolls a 5 for tens and a white die rolls a 3 for ones, the number 53 has been generated.

3. Have teams generate 25 numbers by rolling their 2 dice. They should record their numbers on Worksheet 4–3c to form a stem-and-leaf plot. The ones digit rolled should be recorded in the row that shows the tens digit (a stem) in the left-most column. The ones digits in the same row (the leaves of the stem) should be recorded in nondecreasing order from left to right. Repeated numbers should be included. The key for the stem-and-leaf plot, for example, "5|3 means 53," should be recorded below the completed plot on Worksheet 4–3c.

4. Have students transfer their data to the 5-mm grid paper to make a scatter plot. The lower left corner should be the origin of the plot or graph. The horizontal axis should be labeled for the numbers rolled with the dice, using an appropriate scale. The vertical axis should be labeled for the number of times (0–25) each number was rolled. Each point on the grid will represent an ordered pair: (number rolled, number of times it was rolled). Students should *not* connect the points that are plotted.

5. Ask students questions about their results. Compare the appearances of the two forms. For example, how does the number with the most rolls (the mode) look on one form compared to the other form? (That number will have the most leaves on the stem-and-leaf plot and the highest point on the scatter plot.) Both types of graphs show the specific numbers and their frequency in the data set, which would not be the case for a histogram or a box-and-whiskers plot. Ask if the scatter plot shows a possible *trend line*; that is, the points appear to be aligning themselves together to form a "straight path" that slopes upward or downward to the right. Most likely a trend line will not appear in these particular data because of the random nature of the generated numbers. Encourage teams to create questions about their own graphs or plots that other students might try to answer.

Here are possible examples of a completed stem-and-leaf plot and its scatter plot. The scatter plot is partially shown:

1	2	2	5	6			
2	1	1	3	5	5	5	
3	3	6	6	6	6		
4							
5	3	4	4	4	6	6	
6	1	1	5	5			

5|3 means 53 has been rolled.

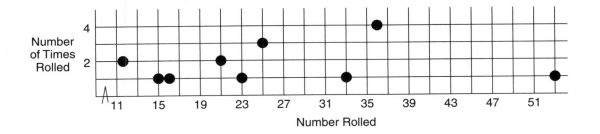

WORKSHEET 4–3c

Stem-and-Leaf Plot

Name _____

Date _____

Collect data by rolling 2 dice (2 different colors). Record the results in the chart provided to make a stem-and-leaf plot.

1							
2							
3							
4							
5							
6							

Activity 3: Independent Practice

Materials

> Worksheet 4–3d
> Regular pencil

Procedure

Give each student a copy of Worksheet 4–3d to complete. It is assumed that students have had previous experience with a variety of graphs like those discussed in Activities 1 and 2. After all have finished, have several students share their answers and reasoning with the entire class.

Answer Key for Worksheet 4–3d

1. B

2. A

3. B

4. D

Possible Testing Errors That May Occur for This Objective

- Students match a few entries on one graph to corresponding entries on another graph, but fail to test the remaining entries for similar matches.

- Students match only the maximum value (or minimum value) indicated on a graph to that value in another graph when comparing the two graphs, ignoring all other values on the graphs.

- Students incorrectly apply the key to interpret entries of a stem-and-leaf plot.

- Students do not correctly apply the scale when reading a single or a double bar graph.

310

Complete the exercises provided.

1. A dentist kept a record of the number of new cavities her patients had per year for the past 5 years. The scatter plot below shows the average number of new cavities per year for her patients in the 5- to 25-year age range. Which statement best describes the relationship reflected in the dentist's data?

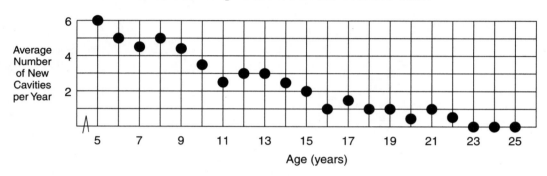

A. No trend   C. Cannot be determined

B. Downward trend   D. Upward trend

2. Eight stores were surveyed regarding their price for a certain bracelet. The survey results are shown on the stem-and-leaf plot below.

2					
3	8				
4	3	7			
5	3	4	5	5	
6	0				

5|3 means $5.30 for one store's price for the bracelet.

Which set of data matches the prices shown on the plot?

A. $3.80, $4.30, $4.70, $5.30, $5.40, $5.50, $5.50, $6.00

B. $2.00, $3.80, $4.30, $4.37, $4.70, $5.34, $5.55, $6.00

C. $2.00, $3.80, $4.30, $4.70, $5.30, $5.40, $5.50, $6.00

D. None of these

WORKSHEET 4-3d Continued

Name _____

Date _____

3. The heights of 25 eighth graders are shown in the bar graph.

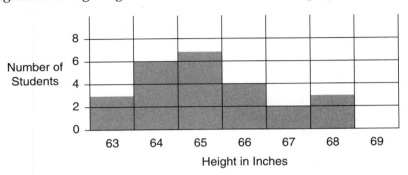

Which set of data best matches the information in the bar graph?

A.

Number of students	||||	⊬⊦	||||	⊬⊦	|||	||
Height (in.)	63	64	65	66	67	68

B.

Number of students	|||	⊬⊦|	⊬⊦||	||||	||	|||
Height (in.)	63	64	65	66	67	68

C.

Number of students	⊬⊦	||	||||	⊬⊦	|||	||||
Height (in.)	63	64	65	66	67	68

D.

Number of students	|||	⊬⊦|	⊬⊦|	|||	||	|||
Height (in.)	63	64	65	66	67	68

4. Based on the graph, which is the best estimate of how many more girls than boys were surveyed about their favorite food?

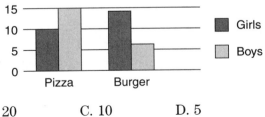

A. 25   B. 20   C. 10   D. 5

Objective 4

Find the mean of a given set of data, using different representations such as tables or bar graphs.

Often students can carry out the procedure of "adding all quantities given, then dividing their sum by the number of quantities used as addends." If asked, they define the *mean* in this way. Students do not, however, realize that finding the mean is equivalent to finding what the equal share will be when an existing distribution of unequal quantities is redistributed equally. For example, if three people had different amounts of money and they were to redistribute what they had so that each person had the same amount of money, then each person's fair share would be the mean of the original three amounts of money. Students need to understand the "equal distribution" idea of the mean.

The activities for this objective focus on the idea of equal redistribution. Decimal numbers and whole numbers are used in the examples, and they will be provided in tables or graphs instead of lists. It is assumed that the addition and division algorithms for whole numbers and decimal numbers have already been mastered.

Activity 1: Manipulative Stage

Materials

Worksheet 4–4a
Sets of base 10 blocks (1 set per 4 students: 8 flats, 30 rods, and 30 cubes)
Regular pencil

Procedure

1. Give each team of 4 students 4 copies of Worksheet 4–4a and a set of base 10 blocks (8 flats, 30 rods, and 30 small cubes). In order to represent decimal numbers, the flat will equal "one," the rod will equal a "tenth of the one," and the small cube will equal a "hundredth of the one."

2. Call out two to four different decimal numbers, which have ones, tenths, and hundredths, for the groups to practice building with their blocks. Use at most 5 cubes and 5 rods and at most 2 flats in each number. Some of the numbers might have only ones, and no tenths or hundredths, in order to include whole numbers. As an example, for the decimal number 2.53, students should lay out 2 flats (ones), 5 rods (tenths), and 3 cubes (hundredths) on their desktops to represent that amount.

3. For each exercise on Worksheet 4–4a, each team should build from some established baseline a "vertical bar" of base 10 blocks for each amount in the given set. All "bars" should be parallel and aligned at their bottom edges, possibly by using the edge of a table or a line drawn on a sheet of paper as the baseline. The block formation will resemble a bar graph when finished.

4. Have students rearrange the blocks in the bars to make bars of equal value, keeping the same number of bars as built initially. The final bars may not be completely rectangular if cubes are involved. The block value of the new bar should then be found, which will be the *mean* of the amounts in the original bars.

5. Students should record their result as a word sentence below the exercise on Worksheet 4–4a.

6. Discuss Exercise 1 on Worksheet 4–4a with the students before they begin to work. When all have finished the worksheet, have several teams share their results with the rest of the class.

As an example, consider Exercise 1, which lists the 4 numbers: 1.21, 2.04, 1.3, and 2.01. Students should show these numbers on the desktop with their blocks: 1.21 will be represented by 1 flat, 2 rods, and 1 cube; 2.04 will be 2 flats and 4 cubes; 1.3 will be 1 flat and 3 rods; and 2.01 will be 2 flats and 1 cube. The blocks should be arranged as "bars" with the flats being placed first, followed by the rods, then the cubes. Here is a possible arrangement of blocks for this set (the blocks are not drawn to scale, particularly the cubes with respect to the rods):

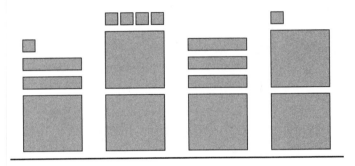

Ask the students to rearrange the 4 "bars" of blocks, redistributing the blocks into 4 "bars" of equal value. From the 6 flats, each new bar will receive 1 flat; the extra 2 flats must be traded for 20 rods. The original 5 rods with the new 20 rods will give 6 rods to each of the 4 bars; the extra 1 rod must be traded for 10 new cubes. Finally, the original 6 cubes with the new 10 cubes will yield 4 cubes to each bar. The equal share for each bar becomes 1 one (flat), 6 tenths (rods), and 4 hundredths (cubes), or 1.64. Have students record their conclusion below Exercise 1 on Worksheet 4–4a: "The mean or equal share for 1.21, 2.04, 1.3, and 2.01 is 1.64." Here is the final arrangement of the blocks:

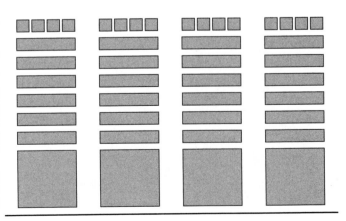

Answer Key for Worksheet 4–4a

1. The mean or equal share for 1.21, 2.04, 1.3, and 2.01 is 1.64.

2. The mean or equal share for 2.34 and 5.62 is 3.98.

3. The mean or equal share for 1.43, 2.31, and 1.15 is 1.63.

4. The mean or equal share for 0.42, 0.29, 0.45, 0.26, and 0.18 is 0.32.

5. The mean or equal share for 2.05, 1.64, 0.84, and 1.27 is 1.45.

WORKSHEET 4–4a

Building Equal Shares

Name _____

Date _____

For each exercise, show the given amounts as vertical bars with base 10 blocks. Redistribute the blocks to make equal vertical bars. The new bar value will be the *mean* of the given amounts. Write a word sentence about the mean and the original amounts below the exercise.

1. Amounts: 1.21, 2.04, 1.3, and 2.01

2. Amounts: 2.34 and 5.62

3. Amounts: 1.43, 2.31, and 1.15

4. Amounts: 0.42, 0.29, 0.45, 0.26, and 0.18

5. Amounts: 2.05, 1.64, 0.84, and 1.27

Activity 2: Pictorial Stage

Materials

Worksheet 4–4b
Red pencil and regular pencil

Procedure

1. Give each pair of students two copies of Worksheet 4–4b and a red pencil.

2. For each exercise on Worksheet 4–4b, have students transfer the data from the table to the grid to make a bar graph.

3. Have students compute the mean for the given data, recording the equations for the addition and division steps below the table of the exercise.

4. Students should then draw a line across the bar graph to mark the level of the computed mean value. Using the red pencil, they should color those portions of the bars of the graph that lie above the mean line and color those blank portions of columns that lie between shorter bars (those bars below the line) and the mean line. Ask students to determine the values represented by these two colored portions on the graph and to record these two totals on the graph, one above the line (a positive value) and one below the line (a negative value). The two amounts should be equivalent in absolute value (that is, opposites), since the mean line is the equalizer of all the bar amounts.

5. Discuss Exercise 1 on Worksheet 4–4b with the class before allowing students to work the second exercise independently.

Consider Exercise 1, which shows the following amounts on the table: $10, $12, $9, and $9, which are prices for a CD at four different stores.

Students should prepare a bar graph for the data and then compute the mean of the four prices. Below the table they should record the following equations: "10 + 12 + 9 + 9 = $40," and "40 ÷ 4 = $10, the average price for the CD."

Have students draw a line across the bars of the graph at the $10 mark on the vertical scale. Then with red pencil, they should color the portion of the $12 bar that extends above the line, and determine the total value of this portion, which is +$2, recording this total above the line on the graph. Students should also color the blank space between each $9 bar and the line. The total value of these two portions will be $2 \times (-\$1)$, or –$2. This total should be recorded below the line. Students should notice that the two totals, +$2 and –$2, are opposites and add to 0. This is the result of the equalizing process used to find the mean. Here is the completed bar graph for Exercise 1:

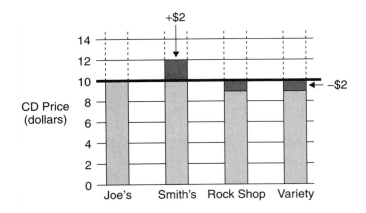

Answer Key for Worksheet 4–4b

1. 10 + 12 + 9 + 9 = $40

    40 ÷ 4 = $10, the average price for the CD

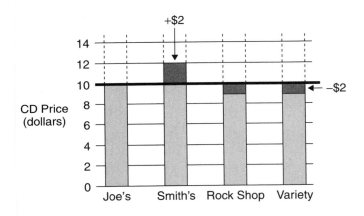

2. 40 + 45 + 47 = 132

    132 ÷ 3 = 44%, average percent of voters over 3 months

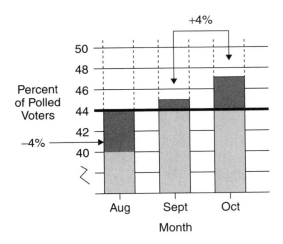

318

Finding the Mean on a Bar Graph

Date _____

For each exercise, make a bar graph for the data in the table. Compute the mean for the data, and draw a line across the graph to indicate the mean's value. Compare the bar values shown above that line to the missing bar values below the line.

1. Four stores have the following prices for the same music CD. Find the average price for the CD.

Store	Price
Joe's Music	$10
Smith's	$12
Rock Shop	$9
Variety	$9

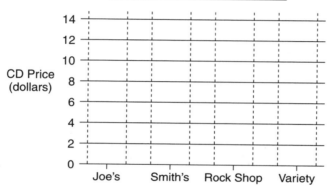

2. Preelection polls were taken for Jan Dean for the mayoral race, with the 3-month results given in the table. Find Dean's mean percent of the polled voters for the 3 months.

Month	Percent
August	40%
September	45%
October	47%

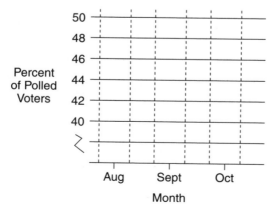

Activity 3: Independent Practice

Materials
Worksheet 4–4c
Regular pencil

Procedure
Give each student a copy of Worksheet 4–4c. It is assumed that students already know how to find the mode and the median, as well as the mean, of a set of data. When all have finished, have several students share their methods and answers with the entire class.

Answer Key for Worksheet 4–4c
1. B

2. A

3. D

4. C

5. B

Possible Testing Errors That May Occur for This Objective
- Students make various errors in their adding and dividing while trying to find the mean.
- Students do not understand the averaging process as a redistribution, so they do not read the values from a given bar graph in order to apply them to find the average for the data represented by the bar graph.
- Students do not understand the steps involved in finding the mean; hence, they are unable to reverse the steps to find missing values, such as the sum of the data or an adjusted mean when a number in the original data is removed.

WORSHEET 4–4c

Name _____

Finding the Mean from Tables
and Bar Graphs

Date _____

Complete each exercise provided.

1. The following table shows the number of pages in novels that George read for
   pleasure each month for 5 months.

Month	Sept.	Oct.	Nov.	Dec.	Jan.
Number of pages	358	367	395	380	374

   If George reads only 160 pages during February, which measure of the original
   data will change the most?

   A. Median   B. Mean   C. Mode   D. All measures will change equally.

2. After playing 7 basketball games of the season, Delia has a scoring average of 15
   points per game. If she scores 20 points in the next game, what will her average
   be for the 8 games?

   A. 15.6   B. 16.0   C. 16.4   D. 17.0

3. Cesar has an average of 88 on 9 quiz grades. If his teacher drops the lowest
   grade, a 70, which equation can be used to find N, Cesar's new quiz average?

   A. $N = \dfrac{88(70-9)}{8}$ B. $N = \dfrac{88-70}{8}$ C. $N = \dfrac{(88 \times 9)-70}{9}$ D. $N = \dfrac{(88 \times 9)-70}{8}$

4. The heights of four mountains are shown in the table. What is the mean height, to
   the nearest foot, of the 4 mountains?

Mountain	Capstone	El Matador	Blacktop	Sawtooth
Height	6,548 ft.	7,087 ft.	5,490 ft.	5,882 ft.

   A. 5,973 ft.   B. 6,153 ft.   C. 6,252 ft.   D. None of these

5. Find the average number of students per class for classes I–IV.

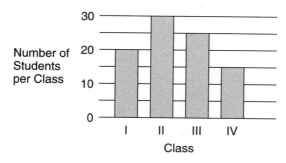

   A. 25.0   B. 22.5   C. 20.0   D. 18.5

Objective 5
Find the probability of a simple event and its complement.

Prediction, based on limited information, is a major topic in probability. Because existing relationships must be extrapolated to a future setting, young students have great difficulty with this topic. Experience is needed, as well as increased logical reasoning. The activities described below provide such experience for students using simple events. For activities that apply proportions to solve word problems involving probability, see Objective 1 in Section 2.

Activity 1: Manipulative Stage

Materials

      Plastic bags of 10 to 20 small objects
      Regular pencil and paper

Procedure

1. Give each team of 4 students a bag of 10 to 20 small objects. Objects in the same bag should be about the same size but be different in color or some other aspect. Some possible items that might be used are colored buttons, colored paper clips, baseball cards, assorted candy tarts, assorted earrings, plastic squiggly worms, plastic animals, toy cars, or erasers. If possible, no two teams should have the same number and type of materials.

2. Ask teams to find three or four different ways to separate their set of objects into small piles. One way might be by color: all red objects go into one pile, all blue objects into another pile, and so on. Other ways might be by shape, flavor, or function. Each of these ways is called a *characteristic*, by which the larger set of objects may be separated into smaller, disjoint piles. Each disjoint pile represents a *quality* or *kind* of the characteristic used for the separation—for example:

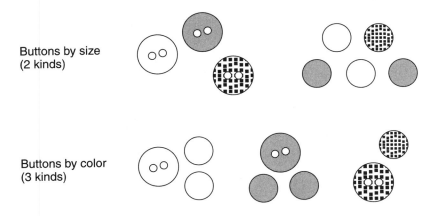

3. For each way a team finds to separate their set of objects, have students write on their own papers comparison statements about their piles. For example, if there are 15 candy tarts in the set or bag, students might write the following, using color as the characteristic: "6 out of 15 are green," "4 out of 15 are pink," and "5 out of 15 are purple." Each disjoint pile formed with respect to a characteristic should have its own statement.

4. After students have recorded their statements for each characteristic used, ask them to find the sum of the numbers they found for the different kinds (piles) of a particular characteristic. The sum should be the same as the total number of objects in their bag. In the example with the candy tarts separated by color, the sum would be 6 + 4 + 5 = 15, which also was the total number of candy tarts in the bag. Tell students that each pile they make for a characteristic also represents an *event* of the characteristic.

5. Tell students that their comparison statements are called *probabilities* and sometimes are written as fractions. A *probability* is a number that simply indicates that if a person takes one object out of a bag without looking, he or she has a specific number of ways to get a particular kind of a characteristic. In the case of the candy tart, a person would have a "probability of $\frac{6}{15}$" to draw a green candy (the event) out of the bag without looking. This may be written in the following way: "Probability of green = $\frac{6}{15}$." Have students rewrite each of their previous comparison statements in this new format.

6. Now introduce students to the idea of the *complement of an event*. That is, if the *event* is green (the pile of green candy tarts) in the separation of candies by color, then the *complement* of the green candies consists of all the candies in the nongreen piles. There are 4 + 5, or 9, such candies. Hence, this new probability might be written as follows: "Probability of not green = $\frac{9}{15}$." For each characteristic they used, have students write a *complement* statement for each probability statement they have written on their papers.

7. If time permits, have each team exchange their bag of objects with another team and repeat the separation process.

Activity 2: Pictorial Stage

Materials

Worksheet 4–5a

Regular pencil

Procedure

1. Give each student a copy of Worksheet 4–5a.

2. For each exercise, have students use the given set of letters or shapes to find the required probabilities. They should write each probability as a fraction. If the initial fraction can be reduced, encourage students to record the reduced form as well.

3. After all are finished, have students rewrite their probabilities in a more abbreviated format. For example, for "Probability of shaded = $\frac{3}{8}$" in Exercise 1 on Worksheet 4–5a, have students write "P(shaded) = $\frac{3}{8}$." This should be read as "the probability that a shape will be shaded is 3 out of 8 ways." Encourage students to read the probability statements in this expanded manner.

Answer Key for Worksheet 4–5a

1. Probability of shaded = $\frac{3}{8}$

   Probability of rectangles = $\frac{2}{8}$ or $\frac{1}{4}$

   Probability of quadrilaterals = $\frac{4}{8}$ or $\frac{1}{2}$

   Probability of not striped = $\frac{6}{8}$ or $\frac{3}{4}$

2. Probability of checked = $\frac{2}{16}$ or $\frac{1}{8}$

   Probability of striped = $\frac{1}{16}$

   Probability of white = $\frac{8}{16}$ or $\frac{1}{2}$

   Probability of not shaded = $\frac{11}{16}$

3. Probability of **M** = $\frac{2}{11}$

   Probability of **T** = $\frac{2}{11}$

   Probability of **K** = $\frac{0}{11}$ or 0

   Probability of not **A** = $\frac{9}{11}$

4. Probabilities will vary depending on the name used.

324

WORKSHEET 4–5a
Finding Probabilities

Name _____

Date _____

For each exercise, find the requested probabilities, using the given figure or set of figures. Write each probability as a fraction.

1.

    Probability of shaded =

    Probability of rectangles =

    Probability of quadrilaterals =

    Probability of not striped =

2. Consider the separate *parts* of the dart board pattern:

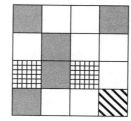

    Probability of checked =

    Probability of striped =

    Probability of white =

    Probability of not shaded =

3. Letters: **M A T H E M A T I C S**

    Probability of **M** =

    Probability of **T** =

    Probability of **K** =

    Probability of not **A** =

4. Letters of your first name: _____

    Probability of **E** =

    Probability of **S** =

    Probability of **Z** =

    Probability of not **R** =

Activity 3: Independent Practice

Materials
Worksheet 4–5b
Regular pencil

Procedure
Give each student a copy of Worksheet 4–5b to complete. Remind students that fractions for probabilities may appear in reduced form. When all have finished, have several students share their methods and answers.

Answer Key for Worksheet 4–5b
1. B

2. A

3. D

4. C

5. A

Possible Testing Errors That May Occur for This Objective
- Students fail to identify all outcomes in the sample space, so all the probabilities found will have the wrong denominator, even though the numerator (number of outcomes for a particular event) may be correct.

- Students use the total outcomes for an event as the denominator in the probability ratio instead of using the total outcomes in the sample space. For example, in a set of 12 colored cubes, 6 cubes are yellow. The probability of drawing a yellow cube is incorrectly stated as 1 cube selected out of 6 yellow cubes, instead of 6 yellow out of 12 total.

- If a set of objects is separated by a certain characteristic, students use the number of qualities or kinds for the characteristic as the denominator of the probability ratio, instead of using the total outcomes in the sample space. For example, if color is used to separate a set of 18 cubes and there are 4 different colors of cubes involved, the probability of drawing a red cube is incorrectly stated as 1 cube selected out of 4 colors of cubes, instead of 5 red out of 18 total.

326

WORKSHEET 4–5b

Finding Probabilities

Name _____

Date _____

Complete the exercises provided.

1. Juan has a box containing 15 colored cubes. There are 6 blue cubes, 2 red cubes, and 3 green cubes, and the rest of the cubes are orange. If Juan reaches into the box and selects 1 cube at random, what is the probability that he will select an orange cube?

   A. $\frac{1}{4}$ B. $\frac{4}{15}$ C. $\frac{11}{15}$ D. None of these

2. A random survey of 80 people showed that 42 people plan to vote for Smythe, 28 for Davis, and 10 for Carroll for the same city council position. Based on these results, what is the probability that Smythe will be elected?

   A. $\frac{21}{40}$ B. $\frac{7}{20}$ C. $\frac{5}{14}$ D. $\frac{1}{8}$

3. For the spinner shown here, what is the probability that the needle will not land on a 5 on the next spin?

   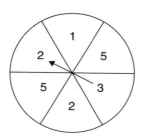

   A. $\frac{1}{2}$ B. $\frac{1}{3}$ C. $\frac{3}{4}$ D. $\frac{2}{3}$

4. In Ralph's desk there are 2 pencils with erasers and 5 pencils without erasers. Three of these pencils are red, and the others are yellow. If Ralph reaches into his desk to pull out a pencil without looking, what are his chances (or probability) for pulling out a pencil without an eraser?

   A. $\frac{3}{7}$ B. $\frac{3}{5}$ C. $\frac{5}{7}$ D. None of these

5. The 11 letters for MISSISSIPPI are written on individual cards, and the 11 cards are randomly placed in a stack. If one card is drawn from the stack of cards, what is the probability that the letter on the card will not be an S?

   A. $\frac{7}{11}$ B. $\frac{2}{11}$ C. $\frac{4}{11}$ D. $\frac{1}{11}$

Objective 6
Find the probability of a compound event (dependent or independent).

A *compound* event occurs when more than one characteristic is being used to describe a set of outcomes. The event may be described with the connectors AND, OR, or NOT, using a list of qualities found in the same sample space (for example, red AND striped). Sometimes the situation involves more than one action, such as turning a spinner and rolling a die simultaneously, so that an outcome consists of two or more actions. In any case, students need to be able to identify the outcomes in the sample space. Once that is done, they should be able to find the outcomes that satisfy a particular event description. The following activities provide experience with sample spaces that allow for compound events. Special formulas will not be emphasized.

Activity 1: Manipulative Stage

Materials
Bags of colored square tiles (1 bag per pair of students; 4 tiles per bag: red, blue, yellow, green)
Worksheet 4–6a
Regular paper and pencil

Procedure
1. Give each pair of students a bag of 4 colored tiles (1 red, 1 blue, 1 yellow, and 1 green) and two copies of Worksheet 4–6a.

2. Have students draw 2 tiles out of the bag without looking, drawing out 1 tile at a time and *not replacing* the first tile into the bag after it is drawn. They should record the colors of the pair after each draw. For example, a red tile may be drawn first, followed by a blue tile. The pair of tiles should be recorded in the order drawn: (red, blue). After the pair is recorded, the 2 tiles should be returned to the bag and another drawing made. The list of pairs drawn will form sample space 1 to be used with Worksheet 4–6a.

3. Students should continue drawing until they no longer draw out a new pair. No repeats should be recorded in the list for the sample space. Because the order of the draw is considered, (red, blue) and (blue, red) do not represent the same pair.

4. When a pair of students thinks they have a complete sample space, confirm that they have 12 pairs in their list. Then have them find the probabilities on Worksheet 4–6a that apply to sample space 1.

5. Now have students repeat the above process, but this time the first tile of the drawing should be *replaced* into the bag before the second tile is drawn. This allows the pairs, (red, red), (blue, blue), (yellow, yellow), and (green, green), to be counted. The new list of pairs found will represent sample space 2 on Worksheet 4–6a.

6. When students think they have a complete sample space 2, confirm that their list has 16 pairs. Then have them find the probabilities on Worksheet 4–6a that apply to sample space 2.

7. After all students have completed the worksheet, have them compare the probabilities for the same event description but from different sample spaces. When the probabilities differ, discuss the reason for the difference (the replacement of the first tile before drawing the second tile changes the choices for the second draw, thereby changing what the final pair might be). Have students write a statement at the bottom of Worksheet 4–6a about why these probabilities differ. When the first tile is replaced, the drawing of the second tile is *independent* of the drawing of the first tile. If the first tile is not replaced, the drawing of the second tile is *dependent* on the drawing of the first tile.

As an example of a probability, consider Exercise 1 on Worksheet 4–6a: "P(1st red or 2nd blue) = _____." The notation for the event means that the first tile will be red OR the second tile will be blue in the outcomes (pairs) being sought.

This exercise applies to sample space 1, where the first tile was not replaced before the second tile was drawn out of the bag. Have students look at their list of pairs for sample space 1. They should find all pairs that show the *first tile to be red*: (red, blue), (red, green), and (red, yellow).

Since the connector OR is used, the outcomes (pairs, here) that satisfy each separate description should be combined together without any repeats. Therefore, students also need to find all pairs that show the second tile to be blue, but they should not include any pairs already counted in the set where the first tile is red. So (red, blue) will not be counted in this second set. New pairs to include will be (green, blue) and (yellow, blue).

Combining the pairs from the two sets, there will be 3 + 2, or 5, pairs from sample space 1 that satisfy the event: first tile red or second tile blue. Since there are 12 pairs in the sample space, the probability for this event will be $\frac{5}{12}$, that is, there will be 5 ways out of 12 ways that a drawn pair might have red for the first tile or blue for the second tile. Students should record $\frac{5}{12}$ in the blank for Exercise 1 on Worksheet 4–6a.

Answer Key for Worksheet 4–6a

1. $\frac{5}{12}$
2. $\frac{6}{12}$ or $\frac{1}{2}$
3. $\frac{1}{12}$
4. $\frac{2}{12}$ or $\frac{1}{6}$
5. $\frac{0}{12}$ or 0
6. $\frac{9}{12}$ or $\frac{3}{4}$
7. $\frac{7}{16}$
8. $\frac{8}{16}$ or $\frac{1}{2}$
9. $\frac{1}{16}$
10. $\frac{2}{16}$ or $\frac{1}{8}$
11. $\frac{1}{16}$
12. $\frac{12}{16}$ or $\frac{3}{4}$

WORKSHEET 4–6a

Finding Probabilities Using AND, OR, and NOT

Name _____

Date _____

Use 4 colored tiles to build sample space 1 and sample space 2. Find the required probabilities for each sample space, using fractions. Reduce the fractions when possible.

For sample space 1 (drawing without replacement):

1. P(1st red or 2nd blue) = _____

2. P(1st blue or 1st yellow) = _____

3. P(1st green and 2nd red) = _____

4. P(one is red and one is yellow) = _____

5. P(both are blue) = _____

6. P(2nd not yellow) = _____

For sample space 2 (drawing with replacement):

7. P(1st red or 2nd blue) = _____

8. P(1st blue or 1st yellow) = _____

9. P(1st green and 2nd red) = _____

10. P(one is red and one is yellow) = _____

11. P(both are blue) = _____

12. P(2nd not yellow) = _____

Explain in your own words why probabilities for the same event seem to differ for sample space 1 and sample space 2.

_____

_____

_____

Activity 2: Pictorial Stage

Materials

    Cards Pattern 4–6a (1 per pair of students)
    Scissors (1 pair per 2 students)
    Worksheet 4–6b
    Regular pencils

Procedure

1. Give each pair of students a copy of the Cards Pattern 4–6a and one pair of scissors. Also give each student a copy of Worksheet 4–6b.

2. Students should cut apart the cards on the pattern sheet, then sort them according to the characteristics described on Worksheet 4–6b. Each card is labeled with a letter to help students communicate about the cards easily.

3. For each event stated in an exercise on Worksheet 4–6b, students should find which cards satisfy the event and then determine the probability that this event will occur when one card is randomly drawn from the set. A fraction comparing the number of cards for the event to the 12 cards total in the set should be written in the blank provided on Worksheet 4–6b. Fractions may be reduced when possible.

4. After all student pairs have completed the worksheet, have several students share their results with the entire class.

5. Exercise 6 on Worksheet 4–6b is discussed below as an example.

Exercise 6 on Worksheet 4–6b asks students to find P(striped OR shaded) and P(not striped AND not shaded), using the card set.

Students must first sort their set of cards according to the two characteristics in the event: "striped OR shaded." They should form one pile of cards that contain stripes, along with any additional cards that are shaded but not striped. If a card has stripes or if it is shaded, it will go in this pile. There will be 7 cards in this pile (cards A, B, C, F, G, H, and K), so P(striped OR shaded) will equal $\frac{7}{12}$. Students should record $\frac{7}{12}$ in the first blank for Exercise 6 on Worksheet 4–6b.

The remaining cards will form another pile where each card does NOT belong to the "striped OR shaded" group. That is, they are the *complement* of the first group of cards. Have students confirm that each card in this second group will also satisfy the second event listed in Exercise 6; that is, each card will simultaneously not have stripes AND not be shaded. There are 5 cards (cards D, E, I, J, and L) in this second group, so P(not stripes AND not shaded) will equal $\frac{5}{12}$. Students should record $\frac{5}{12}$ in the second blank for Exercise 6 on Worksheet 4–6b.

The two disjoint card groups used to find the two probabilities for Exercise 6 demonstrate that one group is the complement of the other. Together they form the entire card set. Thus, the two events that those cards satisfy are complements of each other. The results of this exercise also indicate that "NOT (striped OR shaded)" is equivalent to "not striped AND not shaded." Exercises 4, 5, and 7 show similar results.

At this grade level, this is an exploratory activity. Therefore, do not require students to memorize the logical relationship: Not (striped OR shaded) = (Not striped) AND (Not shaded), or other similar ones. Such generalizations will be studied in later grades.

Answer Key for Worksheet 4–6b

1. $\frac{2}{12}$ or $\frac{1}{6}$ (card L is considered plain, no dots); 10/12 or 5/6

2. $\frac{5}{12}$; $\frac{7}{12}$

3. $\frac{7}{12}$; $\frac{5}{12}$

4. $\frac{1}{12}$; $\frac{11}{12}$

5. $\frac{2}{12}$ or $\frac{1}{6}$; $\frac{10}{12}$ or $\frac{5}{6}$

6. $\frac{7}{12}$; $\frac{5}{12}$

7. $\frac{5}{12}$; $\frac{7}{12}$

CARDS PATTERN 4–6a

A	B	C
D	E	F
G	H	I
J	K	L

WORKSHEET 4–6b

Name _____

Date _____

**Compound Events with
AND, OR, and NOT**

Cut the cards in Cards Pattern 4-6a apart. Assume one card is to be drawn randomly from the given set of cards. Find the cards that satisfy each event's descriptors in order to find the probability for that event to occur when one card is drawn. Record the probability as a fraction in the blank provided.

1. P(dotted) = _____

    P(not dotted) = _____

2. P(shaded) = _____

    P(not shaded) = _____

3. P(more than 3 sides) = _____

    P(not more than 3 sides) = _____

4. P(plain AND 3 sides) = _____

    P(not plain OR not 3 sides) = _____

5. P(striped AND shaded) = _____

    P(not striped OR not shaded) = _____

6. P(striped OR shaded) = _____

    P(not striped AND not shaded) = _____

7. P(dotted OR plain) = _____

    P(not dotted AND not plain) = _____

Activity 3: Independent Practice

Materials
Worksheet 4–6c
Regular pencil

Procedure
Give each student a copy of Worksheet 4–6c to complete. Encourage students to identify a sample space first before finding probabilities based on that sample space. Remind students to reduce fractions to the lowest terms when possible. When all have finished, have several students share their reasoning and answers with the entire class.

Answer Key for Worksheet 4–6c
1. C

2. B

3. D

4. B

Possible Testing Errors That May Occur for This Objective
- When OR is used in an event, students count the outcomes for each characteristic listed, then add the two amounts together without deleting the repeated outcomes. This results in a probability that is too high.

- When the word NOT is included in the event description, students ignore it and select an outcome that has the stated characteristic. For example, if the event requires shapes that are not rectangles, students count the rectangles instead to find the probability.

- When an event describes outcomes that satisfy two or more characteristics, students choose outcomes with only one of the required characteristics. For example, if "red AND square" is required, students select a red shape that is not a square or select a square that is not red.

WORKSHEET 4–6c   Name _____

Probabilities of Compound Events   Date _____

Complete the following exercises.

1. The faces of a cube are labeled 1 through 6. A spinner has 4 equal sectors, each sector labeled with a color: red, purple, blue, or yellow. If the spinner and the cube are used together in a game, what is the probability that a player will spin the color blue and then roll a 3 or 4 during a turn at play?

   A. $\frac{1}{2}$ B. $\frac{1}{4}$ C. $\frac{1}{12}$ D. $\frac{1}{24}$

2. The Venn diagram shows how many of the 300 students at Wells Middle School have a scooter only, a skateboard only, or both a scooter and a skateboard. Use the information in the diagram to find the probability that 1 student chosen randomly will not have a scooter or a skateboard.

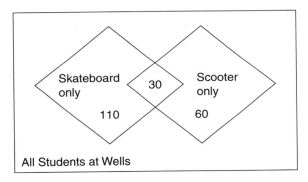

   A. $\frac{1}{30}$ B. $\frac{1}{3}$ C. $\frac{2}{3}$ D. $\frac{6}{11}$

3. A box contains 12 colored disks. There are 3 red disks, 7 yellow disks, and 2 blue disks. If one disk is randomly drawn from the box, what is the probability that the disk will be blue or yellow?

   A. $\frac{1}{12}$ B. $\frac{5}{12}$ C. $\frac{2}{9}$ D. $\frac{3}{4}$

4. If two coins are tossed together without order, find P(two heads tossed).

   A. 0   B. $\frac{1}{3}$ C. $\frac{2}{3}$ D. None of these

Section 4

Name _____

Date _____

GRAPHING, STATISTICS, AND PROBABILITY PRACTICE TEST ANSWER SHEET

Directions: Use the Answer Sheet to darken the letter of the choice that best answers each question.

1. ○ A   ○ B   ○ C   ○ D   7. ○ A   ○ B   ○ C   ○ D

2. ○ A   ○ B   ○ C   ○ D   8. ○ A   ○ B   ○ C   ○ D

3. ○ A   ○ B   ○ C   ○ D   9. ○ A   ○ B   ○ C   ○ D

4. ○ A   ○ B   ○ C   ○ D   10. ○ A   ○ B   ○ C   ○ D

5. ○ A   ○ B   ○ C   ○ D   11. ○ A   ○ B   ○ C   ○ D

6. ○ A   ○ B   ○ C   ○ D   12. ○ A   ○ B   ○ C   ○ D

SECTION 4: GRAPHING, STATISTICS, AND PROBABILITY: PRACTICE TEST

1. Which point has the coordinates (–2,–1.5)? (1 segment = 1 unit)

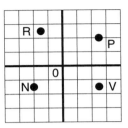

   A. Point R   B. Point N   C. Point P   D. Point V

2. Which statement correctly applies to the triangle on the grid?

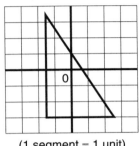

(1 segment = 1 unit)

  A. One vertex is in the second quadrant and another vertex is at coordinates (–1.5,–3).

  B. One vertex is in the second quadrant and another vertex is at coordinates (+2.5,+3).

  C. One vertex is in the third quadrant and another vertex is at coordinates (+2.5,+1).

  D. One vertex is in the third quadrant and another vertex is at coordinates (0,+1).

3. In a survey, 200 students were asked about the type and number of pets they owned. Which circle graph frame (A, B, C, or D) best matches the survey data shown in the table?

Type of Pet	Cat	Dog	Bird	Fish
Number of pets	75	25	25	75

A.   B.   C.   D.

SECTION 4: GRAPHING, STATISTICS, AND PROBABILITY:
PRACTICE TEST (Continued)

4. Three sectors on a circle graph compare as follows: P = Q, and P is twice R. Which of the following figures (A, B, C, or D) will their respective bars look like when shown in P, Q, R order on a bar graph?

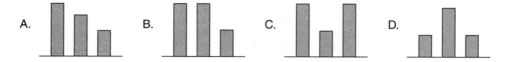

5. Eight stores were surveyed regarding their price for a certain bracelet. The survey results are shown on the stem-and-leaf plot below:

2	9				
3	8				
4	3	7	7		
5	0	4	5		
6					

5|3 means $5.30 for one store's price for the bracelet.

Which set of data matches the prices shown on the plot?

A. $2.90, $3.80, $4.30, $4.70, $4.70, $5.00, $5.40, $5.50

B. $2.90, $3.80, $4.30, $4.37, $4.70, $5.00, $5.55, $6.00

C. $2.90, $3.80, $4.30, $4.70, $5.00, $5.40, $5.50, $6.00

D. None of these

6. Based on the graph below, which is the best estimate of how many more girls than boys said burgers were their favorite food?

A. 25   B. 20   C. 10   D. 5

7. After playing 9 basketball games of the season, Delia has a scoring average of 15 points per game. If she scores 18 points in the next game, what will her average be for the 10 games?

A. 18.0   B. 17.3   C. 16.5   D. 15.3

SECTION 4: GRAPHING, STATISTICS, AND PROBABILITY: PRACTICE TEST (Continued)

8. Find the average number (to the nearest tenth) of students per class for classes I, II, III, and IV shown on the graph.

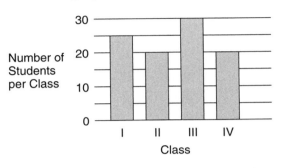

    A. 23.8   B. 22.5   C. 21.4   D. 20.0

9. Karyn has a box containing 20 colored cubes. There are 8 blue cubes, 3 red cubes, and 2 green cubes, and the rest of the cubes are orange. If Karyn reaches into the box and selects 1 cube at random, what is the probability that she will select an orange cube?

    A. $\frac{1}{20}$ B. $\frac{7}{20}$ C. $\frac{13}{20}$ D. None of these

10. For the spinner shown here, what is the probability that the needle will not land on a 2 on the next spin?

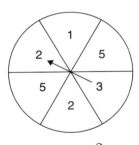

    A. $\frac{1}{2}$ B. $\frac{1}{3}$ C. $\frac{3}{4}$ D. $\frac{2}{3}$

11. A box contains 15 colored disks. There are 5 red disks, 3 yellow disks, and 7 blue disks. If one disk is randomly drawn from the box, what is the probability that the disk will be red or yellow?

    A. $\frac{1}{15}$ B. $\frac{1}{8}$ C. $\frac{5}{8}$ D. $\frac{8}{15}$

12. The faces of a cube are labeled 1 through 6. If a coin and the cube are tossed together in a game, what is the probability that a player will toss heads with the coin and then roll a 5 or 6 during a turn at play?

    A. $\frac{1}{2}$ B. $\frac{1}{4}$ C. $\frac{1}{6}$ D. $\frac{1}{12}$

Section 4: Graphing, Statistics, and Probability:
Answer Key for Practice Test

The objective being tested is shown in brackets beside the answer.

1. B [1]	7. D [4]
2. A [1]	8. A [4]
3. C [2]	9. B [5]
4. B [2]	10. D [5]
5. A [3]	11. D [6]
6. C [3]	12. C [6]

Hands-On Algebra:
Ready-To-Use Games & Activities
For Grades 7-12

Paper/ 640 pages
ISBN: 0-87628-386-5

For grades 7-12 teachers, here's an extensive collection of 159 ready-to-use games and activities to make algebra meaningful and fun for kids of all ability levels!

Through a unique three-step approach, students gain mastery over algebra concepts and skills one activity at a time:

- Activity 1 offers **physical models** (using available materials) and easy-to-follow instructions to help learners seek patterns.
- Activity 2 uses **pictorial models** like diagrams, tables, and graphs to further help students retain and test what they have learned.
- Activity 3 encourages **exploration** and **application** of newly learned concepts and skills through cooperative games, puzzles, problems, and graphic calculator or computer activities.

For quick access and easy use, all materials are organized into five major sections and printed in a big 8 1/4" x 11" lay-flat binding for easy photocopying. Following is just a small sample of the many activities featured in each section:

1. **REAL NUMBERS, THEIR OPERATIONS, AND THEIR PROPERTIES:** Array Build-Up (Multiplication) . . . Splitting Things Apart (Applying Distributive Property) . . . No Sign Posts! (Ordering Operations) . . . Rectangle Mangle (Applying Absolute Value)

2. **LINEAR FORMS:** Make-and-Replace (Evaluating Algebraic Expressions) . . . A Whole in One! (Linear Equations Involving Fractions) . . . Switching Tracks (Solving aX + b = cX + d)

3. **LINEAR APPLICATIONS AND GRAPHING:** How Much Additional Fencing? (Modeling Linear Relationships) . . . Mix It Up! (Ratio & Proportion) . . . Graphing Capers (Solving for Y in terms of X)

4. **QUADRATIC CONCEPTS:** Factor Draw (Factoring Second-Degree Polynomials) . . . Sliding Curves (Exploring Quadratic Functions) . . . Squaring with Tiles (Solving by Completing the Square)

5. **SPECIAL APPLICATIONS:** Great Divide (Transforming Linear Inequalities) . . . Which Sum Works? (Pythagorean Theorem) . . . Growth Patterns (Exponential Functions)

You'll find each activity has complete teacher directions, materials needed, and helpful examples for discussion, homework, and quizzes. And to make your job easier, most activities include time-saving reproducible worksheets or game pieces for use with individual students, small groups, or an entire class!

Frances M. Thompson, Ed.D. (University of Georgia) has taught mathematics at the junior and senior high school levels, served as a K-12 math specialist, and is currently professor of mathematics at Texas Woman's University, Denton.

Other Books by Frances McBroom Thompson

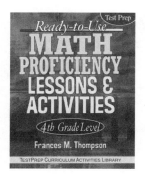

Ready-to-Use Math Proficiency Lessons and Activities 4th Grade Level

Paper/ 400 pages
ISBN: 0-7879-6596-0

Ready-to-Use Math Proficiency Lessons and Activities 4th Grade Level offers teachers a collection of 40 key objectives that help students master the standard mathematics curriculum that they are expected to have learned in grades 1 to 4. Each of these objectives includes three developmental activities.

- Activity 1 provides physical models and the materials that are described in detail, including pattern sheets, building mats, and worksheets with answer keys.

- Activity 2 uses pictorial models such as pictures or diagrams that help students retain and assess what they have learned.

- Activity 3 encourages exploration and application of newly learned lessons. Worksheet items for this third stage give students more opportunities to prepare for the testing experience.

For quick access and easy use, all materials are organized into five major sections and printed in a big 8 1/2" x 11" lay-flat format for easy photocopying. The following is just a small sample of the many activities featured in each section.

1. **NUMERATION AND NUMBER PROPERTIES:** Identify odd and even whole numbers . . . Represent a proper fraction with various models (physical and pictorial) . . . Find equivalent fractions that are less than one.

2. **COMPUTATIONAL ALGORITHMS AND ESTIMATION IN PROBLEM SOLVING:** Add or subtract whole numbers (two-digit to four-digit) to solve a word problem . . . Divide two-digit or three-digit whole numbers by one-digit whole numbers (as divisors) to solve a single-stepped word problem . . .Solve multistepped word problems, using addition, subtraction, multiplication, or division of whole numbers.

3. **GRAPHING, STATISTICS, AND PROBABILITY**: Complete a two-column (or two-row) numerical table, using recognized patterns in the column (or row) entries, in order to solve word problems . . . Find the mean of a set of data . . . Identify possible two-member or three-member outcomes of a situation (multistaged experiment without order).

4. **GEOMETRY AND LOGICAL OR SPATIAL REASONING:** Make generalizations from geometric sets of examples and nonexamples . . . Identify polygons by their generic names . . . Apply logical reasoning to solve a word problem (with or without computation).

5. **MEASUREMENT:** Estimate the length of an object, using an appropriate measuring unit (inch, foot, yard, millimeter, centimeter, meter) . . . Solve problems that involve the passing of time and the notation for time on a clock . . . Find the area of a rectangular region.

Other Books by Frances McBroom Thompson

Hands-On Math: Ready-To-Use Games & Activities For Grades 4-8

Paper/ 544 pages
ISBN: 0-7879-6740-8

Here's a super treasury of 279 exciting math games and activities that help students learn by engaging both their minds and their bodies. Dispensing with tired "rote" learning and memorization, Hands-On Math! uses fun-filled exercises that encourage your students to think and reason mathematically.

In line with NCTM guidelines, this invaluable teacher's aid develops basic and advanced math skills through an effective combination of three components for each lesson: a concrete exercise (manipulatives), a pictorial model, and a cooperative learning experience.

Organized into eight sections, each covering concepts from a different area of mathematics, Hands-On Math! provides scores of reproducible record sheets, workmats and other student handouts to use as often as needed. Sections include:

Number and Number Relationships
Patterns, Relations and Functions
Development of Written Algorithms
Geometry and Spatial Sense (including Symmetry)
Measurement
Statistics and Probability
Number Theory
Algebraic Thinking

Other Books of Interest

Algebra Out Loud: Learning Mathematics Through Reading and Writing Activities

Pat Mower, Ph.D.

Paper/ 256 pages
ISBN: 0-7879-6898-6

Algebra Out Loud is a unique resource designed for mathematics instructors who are teaching Algebra I and II. This easy-to-use guide is filled with illustrative examples, strategies, activities, and lessons that will help students more easily understand mathematical text and learn the skills they need to effectively communicate mathematical concepts.

Algebra Out Loud gives teachers the tools they need to help their students learn how to communicate about math ideas between student and teacher, student and peers, and student and the wider world. The book offers proven writing activities that will engage the students in writing about algebraic vocabulary, processes, theorems, definitions, and graphs. The strategies and activities in Algebra Out Loud will give students the edge in learning how to summarize, analyze, present, utilize, and retain mathematical content.

For quick access and easy use, the activities are printed in a big 8 1/2" x 11" lay-flat format for easy photocopying and are organized into eight chapters.

PREREADING STRATEGIES AND ACTIVITIES: Knowledge Ratings . . . Anticipation Guides . . . Problem Solving Prep . . . Wordsmithing.

READING AND VOCABULARY BUILDING STRATEGIES AND ACTIVITIES: Magic Square Activity . . . Concept Circles . . . K-W-L . . . Semantic Feature Analysis . . . Graphic Organizers . . . Reading Math Symbols . . . Proof-Reading . . . Semantic Word Map.

POSTREADING STRATEGIES AND ACTIVITIES: Group Speak . . . Concept Cards . . . Fryer Model . . . Question-Answer Relationship (QAR) . . . Comparison and Contrast Matrix.

READINGS IN MATHEMATICS: The Secret Society of Pythagoreans: An Ancient Cult . . . Marathon Math . . . Egyptian Multiplication.

WRITING TO UNDERSTAND ALGEBRA: In Your Own Words: Paraphrasing Activity . . . Methods of Operation . . . Graph Description Activity . . . Crib Sheets . . . Math Story Activity . . . Math Ads . . . The Writing Is on the Wall . . . Creating a Math Mnemonics . . . Creation of Written Problems (or Fat Men in Pink Leotards) . . . Math Concept Paragraphs . . . Math Biographies . . . Experimenting to Learn Algebra Reports . . . Concept Math . . . Learning Log.

WRITING TO COMMUNICATE ALGEBRA: Writing Across Campus . . . Group Exposition . . . Guided Math Poetry . . . Math Letters . . . Math Poetry . . . Math Journals . . . Mathematical Investigator.

WRITING AS AUTHENTIC ASSESSMENT: Muddiest Point . . . Math Analogies . . . One-Minute Summary . . . Math Is a Four Letter Word . . . E-Writing . . . Math Similes, Metaphors, and Analogies . . . Targeted Problem Solving Assessments.

WRITING FOR ASSESSMENT: Math Portfolio . . . Math Essay . . . Write Question . . . Math Posters.

Pat Mower, Ph.D., is an associate professor in the Department of Mathematics and Statistics at Washburn University in Topeka, Kansas. Dr. Mower prepares preservice teachers to teach mathematics in elementary, middle, and secondary schools. Her interests include reading and writing in mathematics, and alternative methods for the teaching and learning of mathematics.

Other Books of Interest

The Math Teacher's Book Of Lists, 2nd Edition

Judith A. Muschla and Gary Robert Muschla

Paper/ 250 pages
ISBN: 0-7879-7398-X

The Math Teacher's Book of Lists, 2nd Edition is a one-stop math resource with exciting, challenging, and quick reference materials, all supporting NCTM standards. It includes comprehensive and updated content from general mathematics through algebra, geometry, trigonometry, and calculus, useful in 5-12 classrooms as well as community college classes.

Part I contains nine sections of reproducible lists and offers essential, time-saving and relevant information on over 300 topics. Part II contains a variety of reproducible teaching aides and activities to support the instructional program.
The original lists have been substantially updated, a new section, "Lists for Student Reference," has been added, along with approximately twelve new lists, including "Fractals," "Topics in Discrete Math," "Math Websites for Students," and "Math Websites for Teachers."

This new edition, like the original, is designed for easy implementation. Each list is written in clear, simple-to-read language, stands alone, and may be used with students of various grades and abilities; materials can be customized to your needs. These lists are linked through cross references and can serve as the basis for developing supplementary materials for the classroom, expanding topics in the curriculum, or extending lessons with related topics.

The Math Teacher's Book of Lists provides:

- An invaluable resource for effective mathematics instruction.
- An imaginative way to help students understand the grand scope, practicality and intriguing intricacies of mathematics.

The Authors

Judith A. Muschla has taught middle and high school mathematics in South River, NJ, for the last 27 years, and received the governor's Teacher Recognition Program Award in New Jersey. **Gary Robert Muschla** taught reading and writing for more than 25 years in Spotswood, NJ. This is their eight co-authored mathematics book.

Other Books of Interest

Math Starters: 5 To 10 Minute Activities That Make Kids Think, Grades 6-12

Judith A. Muschla and Gary Robert Muschla

Paper/ 336 pages
ISBN: 0-87628-566-3

Here is a super collection of over 650 ready-to-use math starters that get kids quickly focused and working on math as soon as they enter your classroom! Perfect for any math curriculum, these high-interest problems spark involvement in the day's lesson, help students build skills, and allow you to handle daily management tasks without wasting valuable instructional time.

For easy use all of the math-starter problems are printed in a big 8 1/4" x 11" lay-flat format for photocopying and organized in two parts:

Part I—Making Math Starters a Part of Your Program gives you practical suggestions for implementing math starters in your teaching routine, including tips on evaluation, class management, setting up cooperative groups, and more.

Part II—Math Starters provides six collections of math-starter problems related to six major areas of secondary math. Following is a brief overview of what you'll find for each math areas:

WHOLE NUMBERS: THEORY & OPERATIONS: 86 problems like "Perfect Squares," "Emirps," "Divisibility by 11," and "Symbols" covering types of numbers, basic operations, rules for divisibility, multiple, greatest common factors and other topics

FRACTIONS, DECIMALS & PERCENTS: 122 starters such as "Comparing Fractions & Decimals," "Equivalencies" and "Finding a Number When the Percent of It Is Unknown"

MEASUREMENT: 76 problems using English and metric measurements, time temperature and other measures, including "Obsolete Units" (cubics & spans), "The 24-Hour Clock," "Cords of Wood," "Parsecs and Light Years," and "Computer Memory"

GEOMETRY: 130 starters such as "Types of Angles," "Convex Polygrams," "Generating Pythagorean Triples," and "Identifying Trapezoids and Parallelograms"

ALGEBRA :128 problems, pre-algebra and up, such as "The Number Line," "Adding and Subtracting Integers," "Finding the Slope," and "Finding the GCF of Monomials"

POTPOURRI: 112 math starters on data analysis, probability, fractals, codes, vectors and more, such as "Number Ciphers," "Finding Simple Probability" and "Magic Squares."

The skills in each of the six sections of math starters follow a sequence common to most math curriculum; the difficulty level of each starter is denoted by one, two, or three stars; and a complete answer key for all math starters is provided at the end of the book.